Social Networks

Humans are the most social of all animals, learning from and being interdependent with many others, thereby forming relationships that span our complex world-society. Understanding humans and humanity therefore requires comprehending social relations, which may be hard to grasp systematically. Fortunately, the variety and turmoil of social relations can be mapped out as clear-cut networks. With the aid of network theory, characteristics of social life, such as small worlds, highly skewed distributions of sexual and other social contacts, and the structure of social inequality and cohesion, can be explained for the first time. Furthermore, not yet well-understood phenomena can be grasped more clearly, such as organizations, and the growth and diffusion of knowledge. Many social network models are also applicable to, or inspired by, other fields, such as economics, biology, political science, statistical physics, and organization science.

This book introduces social networks to a general audience – from novices in all kinds of fields to experts wanting to catch up, and from academics to practitioners in consultancy, management, policy, and social work. Sophisticated models are clearly explained without the use of math (which is further clarified separately in boxes, footnotes, and references), and are illustrated with network diagrams and examples ranging from anthropology to organizational sociology. A free and easy-to-use software tool is explained in the final chapter so readers themselves can depict and analyze networks of their interest.

Jeroen Bruggeman is Assistant Professor in the Department of Sociology and Anthropology at the University of Amsterdam.

Social Networks

An introduction

Jeroen Bruggeman

Routledge
Taylor & Francis Group

LONDON AND NEW YORK

First published 2008
by Routledge
2 Park Square, Milton Park, Abingdon, Oxon, OX14 4RN
Simultaneously published in the USA and Canada
by Routledge
270 Madison Avenue, New York, NY 10016

Routledge is an imprint of the Taylor & Francis Group, an informa business

© 2008 Jeroen Bruggeman
Typeset in Perpetua and Bell Gothic by Prepress Projects Ltd,
Perth, UK
Printed and bound in Great Britain by Antony Rowe Ltd,
Chippenham, Wiltshire

British Library Cataloguing in Publication Data
A catalogue record for this book is available from the British Library

Library of Congress Cataloging in Publication Data
Bruggeman, Jeroen.
Social networks : an introduction / Jeroen Bruggeman.
p. cm.
Includes bibliographical references.
1. Social networks. I. Title.
HM741.B78 2008
302.4072—dc22
2007051263

ISBN 13 978–0–415–45803–0 (pbk)
ISBN 13 978–0–415–45802–3 (hbk)
ISBN 13 978–0–203–93046–5 (ebk)

ISBN 10 0–415–45803–X (pbk)
ISBN 10 0–415–45802–1 (hbk)
ISBN 10 0–203–93046–0 (ebk)

Photograph on the cover by the author (2007), Saint-Louis, Senegal.

Contents

Illustrations

FIGURES

TABLES

Acknowledgements

In the course of teaching social networks and writing this book, I posed questions to numerous scholars. For their answers and comments I am indebted to Albert-László Barabási, Jörg Reichardt, Mark Newman, James Moody, Ron Burt, Gianluca Carnabuci, Eugene Johnsen, Andrej Mrvar, Joost Beuving, Eelke Heemskerk, Devon Brewer, Tamas Vicsek, Tom Snijders, Meredith Rolfe, Aljaž Ule, Michael Kearns, Vincent Traag, Rob Mokken, Lada Adamic, Herman van der Werfhorst, Johan de Deken, Gerben Korthouwer, Oana Postolache, Beate Völker, Javier Augusto Loaiza, Thomas Valente, Giuseppe Labianca, Catarina Dutilh Novaes, and Natalie Glance. Douglas White and Duncan Watts also gave invaluable moral support, in addition to their valuable comments. Gábor Csárdi was fantastic in adapting his igraph package and graphical user interface to my requests. Jörg Reichardt generously donated his spin glass algorithm to Gábor's igraph package, and now everybody can use it. Joost Beuving negotiated us into the car market and harbor of Cotonou (Figure 6.1), an unforgettable experience. Most grateful I am to Rasmata Ziwaga, for bringing me to her village (Figure 3.1), and for her love.

Chapter 1

Introduction

SOCIAL RELATIONS

Humans are more cooperative with non-kin and exchange more information than all other animals, with large ramifications for their societies, which eventually became a globe-spanning network. Their pro-sociality enables them to specialize in few activities, and renders them dependent on others for their remaining needs and desires to be fulfilled (Smith 1986). Consequently, one might think of individuals as free-floating atoms in markets where they exchange goods and services. On closer inspection, however, humans rather prefer to affiliate themselves with others in groups and communities of all sorts, such as families, settlements, religions, organizations, and sometimes virtual communities as well. Even if they engage in seemingly free market transactions, these transactions are embedded in institutions beyond bilateral relations, e.g. property rights (Granovetter 1985; North 1990). As part of their gregariousness, humans also learn most of what they know from others, including from the media these others may use. Humans are able collectively to support each other and to invent and produce on an unprecedented scale, but also to harm each other and their natural environment (Tinbergen 1968). For better and for worse, people are profoundly influenced by others for most of what they have, know, and do. These interdependences imply neither that people react to information or influence in a uniform way nor that everybody becomes similar. They do imply, however, that, when we attempt to comprehend humans, studying them in their social environment is much more illuminating than seeing them only as individuals. We should therefore focus on social *relations* in the most general sense (Emirbayer 1997; Elias 1970). Without studying these relations, social phenomena such as religious practices, collective violence, technological innovations, searching resources, and tastes in music and fashion would not be comprehensible, since they cannot be reduced to properties of individuals (Hedström 2006), just as music cannot be appreciated if it is perceived as a series of individual notes. Therefore only the study of social relations can help to reveal the mechanisms that determine social developments, which in their turn set the conditions for continuing, interrupting, and newly establishing relations, as well as the personal experiences these relations bring about.[1] The meanings assigned to these experiences, in turn, are also of interest to social workers, consultants, and other practitioners.

RELATIONS REPRESENTED AS NETWORKS: OVERVIEW

Comprehending the raw complexity of social relations beyond a very small number of people is not feasible without conceptual tools. In this book we will see how social relations can be systematically and clearly represented as networks. A network can depict in a single graph a multitude of interactions between many people, which might have taken place at different times and places. In the words of Jeremy Boissevain (1979), "Network analysis asks questions about who is linked to whom, the content of the linkages, the pattern they form, the relation between the pattern and behaviour, and the relation between the pattern and other social factors." From a network perspective we will investigate human society. We will see that there exist patterns of relations that are crucial for the flows of information, influence, goods, and contagious diseases, that hardly anyone could imagine before they were discovered. We will focus in particular on communities in the broadest sense, because they lie at the core of human sociality. Communities and their overlaps can be detected on the basis of relational data only, without information about individuals' attributes. A case in point is a group partitioned into two opposing coalitions by conflict. We will also see how a community's social cohesion can be measured. From a cultural-evolutionary perspective we will then discuss why people engage extensively in communities and in the maintenance of seemingly inefficient social relations, in contrast to living by arm's-length market relations alone. Then we will shift our focus from communities to individuals and see how people can get access to resources by being connected to others. People as community members can at the same time collaborate for collective goals, while their network positions enable them to broker information and to achieve power and status, leading to social inequality. In these network positions they have certain roles, seen as typical patterns of relations, which can be assessed precisely. Our focus on individuals will also point out why new culture is most likely to be created at the interstices of (sub) communities, where information brokers reside. Newly created knowledge can diffuse through communities by several mechanisms of transmission that we will point out. Organizations, which may be regarded as "special-purpose" communities, are treated at greater length than other kinds of community because many of us work in or for them, and everybody has to deal with them sometimes. Finally, we will show how to use the computer to analyze social networks, and will provide guidelines for data collection. For those who are new to networks, the approach taken might be an unfamiliar but hopefully illuminating way to look at familiar social and sociological problems.

The field of social network analysis up to the mid 1990s was covered extensively in a voluminous handbook by Stanley Wasserman and Katherine Faust (1994). Then two papers by the physicists Duncan Watts and Steven Strogatz (1998) and Albert-László Barabási and Réka Albert (1999) revolutionized the field, and in their trail a highly interdisciplinary and rapidly growing literature transformed it into a broader science of complex networks (Boccaletti *et al.* 2006). Meanwhile, the sociological approach evolved in its own way (Carrington, Scott, and Wasserman 2005). In this book, one will find a selection from both streams of literature and from their cross-fertilizations. The purpose of this book is introductory, and I chose those subjects that most people deal with, rather than attempting to be comprehensive in my overview of substantive research areas where network analysis is applied, or of models it has to offer. My selection is organized around sociological rather than network subjects, a subtle but important distinction with handbooks, while acknowledging that developments in the field of networks shape our perceptions and categorizations of the subject matter. As a consequence of my focus, this book is as much an introduction to social networks as it is an (advanced) introduction to sociology from a network perspective. I assumed that readers might first want to see what network analysis has to offer before they would get interested in its history, and therefore left out the latter. Just in case, there is a short review by Charles Kadushin (2005) of Linton Freeman's (2004) book-length history, while the science of complex networks is described by Barabási (2002).

OTHER APPROACHES

Social network analysis is not the only approach that focuses on interdependent actors at the micro level and the consequences of their behavior at the macro level. Of other approaches that do so, game theory (Szabó and Fáth 2007) is probably the most well known; it analyzes how macro outcomes of individual decisions, based on self-interested motives, result from the interdependent decisions of all players in a game – another way to model social situations. Social network analysis has a different but complementary focus on patterns of relations, and one could say, paraphrasing the title of Thomas Schelling's classic (1978), that it deals with micro *motifs* and macro behavior.[2] In general, the network approach complements other approaches to social phenomena in its systematic treatment of social relations, e.g. in sociology (H. White 1992), anthropology (D. White and Johansen 2005), history (Bearman, Moody, and Faris 2003), economics (Goyal 2007), social psychology (Moreno 1934), communication (Monge and Contractor 2003), political science (Mutz 2002), and organization science (Powell 1990). These fields in their turn provide valuable ideas and data for network analysis, as well as contexts for interpretation of results. For models and methods, the field of social networks traditionally cross-fertilizes with graph theory (Harary 1969), and more recently with physics (Strogatz 2001), biology (Ravasz *et al.* 2002), statistics (Snijders *et al.* 2006), linguistics (WordNet),[3] engineering (Albert, Jeong, and Barabási 2000), and computer science (Dorogovtsev and Mendes 2002), blurring the boundaries between these fields.[4]

SELECTION CRITERIA

To choose material for this book from the vast literature, I applied four criteria that go beyond recent developments of various subfields: testability, clarity, parsimony, and relevance. First, human ideas are fallible, and science distinguishes itself from other fields by requiring that ideas be empirically *testable*, or yield testable predictions, as Willard Van Orman Quine (1990) would say. Testability extends to data and software, which should be open to inspection by other researchers. Obviously, this makes sense only if a falsehood or mistake exposed receives proper recognition. Sifting true from false scientific ideas is now taken for granted, and the struggles to get this practice accepted are long forgotten. However, it is important to realize that this was a great achievement, which can be recognized if we notice how hard it is to get rid of false beliefs in other realms of society, e.g. ethnic prejudice. We may thus acknowledge testability, but many ideas, even scientific ones, are not testable straight away. Scientific concepts, for instance social cohesion, usually have multiple meanings, some of which are more useful than others – if they can be made *clear*. Without guidance on which interpretations out of many make sense, theory testing and knowledge accumulation are not feasible and, on the basis of unclear concepts, computations – essential for grasping complexity – are impossible. In network research, as in many other areas of science, ideas can be made clear by expressing them in a formal language (Peirce 1878; Suppes 1968). Mathematics is used to explicate ideas and intuition in a concise manner, and may therefore be regarded as "the poetry of science" (De Swaan 1995). It is also used to model complex phenomena in a precise manner, and through computations it enables us to reach conclusions that would be too complex for unaided reason (Farquharson 1969). This book, however, can be read and understood without math, which has been put in text boxes and footnotes. Either way, actual computations we will do by computer.

No matter how much computer power is applied, however, science is a human activity and its results should be made understandable for humans as much as possible. Scientific theories should therefore be *parsimonious*. Before the digital age, theories were required to be outright simple (Quine and Ullian 1978), whereas nowadays one might say that the "computational complexity" of theories should be amenable for the human brain to digest. Digestibility depends partly on the amount of prior training of the brain, and therefore some network theories and models that require more mathematical background than can be laid out here are treated at an elementary level. In these cases, however, the basic principles are still simple and can be understood by non-experts, although the subsequent computations or algorithms based on these principles may be complex.

Along with simplicity, parsimony has a second and equally important meaning: that more phenomena can be explained by less theory, or captured by fewer models – generality for short. For example, the concept of hierarchy is very general because it applies to a great many phenomena, such as language structures, and rank orders in business firms, groups of apes, and Web directories. If parsimony were to be carried out to its extreme, however, it would yield an empty theory, perfectly simple and applicable to everything. Obviously, the empty theory provides no comprehension at all, and parsimony should be traded off with other requirements with which it is meshed (Goodman 1961). When shifting our focus to the phenomena to be understood, we may realize that not only their general patterns matter but also their variation. As linguists are interested not just in universal language structures but also in descriptions of different languages and their evolution, social scientists know that formal network models are often preceded, complemented, or otherwise enriched by ethnographic and historical studies. Comparing different variants of a phenomenon, often qualitatively described, can help us considerably to generalize. In a similar vein, applicants of statistical models have to trade off simplicity with more variation explained by more complex models. Furthermore, formalization is an enduring process, unfinished for many concepts, and some phenomena not yet properly cast in a precise language, e.g. culture, are too important to leave undiscussed. In general we should regard all approaches that stretch our imagination or increase our comprehension as *relevant*. In sum, when selecting scientific contributions or developing our own, we should aim at clarity, testability, relevance, and reasonable parsimony. These four criteria do not nearly exhaust all good lessons from philosophy of science but, as it seems, they cover the most important and most arduous problems in scientific practice, or of thought in general, as one might argue. To wrap up with the words of the Nobel laureate Herbert Simon (1996: x), "The goal of science is to make the wonderful and complex understandable and simple – but not less wonderful." On this note, we may get started with social networks.

SUGGESTED BACKGROUND READING

General history of mankind, Diamond (1997, 2002); introduction to social science, De Swaan (2001); embeddedness of social action in relations, Granovetter (1985); relational thinking in sociology, Emirbayer (1997); a brief historical overview of the field of network analysis, Kadushin (2005); an introduction to philosophy of science, Quine and Ullian (1978); finally, a delightful book on the beauty of mathematics is Aigner and Ziegler (2003), which suggests a fifth criterion that we might want to add to the four above.

Chapter 2

Representation and conceptualization

NETWORKS AS REPRESENTATIONS OF SOCIAL RELATIONS

Social relations exist in a large variety. Criminal contacts are kept secret, whereas presidential encounters are conspicuously shown on television for millions to watch. Friendships are mostly between (approximate) equals, whereas employment relations are authoritarian, and in some places involve force, at an opposite extreme from equality. Lovers have mutual trust, emotional involvement, and frequent interactions, whereas "arms length" market transactions are brief and emotionally shallow. Although many relations are reciprocated, they are not necessarily so, like fleeting glances in a subway. The last example shows that some relations are not even noticed by all participants but can still be influential: someone saw somebody with an appealing product and now wants to have it too. In strength, relations vary as well, often associated with the kind of relation. Strength varies as a function of (1) emotional intensity, (2) trust, (3) time spent, and (4) reciprocity (Granovetter 1973).[1] The more two people are emotionally involved with each other, trust each other, spend time on or with each other, and reciprocate each other's actions, the stronger their relationship will be. However, the stronger relationships are, the more ambivalent people tend to feel about each other (Smelser 1998), which can sometimes result in conflict.

GRAPHS

In searching for relational patterns to explain social phenomena, as motivated by Chapter 1, it seems that we have gone astray, by tumbling into a bewildering variety of relations seemingly out of control. Continuing to study what we can hardly grasp seems not to be a very useful pursuit. What we need instead is a clear-cut representation or model of these social relations, in order to see what we are talking about. Subsequently, we need tools and theory[2] to analyze these relations, in order to develop a meaningful understanding. On both counts, social network analysis can help us to get ahead. *Actors*, i.e. intentional objects such as humans or organizations, represented as nodes (*vertices*) and their relations as lines (*edges*), can be drawn as a *graph*, or social *network*. The problem of getting empirical data to draw such a graph can then be treated separately. The resulting graph makes possible visual inspection of relations beyond anything possible by observing the actual relations, and a graph can be a great deal more complete and less ambiguous than the ephemeral encounters on which it is based.

As an example of a social network, let us look at a pattern of sexual relations (Figure 2.1). The data for this graph were obtained at a high school in a rural area in the United States, where over half of the students reported romantic or sexual contacts with fellow students of the opposite sex during a one-and-a-half-year period. Neither the students nor the researchers were initially aware of the larger pattern of these encounters. The giant component contains 288 students, which is about half of those romantically involved. A *component* is a set of nodes in which each node can be reached from any other through a path, i.e. a concatenation of lines; a component is therefore a so-called *connected graph*. The smaller components depict smaller sets of students disconnected to the remainder students in their sexual contacts; 63 isolated couples are not depicted. How the actual pattern unfolds over

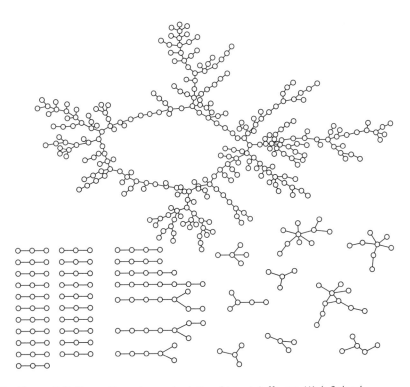

Figure 2.1 *Romantic and sexual relationships at Jefferson High School (Bearman, Moody, and Stovel 2004). Kindly provided by James Moody.*

7

time can be seen on a website (see Bearman, Moody, and Stovel 2004) in a sequence of networks collected by the researchers. Such a sequence presents a stroboscopic image of a network's evolution, whereas a static image, such as the one above, is a cognitive aid to grasp a complex social pattern at a moment in time.[3]

By now you might feel inclined to draw a graph of a social network. To do this well, sufficient precision of terminology is required first.[4] In this precise language, a social network or graph has a non-empty set of objects, e.g. actors, industries, or even countries. The members of this set can be drawn as nodes – vertices, or vertex in the singular – and written down by their names or by numbers if respondents' anonymity was promised. An example is a set of four people, Ciprian, Andra, Milena, and Pachanga. The order in which their names are written is unimportant. It may seem that actors represented as network nodes have now become immutable substances, but that is not at all assumed. Only their name (or number) as identifying mark must remain stable for the duration of the study.

The members of the set are in some sort of social relation with each other, such as friendship, colleague, love, or whatever is of the researcher's interest. A *relation* is a (possibly empty) set of *ordered pairs* of objects, and the order in which these objects are put does make a difference. Perhaps Ciprian is in love with Andra, but Andra is not in love with Ciprian. In the visual representation, an *arc* (arrow) is then drawn from Ciprian to Andra, not necessarily the other way around, resulting in a directed graph, or *digraph* for short. When making a data file for a graph, one writes on a single line the names Ciprian and Andra, in the first and second column of a spreadsheet respectively, or just separated with a space or tab in a file without format. The computer coming across this information will *not* assume that the pair Andra and Ciprian is in the same, here love, relation, unless this is *explicitly* said on a subsequent line, as below. Either way, each ordered pair must be on a separate line in the data file.

```
Ciprian      Andra
Andra        Ciprian
```

and so on and so forth.

For high numbers of actors, typing data might be more convenient when using abbreviations of names, or an *index* by assigning a number to each actor in order of appearance. Ciprian will then become "1" and Andra "2," etc., and the lines in the data file become:

```
1      2
2      1
```

The graph pertaining to these data (see Figure 2.2) can be drawn in infinitely many ways, e.g. by varying the positions of the vertices, having somewhat rounded instead of straight lines, or by drawing the lines in a different color or thickness. For as long as the graphs obey the relation(s) specified by the data, all drawing variations have the same *topology* and represent the same network; in other words, these graphs are isomorphic.

When social relations are examined in sufficient detail, they are almost always asymmetric (Carley and Krackhardt 1996), suggesting that one would normally represent them by arcs. However, it depends on the purpose of study, or the research question, how much detail of a relation is important. Many researchers treat relations that are reciprocal, such as friendships or sexual encounters in Figure 2.1, as symmetric, especially if one wants to examine larger network patterns rather than details of the *dyads* (bilateral relations). One may then save typing effort by entering each pair only once in the data file, and tell the computer to deal with the data as an *undirected* graph. The relation is then depicted by *edges*, i.e. lines without arrowheads. Vertices connected by edges are called *neighbors*, although there is no intrinsic need for them to be in the geographic vicinity of each other. They may be continents apart and it is their social relation, by email, phone, or otherwise, that establishes their network proximity. Geography is important for social life and conflict, but geographic distance should be distinguished from social distance. A social network can in fact be regarded as a socio-cultural analogue of space (H. White 2000).

To represent multiple kinds of relations simultaneously, for instance to distinguish a love relation from a professional relation, different symbols or subscripts are used for each, yielding a *multigraph*, or *multiplex* graph. Couples in one kind of relation, e.g. professional, are not necessarily in a friendship relation and vice versa. Using different colors or lines in the pertaining graph will keep two (or more) different relations distinguishable. This can be important, because different relations may have quite different social consequences, and the kind of information passing through will differ as well. When examining relational patterns at a macro or global level, however, it often suffices to say whether people are related or not, abstracting away from the details of the particular relationships.

Furthermore, the strength of relationships may vary and, depending on the purpose of the researcher, this aspect may be relevant too. Perhaps Pachanga considers Milena a very good friend, but Milena sees Pachanga as just a friend. When strength matters, arcs get values, for instance 3 for a very good friend, 2 for a friend, and 1 for an acquaintance; or a plus sign for a positive relationship and a minus sign for animosity. The choice of numbers is all yours, and the result is a *valued graph*. When arcs or edges can be only absent (have value 0) or present (value 1), the graph is *binary*, or non-valued (only having value 1).[5] By slightly stretching the definition of relation above, and speaking about ordered triples rather than ordered pairs, we can write in our data file, either with index numbers or with names:

Milena	Pachanga	2
Pachanga	Milena	3
Andra	Milena	1

9

Bear in mind that in daily life the strength of social relations fluctuates, and a cross-sectional measurement of a tie with value 3 might have had value 2 another day. A *tie* is a generic word for edge or arc, and context determines which of the two applies. The closeness of friendships varies, and in a good friendship a half-year absence of contact doesn't imply it's over. The important question to ask is whether, over and above the distinction between "tie" and "no-tie," the result of a study would improve by collecting data to distinguish tie values or one would mainly collect measurement error.[6]

Valued graphs and multigraphs can be interchanged, which makes it possible to apply network measures designed for binary networks to valued networks, which are then treated as multigraphs (Newman 2004). One can regard an arc of strength 3 as if it were three separate arcs of strength 1, or the other way around. Bear in mind that the data may have to be rescaled to reach a meaningful transition from a valued graph to a multigraph, because an edge of value 0.1 and another one of 0.3 will not be distinguishable in the multigraph unless all edges are multiplied by 10. Sometimes one can even simplify a multigraph with *different* kinds of relations to a valued graph with one kind of relation, if it is meaningful to do so; for example ongoing business relations tend to develop an aspect of friendship (Uzzi 1996), and then the business and friendship edges can be added up to a single "strong" edge. When entering data in a file, it is most convenient to have separate files for each kind of relation, which may later be merged into one if relationships are merged for theoretical considerations.

An important distinction is between a larger network on the one hand and a network of a focal person and his/her direct contacts and the relations among them on the other hand. A network of a focal person is called an *ego network*, which might sound like egocentric but has nothing to do with ego's character; it is only jargon. Ego's contact persons are called *alters*. Notice that an ego network is a component by definition. Also other properties of ego networks can be determined, of which the most straightforward is the number of ego's ties. The jargon word for the number of ties of an actor is *degree*. You are by now equipped with an understanding of tie direction and strength, and of data files to put this information in, and can start drawing an image of ego (or larger) networks, with some help from Chapter 8.

Up to now, we have presumed that ties are either present or absent, but we should realize that there is in fact an ambiguous trajectory from a first (inter)action, or a small number of them (Goffman 1959; Collins 2004), to a possibly ensuing social relation. A similar ambiguity occurs when a relation has no clear ending but slowly fades out. An observer who notices one or a few initial (inter)action(s) might feel like trying to draw a regression line through a very small number of points close to each other. In the longer run, a social relation is more easily identified, and then consists of (1) interactions, often but not necessarily in a symbolic or material form of *exchange* (Cook and Emerson 1978), (2) rules on how to (inter) act, and (3) expectations associated with these rules. Notice that exchange can be indirect as well, beyond the dyad (Lévi-Strauss [1949] 1969); for example a client receives a service from an employee who knows that the client has already paid his boss and expects that the boss will later pay his salary. In this example, the client does not exchange directly with the employee, which is only possible under stable expectations. Of expectations raised in interactions, *trust* – the expectation that the other won't do harm[7] – is arguably the most important, if it develops. Trust has a biological basis (the neuropeptide oxytocin; Kosfeld *et al.* 2005), pointing to an evolutionary origin. Opting for a network representation of social (inter) actions depends on the purpose of the researcher. Nevertheless one may sometimes want to model brief (inter)actions as a network; for example a soccer match can be mapped out as a directed graph of ball passes as arcs connecting players. In any case, the phenomenology of social (inter)actions (Schütz 1932), possibly cast in "thick descriptions" (Geertz 1973) first, can subsequently be represented abstractly as a network (e.g. Mitchell 1969).

Learning to collect network data is best split into three phases. First, by mapping out a part of your own network, as an exercise at the end of this chapter, you can familiarize yourself with making and handling a data file and with the software to draw a graph. You are your own informant, so you don't yet have to come up with ingenious measurement instruments. Second, collect data on a small network in an organization with a clearly defined boundary, and train your analytic skills on already existing larger data sets that can be found on the Web or generated by computer, as exercises in later chapters. To collect data on a small network you need to develop and apply measurement instruments, but in a relatively "safe" setting with a clear boundary. By analyzing existing data sets, in turn, you can set your mind to relating data to theory without at the same time bothering about validity and reliability. All that is well within the abilities of beginning students of networks. If you feel confident there, the third phase is to examine networks in the wild. The problems of validity and reliability out there can be daunting (e.g. collecting the data for Figure 2.1), and you will need background reading and preparatory work well beyond this book, for which some guidelines and references will be provided in Chapter 8.

CONCEPTUALIZATION: EXPLICATION OF IDEAS

The graph in Figure 2.1 might look impressive on first sight but it leaves important questions unanswered. What does the structure mean? How is it generated? Given an individual's position in the network, what is his or her chance of catching or passing on a disease? A picture can say more than a thousand words, but not a great deal more than that. However, a graph is also a precise mathematical object, or model, although its mathematical flipside has not been conspicuously shown yet. As we will see, we can through computations reach conclusions that would be too difficult or counter-intuitive to reach discursively.

To construct a model is to adopt an idealisation. One replaces the subject of one's enquiry, fallibly perceived and imperfectly understood, by an intellectual substitute: a formal structure whose properties are explicitly assumed, or formally deducible from explicit assumptions. Conclusions about this abstract structure are accessible to the unaided reason, and testable logically within a deductive framework. This idealization permits the application of mathematical techniques to the perceptual world. Observation is reduced to order within a system built up from purely formal elements. For such a system to be of use, it must do two things. First, it must confirm crude experience in elementary cases. Second, it must provide conclusions whose scope extends beyond immediate experience, and which can be put to the test as experience is extended. Falsification of any conclusion indicates that at least one assumption of the model must be modified.

(Farquharson 1969: 3)

Before anything meaningful can be deduced or computed, however, we first have to bridge a gap, connecting scientific or other plausible ideas on the one hand to (computations on) a network model on the other hand. These ideas must be conceptualized, i.e. given a precise and at the same time sociologically meaningful interpretation in the model at hand. Conceptualization is so important and so little understood that much attention will be paid to it in this book. Let us start with an example, and try to explicate *social cohesion*, one of the most important concepts in sociology, invented at the end of the nineteenth century by the very first professor in this field, Emile Durkheim (1893, see Coser 1971: 129–143).

Intuitively, cohesion is about relations holding people together and preventing a community from breaking apart. If people in a group or society at large have relations with many others, or have many relations, cohesion is supposedly strong, and if there are many "holes" in the network – absent edges where they could have been present – cohesion is presumably weak. This is true but still too vague; our ambition was to be clear.

We may notice that social cohesion has nothing to do with intimate, secret or strategic information. It is about all relations that pass on or reconfirm more or less generally shared ideas, norms, and values (Granovetter 2005a), which can happen in family relations, and in conversations among neighbors and colleagues as well. As a first approximation, we might say that people either have a social relation or not, and abstract away from whether they relate as friends, colleagues, neighbors, or schoolmates, or by chatting on the Web. If their interactions endure long enough for stable mutual expectations to develop, and small services can be asked and gossip shared, then there is *solidarity* at the dyadic level, which adds up to solidarity, or cohesion, at the group level (Durkheim 1893). If interactions have turned into expectations then there is social structure, of which one property is cohesion. We could thus apply a certain low *threshold* of interaction to distinguish between interactions that are too brief and shallow to contribute to cohesion and interactions that we take for a social relation, in which at least some stable expectations are established and small services can be asked. Empirically, we can use as indicators the duration or some minimal frequency of contact, for example a certain number of emails per half year (group email excluded) provided that these mails are reciprocated (Adamic and Adar 2005). Marsden and Campbell (1984) found in a comparative study that emotional intensity is a better indicator of strength of relationship than frequency of contact (see also Collins 2004), but if the researcher lacks such data, one must do one's best with the data one has. For telephone calls, their duration might be seen as a reasonable proxy for emotional intensity, when taken along with reciprocal contact over a longer period (Onnela *et al.* 2007). If we set edge values based on contacts below the chosen threshold to 0, and above the threshold to 1, we seem to make a reasonable choice (and for now we forget the difficulty of collecting data in practice). Bear in mind that a threshold must be different for other sociological concepts. For the sexual contacts depicted in Figure 2.1 the threshold is obviously much higher, and the graph is less dense than that of students who know each other from class. For cohesion, people should be bound together, which is only possible in more or less symmetric relations, not in strongly asymmetric relations, and in the network representation we should thus opt for edges.

Basically, we could count the number of edges in the network representation of whatever group or society we are interested in, presuming that a low number indicates low cohesion and a high number high cohesion. Suppose the group at hand contains n people, and the total number of edges equals m. Is this high or low? One way to deal with this question is to compare the actual number with the maximum possible, which results in a quantity called density, which always has a value somewhere between 0 and 1. If density is close to 1, cohesion is high; if it's close to 0, cohesion is low. In different contexts, density can also be computed for a network of arcs, taking into account that there can be twice as many arcs as edges.

Density, degree, and adjacency matrix

Density = m/maximum

where m is the actual number of ties. For the maximum to be reached, there is a case distinction between arcs and edges, since there can be only half as many edges as arcs. Furthermore, people are not socially related to themselves, although psychologically one would hope they are, so reflexive ties of people to themselves are excluded. In the case of arcs, each of n people would have an arc to everybody else, again n, minus the reflexive arcs, in total $n(n-1)$ arcs.[8]

In this book, the notation for *degree* of vertex i is k_i, consistent with modern literature. If arcs come into play, a distinction is made between *indegree* and *outdegree* for incoming and outgoing arrows, respectively. For directed networks, degree then becomes *total degree*, the sum of indegree and outdegree.

Network data can be written alternatively in a matrix, as in the example in Table 2.1, which contains the same information as the graph (Figure 2.2) and as the data file, although each presents it in a different form. Matrix notation is a necessary step to understand how in later chapters computations on network data are done. The actors are in the rows, and the order in which they appear is irrelevant, as said earlier. Once an order is picked for the rows, the actors are put in the columns in the *same* order as in the rows. If an actor in row *i* of the matrix has an arc to an actor in column *j*, "1" is written in the relevant cell q_{ij} and, if these two actors are unrelated, $q_{ij} = 0$.[9] The matrix without the names of the actors (or their index numbers) on the sides is called an *adjacency matrix*. If in all cells $q_{ij} = q_{ji}$, then the matrix is symmetric towards the diagonal (where $i = j$); the values on the diagonal are usually 0.[10] In the matrix, indegree of *j* is the summation of q_{ij} over column *j*, $\Sigma_i q_{ij}$, while outdegree of *i* is the summation of q_{ij} over row *i*; the total number of ties is the summation over each column (or row) first plus the summation of all subtotals, hence a double summation sign: $\Sigma\Sigma_i q_{ij}$, and $i \neq j$. Maximum density is the number of rows times the number of columns minus the diagonal.

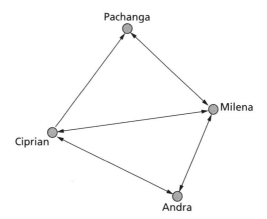

■ *Figure 2.2* Graph of the matrix in Table 2.1.

■ *Table 2.1* Adjacency matrix

	Milena	Andra	Pachanga	Ciprian
Milena	0	1	1	1
Andra	1	0	0	1
Pachanga	1	0	0	0
Ciprian	1	1	1	0

In general it will be true that density values close to 1 indicate high connectivity, hence high cohesion. In a group of friends, family, or in a small village, it is quite possible that density approximates or equals 1; in network jargon, a network with minimally three members and featuring maximal density is called a *clique*; it is maximally connected. In very small networks, as in Figure 2.1, density works fine, and it measures cohesion well. In larger societies, of say a city with 2 million people, it is not possible for an individual to know everybody, and density will always be low. Does this tell us something about cohesion? More importantly, a larger group or society will consist of several subgroups or communities according to kinship, ethnicity, work, or other affiliations, as in Figure 2.3. As a result, the cohesion of each subgroup is higher than that of the entire group, and overall cohesion is inhomogeneously distributed. Density, however, is "blind" for subgroups, and overestimates overall cohesion while it underestimates subgroup cohesion.

What we have learned is that we may compute "something" precisely but, if our conceptualization is done badly and we don't understand what we are doing, the result is misleading at best or plainly wrong. Precision is not the same as conceptual validity or accuracy. Unfortunately there are many studies wherein concepts are precise, but "where the passage from axioms to actualities tends to be rather nonchalantly traversed" (Geertz 1978).[11] A valuable idea sprouted from sociological imagination, on the other hand, might be expressed in an unclear or unsound manner, and not lead to relevant knowledge either. Both extremes miss the point: "Science is a conversation between rigor *and* imagination" (Abbott 2004: 3, italics added).

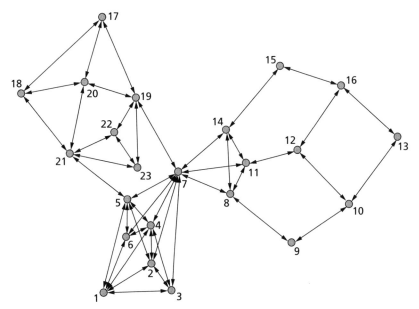

■ **Figure 2.3** Network with locally higher cohesion than the overall network (adapted from Moody and D. White 2003).

Again a network graph turns out to be a useful device, now to protect us from fallacy. Although a graph can't tell us everything we want to know about a social structure, Figure 2.3 shows what it can do very well: refute more than a thousand words.[12] Our conceptualization attempt stranded in the complexity of the subject, and for now we will have to retreat. We will return to cohesion in Chapter 5, better prepared, and then solve the inhomogeneity problem. On the positive side, we have learned a density measure that in the next chapter will get a new and much more useful role. Most importantly, we have learned that we must always be very careful in conceptualizing, and neither conceptualize intuitively appealing notions at the expense of precision, nor develop precision for its own sake.

SUGGESTED BACKGROUND READING

The most influential sociological paper on networks so far is Granovetter (1973), updated and extended a decade later (Granovetter 1983). Communities as "social foci" are introduced by Feld (1981), who also explains "Why your friends have more friends than you do," Feld (1991). Both papers by Feld are stepping stones toward the next couple of chapters.

EXERCISE 2.1

Choose at least 20 people whom you know, but not too many more, preferably from various social "circles" such as family, sport, university, and work. Think in advance if and why weighted or directed relations are called for; then make a file (see Chapter 8 on how to do this) and depict your ego network. Are there noticeable clusters or groups in the graph, which are internally more densely connected than the entire network? Compute the density by hand. Who after you has the highest degree in your network, and what does that mean socially?

EXERCISE 2.2

Rethink a familiar sociological problem from a network perspective, and write a research proposal for it in 2000 words. Add a section on how subjects would be selected and flesh out your measurement instruments. To do this well, bits and pieces from several subsequent chapters will be necessary, but the exercise is presented here because the research problem has to be thought through carefully over a longer time. In contrast to what you might think, this is the hardest exercise of all, and requires a great deal of attention to achieve sufficient coherence, rigor, focus, precision, and definition of the boundary of the network. In case you consider a questionnaire as measurement instrument, examples thereof can be found through the INSNA Website (www.insna.org/) and on Ron Burt's (http://faculty.chicagogsb. edu/ronald.burt/research/), and see Chapter 8.

Chapter 3

Small worlds

When I started studying sociology in 1987, our teachers told us that investigating social relations at large is very hard, because "we can't put society on our desk and examine it." Thanks to modern network analysis, using large data sets and computational power that have become available meanwhile, that statement is no longer true. It is no coincidence that the field of complex networks emerged along with the Internet, and the former uses the latter as a subject of study, not only as a means of communication. We can now investigate large social structures on personal computers and make visible patterns that eluded our predecessors. We can at the same time look at global network characteristics and at their constituting local structures, and see how they interrelate. In this chapter we will examine several important and very general properties of our society by putting it on our desk, so to speak.

To begin with, there are over 6 billion people on earth (and we can get a fairly accurate update of this number if we want to). Out of all these people, how many social contacts does an average person have, above a threshold (Chapter 2) making sure that all acquaintances are included? It turns out that, on average, people know about 750 others (Zheng, Salganik, and Gelman 2006), and not more than about 10,000, even though his number varies greatly from a hermit to a politician. Before actually counting ties, we should set the threshold for distinguishing between 0 (no tie) and 1 quite low and include all *weak ties* (Granovetter 1973). If the threshold were raised to close friendship or family – *strong ties* – the number of ties counted would be a great deal smaller, vary much less between people, and also be much more stable over time since weak ties are more volatile (Kossinets and Watts 2006).

Wherever one sets the threshold for tie strength, a certainty is that every person knows only a tiny fraction of all people on earth, about six or seven orders of magnitude fewer than there are, even for the best connected businessmen and politicians. Hence global density is very low indeed (since it could only approximate 1 if nearly everybody knew nearly everybody else), whereas the number of people on earth is enormous. Individuals are tied to their own clusters of family, friends, and acquaintances, who in turn are to some extent connected with each other, and thus are one step away from each other, or two steps via a focal person (*ego*). Hence it seems very unlikely that an arbitrary person elsewhere on this planet is related to ego through just a few intermediate persons. From a relational view on mankind, a fundamental question to ask is in how many steps, and along which paths, information (that is too subtle or confidential for the Internet) passes from elsewhere to here or the other way around.

Humans are *bounded rational*, which means that, although they wish to optimize their choices, they have limited capacity to search and process information (Simon 1997; Camerer and Fehr 2006; Conlisk 1996; Gigerenzer and Goldstein 1996; see also Gintis 2007). They have difficulty accounting for the future in current decisions (Gilbert and Wilson 2007; Glimcher, Kable, and Louie 2007; Fehr 2002), and have biases in perception and cognition. Although in any but the simplest situations they cannot maximize their decision outcomes, they can satisfice substantially better if they use information from others. But then this information should be accessible and not have to travel too far, otherwise too much gets lost on the way or it takes too long to arrive. Finally, distance is also relevant for the diffusion of influence and of diseases. For a multitude of reasons we want to know how far from each other are two arbitrary strangers. As has become widely known, it's only "six degrees of separation" – a truly small world after all. However, since personal experience is much more strongly influenced by someone's local and relatively dense environment than by more remote people, global short distances pass largely unnoticed. Therefore this small number always surprises people when they hear it for the first time. How are short distances possible? Why isn't average distance, say, a few hundred steps?

The small world phenomenon itself was first noticed in 1929, not by a scientist but by a fiction writer, Frigyes Karinthy,[1] then forgotten, and independently rediscovered by social scientists in the 1960s (see De Sola Pool and Kochen 1978 for an early overview). To explain the small average distance was a problem that haunted scholars for decades, until it was finally solved in 1998 by Duncan Watts. His paper, written together with his thesis adviser Steven Strogatz, has changed the way we look at social networks today, in particular because it was complemented by a large number of interdisciplinary papers in its wake.

A crucial step towards the view that changed the world was the insight that social networks, as well as many other nets, are neither ordered nor random, but are pretty much ordered with a touch of randomness. Order is imposed because people don't choose their close contacts at random, and neither do the contacts. First of all, and independently of cultural or other background, if two humans believe they are family, whether true or not, this belief makes a big difference for their chances of starting or having a social relation. Families are highly structured, i.e. the familiar family tree, and far away from random networks. Friendships, in contrast, are established on the basis of mutual (although possibly unequal) sympathy. Sympathy doesn't emerge between random pairs of people, even though first encounters of friends-to-be may be random. If two persons do not yet know each other but have strong ties with a common third person, however, there is a fair chance that they will subsequently connect with each other (Kossinets and Watts 2006), a phenomenon called *transitivity* (Rapoport 1953; Homans 1950),[2] which expresses the probability that a friend of a friend is a friend. Transitivity is very strong in families, and for siblings and cousins it approximates 1. Also for friends, transitivity is orders of magnitude larger than the probability for randomly chosen pairs of people to know each other. Only status differences, e.g. in a teacher's acquaintanceship with his or her students, hinder transitivity, and in such a case there is not an increased chance that students from separate classes will meet (Kossinets and Watts 2006). In general, transitivity captures the idea that two persons have a higher chance of having a tie because of ties to a common third (and fourth, etc.) person, be it family, friendship, or other types of relations. Furthermore, during the last century, a progressively larger number of people came to work within governmental and business organizations, where a hierarchical structure imposes orderly connections among large numbers of people, enforcing employees to become subordinates to managers and colleagues of each other. Along with work, people have other affiliations, such as sports, clubs, and social meeting grounds they prefer to or must go to. In general, having affiliations, or social foci, in common makes people more similar in terms of shared background and increases the chance that contacts will be established (Feld 1981; Kossinets and Watts 2006). Others argue, seemingly in contrast, that people more easily identify and start social relations with similar others, for example people sharing the same religion, social class or ethnicity, even without knowing them beforehand or having shared foci (McPherson, Smith-Lovin, and Cook 2001; Forsé and Chauvel 1995). It seems that both views are right, however, as follows. If shared foci and experiences happen relatively early on in life with people of distinguishable kind (e.g. ethnic, class, or religious), expectations are formed of these people's prosociality (Eshel and Cavalli-Sforza 1982) and associated with the relevant groups or social categories. In most cases, but not necessarily so, these shared experiences are with people of the same ethnic (or religious, and so on) group that ego comes from, which leads to *assortative mating*, also called "homophily," a preference for others that are similar to ego, at least in some aspect(s). But orphans growing up with families of different ethnicity identify strongly with their new families and friends, showing that homophily, although generally true, is not the ultimate cause of identification or of expected pro-sociality. In sum, transitivity and assortativeness (through shared foci or group identification) contribute to the orderliness of the global network. At the same time there are also random encounters, sometimes with long lasting consequences, for instance a holiday love affair that ends up in a marriage with children.

To show how order and randomness together make the world small, we go to the African savanna for a thought experiment.[3] There (or here, depending on where you read this text), people live in small huts, and a village is spread out over a considerable surface of land. Figure 3.1 illustrates a *cultivateur* in Manéga, Burkina Faso, and in the backdrop three granaries are visible. As a side remark, social networks is a field where *ideographic* approaches (which stress the uniqueness of a phenomenon, e.g. ethnography) and *nomothetic* approaches (stressing law-likeness) can seamlessly blend together (see Boissevain and Mitchell 1973; Mitchell 1969; Schweizer 1997; D. White and Johansen 2005).

For our thought experiment, and in contrast to actuality, we presume that the huts, each represented by a vertex in a graph, are positioned in a large circle constituting the village. We furthermore presume that the villagers are reciprocally related to people in the neighboring huts on each side of them, and with people in huts once removed, as in Figure 3.2a.[4] The implication is that information on one side of the village has to travel along many intermediate steps to the other side, and possibly never arrives because of attrition on the way. Attrition is an important issue in social networks (Granovetter 1973: 1365; H. White 1970), about which will be said more in subsequent chapters. One day, our *cultivateur* (Figure 3.1) receives a bicycle from his brother who lives in the capital. Now he can travel the large distance across the savanna to the opposite side of the village easily, and visit his other brother, with whom he has lost contact owing to the relatively large distance. Along with him he brings the latest gossip and news from his side of the village, and carries gossip and

■ *Figure 3.1* Villager with a bicycle in Manéga, Burkina Faso; granaries in the background. Photograph by the author (2005).

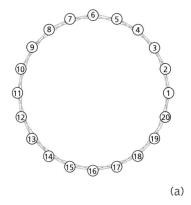

(a)

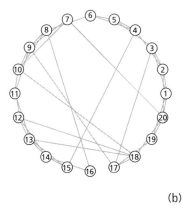

(b)

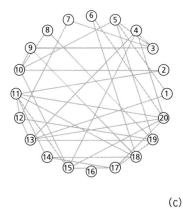

(c)

■ **Figure 3.2** *Increasing randomness, p, of edge rewiring, (a) p = 0, (b) p = 0.1,*
(c) p = 1. Adapted from Watts and Strogatz (1998).

news back to his own side on his return voyage a day later. As a consequence, villagers in both target and home settlements, as well as their neighbors, get news and gossip in much faster and much less distorted form than if the same information had passed the long way along all intermediate settlements. Their world has thus become "smaller."

Now the basic idea has been pointed out, we will follow the more abstract and general argument of the original paper, and start out with an ordered network, the regular lattice of Figure 3.2a. Its symmetry is totally unrealistic, but it has two crucial properties in common with large social networks: it is globally sparse and locally clustered, where the abstract clusters may represent families, organizations, groups of friends, or other foci. As a matter of fact, it is a very fruitful heuristic in general to start out with a simple and therefore comprehensible model that resembles the actual problem under investigation only in its most relevant features. Of course simplicity is no guarantee by itself that the model at hand is correct, but it is a necessary condition to comprehend complexity. Overly realistic models are as incomprehensible as reality itself: *qui trop embrasse mal étreint* (one's reach may exceed one's grasp). Once the simple model is well understood, realism, i.e. complexity, may be added stepwise, but one should stop adding complexity before losing track, bearing in mind that one may have "gained realism, but lost certainty" (Simon 1954: 414). Traits not crucial for explanatory purposes should therefore be left out, and if they are meaningful in other ways they may be dealt with by the ethnographer or by the historian.

In Figure 3.2a, the lattice network has no randomness at all ($p = 0$), and the average distance is relatively large – obviously not for 20 vertices but for thousands or more vertices, the figure would become unclear. In Figure 3.2b, some of the edges in the network are rewired by increasing overall randomness slightly ($p = 0.1$), as if several villagers were sent out to cycle to randomly chosen destinations. In Figure 3.2c, randomness is maximal ($p = 1$).

The effect of increasing randomness on *path length* (i.e. number of steps along a chain of ties, or for a sequence of arcs consecutively in the direction of the arrows, without repeating steps)[5] is demonstrated by focusing on two simple network characteristics that capture the most basic features of the network: local clustering on the one hand, and global connectedness by network paths on the other hand. The third characteristic, low density, is guaranteed by holding constant the number of edges. The first network measure was introduced as (global) density in the previous chapter, but here it gets a new role as *local clustering* (by modifying its index set), the proportion of someone's contacts that are mutually connected with each other. If on average alters are highly interconnected, local clustering is high; if they are mostly disconnected, clustering is low. The difference with density is that the local clustering measure is limited to ego networks and that the ties of the focal actor are left out of the equation, because, by definition, ego has ties with all his or her neighbors, which therefore adds no information. Notice that a cluster is not a clearly defined object, in contrast to a clique. A cluster is a relatively denser area within a sparse network, and the local clustering measure does not deal with cluster boundaries.

Local clustering

Focal actor i has edges with n_i neighbors (if there are arcs, they will here be considered as edges). Only the number of edges between i's neighbors, m_{ij} are taken into account, not the edges between ego and his or her neighbors. As for density, the actual number of edges m_i between i's neighbors, n_i, is divided by the maximum possible, $n_i(n_i - 1)/2$, if all neighbors are mutually connected:[6]

$$Cl_i = 2m_i/n_i(n_i - 1) \qquad\qquad \text{(Def. 3.1)}$$

Taking the mean of all vertices' local clustering values, Cl, yields a measure of local clustering of the entire network, which is used in small world models. An alternative measure of local clustering, which yields slightly different numbers but the same qualitative result, focuses on transitivity: it compares the number *triads* in the entire network (in a triad, i, j, and k are mutually connected) with the number of *triples* (when there is a path from x to y but x and y are possibly unconnected), assuming there is at least one triple (otherwise the denominator equals 0). Since for each triad there are three possible triples wherein the pair (i, j) or (j, k) or (i, k) is possibly unconnected, and to keep the resulting measure between 0 and 1, *transitivity* is defined as follows:

$$T = 3 \times \text{triads/connected triples} \qquad\qquad \text{(Def. 3.2)}$$

Transitivity is not calculated for ego networks first, but directly for the entire network, so there is no mean to be taken. For small world models, local clustering and transitivity can be used interchangeably, and they yield qualitatively the same results.

Along with local clustering, networks are characterized by the number of steps, or edges, information has to travel in the shortest path connecting one person with another. For an arbitrary ego, his or her contacts are at social distance 1 away from him or her, and the friends' friends that ego does not know directly are at distance 2 apart. As said earlier, one friend may live next door and another in another continent, but network researchers abstract away from geographic distance (most of the time). If between actors i and j there are several others, there may be several alternative paths from i to j, but we are after the shortest path. Of shortest paths there may again be several in parallel, each of the same length, but that will not concern us here (it will in later chapters). A chic word for shortest path is *geodesic*, and the mean geodesic of the entire network characterizes an important global property. Now global distance is precisely defined as mean geodesic; we may refer to it informally as average (shortest) path length. The *diameter*, in contrast, is defined as the *longest* geodesic. Of a clique, the mean geodesic is of course 1 (which follows from the definition of clique), but how about the human race?

In a perfectly ordered network without randomness (Figure 3.2a), the average geodesic is long, whereas in a random network (Figure 3.2c), it is short and scales logarithmically with the number of vertices. The most interesting thing is what happens at small to intermediate levels of randomness, as in actual networks that are between order and randomness. If the probability of edge rewiring is just 0.01, the average geodesic plummets to a value close to that of a random network, while local clustering is at almost its initial level of the ordered network (as in Figure 3.2a). In other words, the discrepancy between clustering (high) and distance (low) is very high. Thus with a dash of randomness in otherwise ordered social contacts, e.g. a few bicycle rides in Burkina Faso or a holiday love affair out of your local circle of friends, local clustering remains high, while path lengths become a great deal shorter, characterizing a small world.[7] At increasing randomness, e.g. from 0.01 to 0.1 (Figure 3.2b), the average geodesic decreases further but not nearly as much as in the step from 0 to 0.01, while local clustering, although decreasing, is still at a considerably higher level than in a random network. Only at much higher levels of randomness, above 0.5, does local clustering decrease substantially. This computational result of low average distance and high clustering in a sparse graph has been generalized from lattice networks to empirical networks, initially by Mark Newman (2001, 2003) and later by many others. In fact, the short distance property turned out to be so general that any large sparse network that has some degree of randomness has it (Watts 2004). Also, if weak ties are removed, for many networks the remainder strong-tie network has only modestly longer average distance (Shi, Adamic, and Strauss 2007). The small world model thus provides us a general characterization of our cosmopolitan *Gesellschaft* (society) at large, with our cozy *Gemeinschaften* (communities) within it, and we may conclude that "We are all bound together in a tightly knit social fabric" (Milgram 1967: 67). Rather than networks in plural, there is in fact one global network, albeit with many clusters and many different kinds of relations.[8]

It would be interesting to know how global distance and local clustering have changed over the past 500 years or longer, but lacking data we can only guess. For average distance, several tendencies worked in opposite directions. Globalization shortened distances, but nobody knows how much. For some parts of the world, the consequences of shortening distances are well described historically but data on actual distances are not available. Covering the period from 1870 to 1914, Eugen Weber (1976) showed in an analysis of France how local languages and customs vanished in favor of the French language, during a time when new roads and railroads shortened distances, and nationalistic politics and a uniform school system made inroads into formerly remote provinces. A counter-tendency is the increasing number of people. Its effect on the average distance is modest, however, because, as said, average distance scales logarithmically with the number of people in the network. While the human race has increased to over ten times the numbers it had in 1500, average distance has increased less than a tie's length. Additionally, social contacts made possible by the Internet have a substantial impact on distances.

An interesting application of the small world theory is to the world of corporate governance. Boards of directors control a substantial amount of economic assets and, because of their influence on the global economy, they form an important subject of investigation. Some critics have suggested that company boards have actually too much control of the economy, by forming a dense, collusive network of wealthy people. Using the theories of random networks and small worlds, we can now compare: Is the average distance of the actual network of boards shorter and the clustering higher than what we may expect on the basis of random chance? That might indicate collusion.

A board consists of directors who all know each other, and some directors may function on several boards. If two boards have a director in common, a connecting edge is drawn in the network representation of boards, as a bridge through which rumors and ideas, such as business practices, can pass from one board to another. A *bridge* connects two otherwise unconnected components of a network.[9] The pertaining data matrix, called an *incidence matrix*, has companies in the columns. In Table 3.1, Directors 1 and 2 both sit on the board of Company 1, while Director 2 also sits on the board of Company 2, thereby connecting the two boards. The graph is called *bipartite*, because there are two kinds of entities, persons and their affiliations; a complementary graph can be drawn of all directors and their mutual connections, based on the same incidence matrix. Incidence matrices and their bipartite graphs can be used for whatever affiliations are of interest to the researcher, be it church attendances, sport teams, classrooms, settlements, or armed robberies (see Breiger 1974).[10] Other applications of bipartite graphs are individuals exposed to media, and measures of multigroup affiliations.

The networks of boards and of directors in the US, Germany, and the UK turn out to be very sparse, and therefore suitable subjects of small world analysis. The pertaining statistics applied to bipartite graphs need a little correction with respect to simple graphs, because one wants to discern clustering that goes beyond the cliques already given by the board structure (Newman, Watts, and Strogatz 2002).[11]

■ **Table 3.1** *Incidence matrix of directors and company boards*

	Comp. 1	Comp. 2	. . .	Comp. s
Dir. 1	1	0	. . .	0
Dir. 2	1	1	. . .	0
. . .	. . .	. . .	. . .	. . .
Dir. n	0	. . .	. . .	1

With the corrections put in place, actual and expected clustering turn out to be virtually the same, whereas the actual path lengths are slightly longer than in their random counterparts (Conyon and Muldoon 2006). This result is similar for the three different economies under investigation. Although boards are surely influential, the small world analysis suggests that the "collusion of the elite" hypothesis should go by the board.

Social elite studies from a network perspective have a tradition dating back before the Wattsian small world model (Scott 1991 gives an early overview). Some of the most interesting studies are longitudinal, showing how changes in the corporate directorship network relate to macro-economic developments (for the Netherlands, Mokken and Stokman 1978, replicated by Heemskerk 2007). Other examples are studies of the French financial elite (Kadushin 1995), the Japanese corporate network (Gerlach 1992), and the diffusion and adoption of certain types of contract (golden parachutes and poison pills) in the United States (Davis and Greve 1997).

After speaking only about large and sparse networks so far, it might be useful to end this chapter by pointing out that, paradoxically, some worlds are in fact too small to be small worlds. Cliques, for example, can't possibly be. There is no room for randomness at all, and they are too full of ties, connecting everybody to everybody else at distance 1. It's an insightful exercise to produce more examples.

SUGGESTED BACKGROUND READING

The small world story by Frigyes Karinthy, in Braun (2004); small world experiments before the Internet, Milgram (1967); the solution of the problem, introductory, Collins and Chow (1998), told to sociologists, Watts (1999a), and the landmark paper, Watts and Strogatz (1998); finally, small worlds at book length, Watts (1999b).

EXERCISE 3.1

Analyze the small world nature of a reasonably large undirected network, for instance a large data set from the Web, or a so-called power law network, further explained in the next chapter, generated by computer (see "barabasi-albert" or "barabasi.game," Chapter 8). In the latter case, generate a network with 1 . . . . vertices, where the dots are to be filled in with the last four digits of your student ID or social security number, and an average degree of 20. Compare this network with a random network (see "erdos.renyi," Chapter 8) with the same order (n, number of vertices) and size (m, number of ties). In a small world, the mean geodesic L_{actual} is roughly equal to L_{random}, whereas T_{actual} is much higher than T_{random} (and, as mentioned, Cl and T can be substituted for each other), except in sparse power-law networks. The computation of average path distance may take a few minutes, depending on your computer, although clustering should go faster. There are neither exact values for these variables at which a large world turns small, like $0°$ Celsius for ice to melt into water, nor statistical tests, so one has to compare one's results with those from other studies in the literature. It might be handy to realize that $m/n = \frac{1}{2} \langle k \rangle$, where $\langle k \rangle$ stands for mean degree.

Chapter 4

Searching and fat tails

In the global network spanning mankind, bounded rational people have very limited and mostly only local information about the network. Long distances are in most cases spanned by chains of weak ties, of which people are aware at best dimly, if at all. People's knowledge is mostly about their direct contacts, and they are progressively less aware of what is going on further away from them in the global network. Global network spanning paths (as in Figure 3.2) may be short in theory, but perhaps more relevant is the question if and how people can find such paths in practice. Psychologically, distances to socially distant people are enormous indeed, being not just six or seven steps apart but six or seven social circles or communities apart (Milgram 1967: 67). For a network to be *searchable* by individuals, (1) the distances have to be feasibly small, as in small worlds, but also (2) in each subsequent step along a path, a message should hone in on its target person rather than moving away from it or randomly moving around and overshooting its target (D. White and Houseman 2003). To solve the *searchability* problem, the computer scientist Jon Kleinberg (2000) offered an elegant model, starting out with the assumption of local knowledge. Like Watts, Kleinberg also used an unrealistic lattice network, in his case a grid with clear-cut dimensions (two, in the simplest case, as in Figure 4.1), wherein everybody has four neighbors close by (as in the small world lattices, Figure 3.2a), plus a fifth contact at a distance yet to be established (Figure 4.1).

Our villager in Burkina Faso, now living on a two-dimensional grid, might then know four near neighbors and, with a bit of luck, one person far away in the village, whom he might use to find yet further removed people. For the fifth contact to be established, between a focal person i and a person j, a "luck" parameter determines the probability of the contact proportional to the grid distance, and this probability decays with distance.[1] When the parameter value is large, only a local tie is feasible, at distance 1, which implies that j is a close neighbor, and remote people are too many steps away and stay out of reach. No luck for i. When the parameter equals 0, on the other hand, the tie has a random chance of ending up anywhere in the

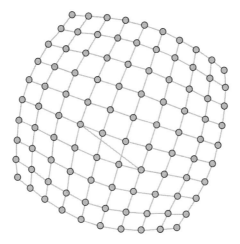

Figure 4.1 *Lattice wherein a focal actor has a fifth contact.*

network, as is also true for the ties of everybody else, but leaping through the resulting messy network will usually not bring i's message closer to j, by overshooting the
target. No luck either. Since in Watts's small world model (i.e. a one-dimensional,
albeit circular, lattice) ties were rewired randomly, his model is in fact unsearchable.
It therefore seems that in his simplification of the real world he had gone too far.
Kleinberg's counter-intuitive result was that the lattice network is only searchable
when the luck parameter equals (or is very close to) the number of dimensions of
the lattice. It was an interesting result because it pointed out that in many possible small worlds, wherein the parameter and the dimensionality diverge too far
from each other, people won't be able to find distant others – presupposing that
Web search engines don't exist in those worlds. How seriously do we have to take
Kleinberg's criticism of the small world model?

Kleinberg's lattice is of course "too" homogeneous, whereas we already noticed
in Chapter 2 that human societies are inhomogeneous on account of ethnic, national,
religious, and other affiliations. How about searchability in the real world? Long
before the Internet existed, Stanley Milgram and others conducted experiments
wherein senders in the United States had to forward a letter to a target recipi-
ent, elsewhere in the United States, by first sending the message to someone that
they thought might be closer to the target (Milgram 1967; Travers and Milgram
1969; De Sola Pool and Kochen 1978). The search task was then handed to that
second person, and so on, until the message arrived at the target person. Nowadays
the Internet, being a global network with a great many users, offers possibilities
for large-scale and global empirical studies. Dodds, Muhamad, and Watts (2003)
conducted a field experiment on the Internet involving 60,000 people. There was a
great deal of attrition of messages along the way, and after the first step, which still
had a reasonable chance of being completed, at each subsequent step only half of the

messages were passed on. Many chains were thus not completed, which was partly a motivational problem, too, because senders might have had "ill temper, business, absent-mindedness, distrust of scientists, lack of inspiration, and other motives or lack of motive" (H. White 1970: 260). Attrition being taken into account, this field experiment confirmed the small world prediction nevertheless: for target and sender in the same country, their distance turned out to be about 5, and for those in different countries it was about 7 (and without attrition it was only 4). This study taught us two things: first, the world is basically searchable even for people having local knowledge only; second, affiliations, countries in this study, do make a difference. In earlier small world experiments, as well as in the Internet experiment, it turned out that people use cues that they think the receiver has in common with the target person, of which geographic *proximity* and *profession* are the two most important (Killworth and Bernard 1978). Watts and his colleagues (2002) showed in a computer simulation that when people with only local knowledge use multiple cues about social affiliations, for instance country in a first step and profession in a subsequent step, small world networks are searchable over a wide range of conditions (see also Watts 2003). This result implied that Kleinberg's constraint (that the luck parameter should equal the dimensionality of the lattice) does not hold for social networks, wherein people usually have multiple affiliations that can be used to search them. People do make mistakes in searching for others, of course, and paths therefore tend to be longer than strictly necessary; in a small network study of $n = 99$, actual paths were about 50 percent longer than the shortest paths, which in this particular case were known to the researchers (Killworth *et al*. 2005). Moreover, searchability is a statistical regularity and implies not that everybody can be found easily by everybody else, but that large social networks are searchable for the average person.

SCALE-FREE DEGREE DISTRIBUTIONS

Although Watts's initial lattice model was too unrealistic, in the sense that it can't explain why the actual world is searchable, it stood up to scrutiny, because its explanation of the world's smallness – for which the model was designed – still holds. But there turned out to be another oddity. As mentioned briefly in Chapter 3, some people have few acquaintances whereas others, such as politicians, have thousands. This high variation in degree was known for a long time, and initially it was believed that it has approximately a normal distribution (a bell-shaped, or Gaussian, curve), with a mean degree and a variance about the mean; a politician would be on the high end of the distribution, a hermit on the low end, and most of us somewhere in between, as in Figure 4.2a. For a random network, this assumption would not be extravagant (in fact it's Poisson, which is pretty close to Gaussian), and in Watts's and Kleinberg's models every vertex is given the same (average) degree accordingly, which sounds like a reasonable first approximation. But is it?

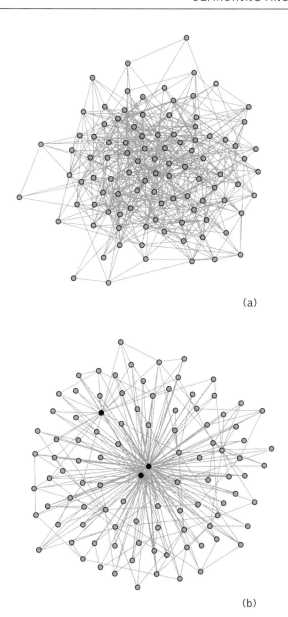

(a)

(b)

■ **Figure 4.2** *A random network (a) and a power law network (b) with same order (number of vertices) and size (number of ties). Hubs (here, vertices with degree above 18) are in black, and are nonexistent in the random network.*

Barabási and Albert (1999) discovered and explained another very general net-work trait. Some people turn out to have incredibly many acquaintances and friends

– substantially more than one would expect in a random network – whereas most people have quite a bit fewer, forming a highly skewed distribution, very different from a normal distribution (as in Figure 4.2b). The same skewed degree distribution holds for many other social (and non-social) relations as well, for instance Web pages and their indegree.[2] On a logarithmic scale on both horizontal and vertical axes, a straight line fits the degree distribution, a hallmark of a so-called *power law*, or *scale-free*, distribution.[3] The vertical axis in Figure 4.3 is a cumulative frequency distribution (and $10^0 = 1$). The straight line is a power law distribution. For comparison, there is a (truncated) Gaussian two lines beneath it, which for clarity of the figure has its mean at 0. In a Gaussian or Poisson distribution, the chances of meeting somebody with many contacts, or with some other value much higher than average, are negligible. In power law distributions, in contrast, the chance of encountering highly connected people, or generally an event with a high value, is considerably higher. The highly connected vertices, with a prominent presence in a network, therefore play an important role, for example if it comes to spreading contagious diseases (Pastor-Satorras and Vespignani 2001). Indeed, the networks of sexual contacts in Sweden, Britain, and Zimbabwe turned out to be power-law distributed (Liljeros *et al.* 2001, 2003; Schneeberger *et al.* 2004).

Power laws turn out to be widespread and are not confined to networks. A century ago, Pareto discovered that income distributions follow a power law (in his time not yet so called), which means that a large portion of all income is received by a small portion of the population. Meanwhile social inequality has increased and the Pareto distribution has become more skewed than it was, but is still power-law distributed. With respect to wealth and income it is important to notice that differences thereof are not predicted by how many friends one has, and more sophisticated centrality measures are necessary, which we will encounter in Chapter 6. Another example of a power law is task completion, such as responding to mail. We have sufficient

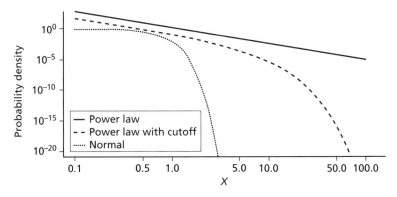

■ *Figure 4.3* Power law (straight line on top), power law with exponential cutoff (in the middle, still fat-tailed), and normal (Gaussian) distribution. Variable x can stand for degree or any other property.

data about a few famous people from the past, and we know about both Albert Einstein and Charles Darwin that they replied very quickly to most letters, but some senders had to wait for months or years before they received an answer, and all response times together form a perfect power law distribution (Gama Oliveira and Barabási 2005).[4] In modern times, people are no different in replying to their email (Barabási 2005). For weighted networks, tie strengths, e.g. the duration of telephone calls, turn out to be power-law distributed (Onnela *et al.* 2007), which means that people have few very strong ties and many weak ties (Barrat *et al.* 2004). Also subjects as diverse as strikes (Biggs 2005) and hospital waiting lists feature power laws, which in the latter case means that some people must wait an extremely long time before they get medical treatment (Smethurst and Williams 2001). Using modern transportation, traveling distances within a time interval of a couple of days are power-law distributed, with most people staying close to their homes and few people traveling far (Brockmann, Hufnagel, and Geisel 2006; for other examples, see Barabási 2002, Ball 2004).

Bear in mind that some researchers have a different custom of representation, mathematically equally sound, and use the horizontal axis for the *rank order* of people according to their degree, or of cities according to their sizes (then called Zipf distribution). Contrary to the regular representation of a power law, the lowest ranks in a Zipf distribution are of those people with the highest degree, and the rank order distribution features a so-called "long tail" along the horizontal axis, of people with few contacts rather than many (Adamic and Huberman 2002).

A last example for now is the power law distribution of citations of scientific papers (Lotka 1926; De Solla Price 1965). Scientific work forms a graph of papers as vertices, and citations as arcs pointing to papers being cited, or, to put it another way, to sources where information is sought. This is a network not of social relations between people but of knowledge sources (papers) pointing to other knowledge sources where ideas came from. This example brings us back to the question whether scale-free networks would refute the small world model by having a very different topology. It turned out that large scale-free networks have short distances indeed, which is in fact easy to comprehend. A few hubs having many ties make distances from and to all other vertices shorter, as in the global airline network with hubs in Beijing and Los Angeles, among others, which also happens to have a power law distribution. This network makes it possible to fly everywhere on earth by changing planes not a vast number of times but only a few times at hubs (Barabási 2002). You should not believe everything you read, though, and should experiment on a computer, generate scale-free networks, and assess if their distances match the small world prediction (see Chapter 8). Power law networks of social relations are easily searchable in principle, because distances are short and by using a few hubs a target can be found. In practice, however, social hubs would get overwhelmed with requests beyond their capabilities, and using hubs in actual searches (if the vertices are not computers) would therefore be inefficient. It turns out that people do not especially look for hubs in their searching behavior (Dodds, Muhamad, and Watts 2003) and if they do, in a large organization where this was investigated, their searches take more steps than the average number (Adamic and Adar 2005).

Explaining the emergence of power laws in networks is quite simple. An informal explanation was provided by the sociologist Robert Merton (1968a), who called it the Matthew effect:[5] put briefly, the rich get richer, resulting in proportional growth. As the population of humans (or that of scientific papers) grows, new members attach themselves to incumbents (or cite already existing papers). Vertices having slightly more ties, which initially happens by random chance, have a proportionally higher chance to receive yet more ties from newcomers. Initially small differences then grow into large differences. In Merton's case, more famous scientists have a higher chance to get funding and other advantages than less famous scientists, and the differences increase. This mechanism was laid out formally for degree by Barabási and Albert (1999), who called it *preferential attachment*, and discovered it for scientific co-authorships (Barabási *et al*. 2002), among others.[6] The principle cast in mathematics does not tell whether sending or receiving actors take the initiative of attachment, which increases the range of sociological applications. Also the following variation of preferential attachment leads to the same outcome. Newcomers, possibly ignorant, attach themselves to incumbents, possibly more knowledgeable, who in turn re-link some of these new ties according to the principle of preferential attachment (Krapivsky and Redner 2001). Preferential attachment is a very parsimonious way to explain the emergence of power laws.

Many networks do have power law distributions but not all of them. For example in the network of scientific collaborations (Newman 2001), email contacts at a university (Guimerà *et al*. 2003), and a number of other cases, if actors have very high degree, they are *less* likely to receive more ties, for example because by then they spend all their time on the ties they have, or because at some point they retire. These distributions better fit a power law with *exponential cutoff*, a cousin of the power law that features a still fatter tail than a Gaussian but not as fat as power laws (Figure 4.3 in the middle).[7] In contrast, distributions of ties that cost considerable effort to maintain, such as close friendships, or of ties that rapidly dissolve if left unattended, are closer to a normal distribution than to a power law (Amaral *et al*. 2000). Nobody has a very high number of very close friends, hence the distribution of close friendships cannot have a fat tail. Distributions of ties that either require a great deal of maintenance or disappear when ties age, or both, feature a (close to) normal distribution. The less maintenance a kind of tie requires, or the less ties age, the more skewed the pertaining tie distribution becomes, and the more closely it approximates a power law. Power laws and their mathematical relatives are not universal but abundant nevertheless, and have also been found for networks that not only grow but also, more realistically, lose some of their vertices and ties (Barabási 2002).

A similar caveat applies to preferential attachment. It is a very simple mechanism but if it were the only mechanism at work it would result in very low values of local clustering, and we know that this isn't the case empirically. Another counter-example is the rank order of cities that follows a power law, but fluctuations in rank order positions refute proportional growth (Batty 2006). In actual networks there are usually multiple growth mechanisms at work simultaneously, which together produce power laws with exponential cutoffs, not exactly power laws. When modeling multiple mechanisms, parsimony has to give in, and growth dynamics of networks then becomes a rather complex issue, which some pursue into the foundations of statistical physics (D. White *et al.* 2006; see Boon and Tsallis 2005) and others through exponential random graph models (Robins, Pattison, and Wollcock 2005).

There is yet another very general feature of large social networks. People with many contacts tend to be related to others with many contacts, as hubs in airline networks are directly connected. A graph with a high correlation of degree is called *assortative*, and ego's preference for alters with similar degree is sometimes called assortative mixing (Newman and Park 2003). The more general notion is assortative mating, e.g. choosing similar friends, where similarity can be gender, social class, or another affiliation, and in the literature assortative mixing and mating are used interchangeably. Assortative gender mating occurs in networks of humans, dolphins (Lusseau and Newman 2004), and monkeys (Silk 2007). However, this general feature is not universal; for example, it does not hold for Internet dating communities (Holme, Edling, and Liljeros 2004) possibly because the way people present themselves on the Internet is unrelated to their pro-social behavior.

If we take random networks as a baseline for comparison (Solomonoff and Rapoport 1951; Rapoport 1957), we can now understand the Jefferson High School network (Figure 2.1) and its underlying mechanisms, which we could not yet grasp when we started off in Chapter 2. Bearman, Moody, and Stovel (2004) pointed out first of all that the network is far from a random network. Although it is sparse, it is too ordered to be a small world, and the mean geodesic is too long. This is obviously an artifact of the data, because the threshold for sexual relations is much higher than it is supposed to be for small world studies; if ties of acquaintanceship were added, the average distance would decrease considerably. As it turned out, the giant component could be generated in a computer simulation by two mechanisms simultaneously at work. First, assortative mixing on the basis of sexual experience, i.e. the less experienced mix with each other, whereas the more experienced look for more experienced partners. Second, the prohibition of cycles of four (C_4); a *cycle* is a path along (at least two) distinct ties through a network that ends at the vertex where it started. Borrowing from Goethe's novel *Elective Affinities*, suppose Eduard is partnered with Charlotte and the Captain is with Ottilie. At some point in time Eduard and Ottilie form a new couple, but according to the ehtos of Jefferson High, it would be humiliating for the Captain and Charlotte to form a second partnership; they would face public scorn if they tied up with each other. Therefore C_4 configurations didn't occur. Outside the confines of the school this prohibition is less strict, possibly non-existent, and assortative patterns are more complex. There is more randomness out there, making the larger world smaller, with the drawback that many people are exposed to a higher risk of catching a sexual disease there than at school.

When using data with an appropriate threshold for tie strength (Chapter 2), all large social networks, although sparse, have short path distances as a consequence of some low degree of randomness (Chapter 3). Moreover, people don't choose their social contacts randomly and, owing to transitivity and assortativeness, social networks are locally clustered (Chapter 3). In this chapter we saw that short paths that are present can in principle also be found, thus the world is searchable for people with only local knowledge who use multiple cues for social affiliations, such as country and profession. Surprisingly, distributions of social contacts turned out to be fat-tailed, which also holds for distributions of tie strength and many other properties. High-maintenance ties, of which nobody can have many, are an exception. Most social networks also exhibit assortativeness, except on the Internet; the rule and the exceptions might be explained by expectations of pro-sociality or the lack thereof, respectively. Taking the exceptions into account, we have identified seven very general structural characteristics of our society: sparseness, short distances, searchability, fat tails, and assortativeness and transivity, which in turn lead to local clustering.

SUGGESTED BACKGROUND READING

The first power law discovered in networks, De Solla Price (1965); the mother paper of the general theory, Barabási and Albert (1999); the general theory popularized, Barabási and Bonabeau (2003); sexual contacts, Liljeros *et al*. (2001); an introduction to grand-scale small world experiments, Granovetter (2003); the actual paper (Dodds, Muhamad, and Watts 2003) is great but might be too technical. An introduction to power laws is Adamic and Huberman (2002).

EXERCISE 4.1

Check out the degree distribution of the network from Exercise 3.1 (see Chapter 8).

Chapter 5

Communities

Detection, conflict, cohesion, and culture

Small world analysis showed that the world is locally clustered, but where the boundaries of the clusters or communities are is yet unclear. We may have information about group identities or assortativeness, but identities often emerge in the course of group processes and are in general not given in advance. When studying social animals like humans, a first task for a social scientist or biologist is to determine in what groups they live on the basis of relational data only, as well as the cohesion that binds group members together. When trying to conceptualize social cohesion in Chapter 2, we came aground on density as a measure, because cohesion is distributed inhomogeneously over society at large, whereas density can turn out only a single value for an entire network, or for an arbitrary subnetwork[1] thereof. In fact we have two distinct problems to solve. One is to find communities or groups within a larger network in which inter-community density is higher than intra-community density. A special case is a community in conflict that is partitioned into two opposing groups. The second problem is to determine cohesion within (and, if one wishes, adhesion between) these communities. Once we have solved these two problems of assessment, there is a deeper question: why there exist cohesive communities at all. Many animals are solitary and, if they collaborate, it is only with close kin, with whom they have many genes in common, e.g. parents and offspring. Nevertheless, these more solitary animals seem to fare well and exist on this planet much longer than we do. Even highly intelligent social animals like apes are not nearly as cooperative with non-kin as humans are, and their communities are smaller and less complex (Herrmann *et al.* 2007).

In this chapter, we will first see how communities can be determined. Subsequently, we will explicate social cohesion, and see how it can be measured precisely. Then we will go into the problem of explaining human cooperation, and see how the network approach can contribute to solving it, complementing insights from biology and evolutionary game theory. As it turns out, culture – information that people acquire from others (e.g. rules, values, symbols, technology) – is crucially important for cooperation, as it is for social life in general. In the last parts of this chapter, we will revisit communities from an evolutionary perspective, which makes it possible to analyze their culture(s), cohesion, and cooperation, or lack thereof, in a unified framework.

COMMUNITY DETECTION

If it is clear in advance what specific kinds of groups one is after, for example of certain professional groups or clans, it is important to use data that are sufficiently specific to these groups, because a mixture of professional ties and kinship and other kinds of ties in the same data set would yield quite different community boundaries from if, say, only professional ties are used, and might ruin the result of the analysis. In general, any kind of positive ties will do for community detection. Some people are connected by random chance, for instance a leader who as representative of her group has many ties and different social activities and is bound to meet other group leaders. Obviously, for two group leaders, having a tie doesn't imply they belong to the same group. Put another way, if a bunch of Mikado sticks is dropped on the table and some fall together in a group, this does not imply there is intrinsically some mechanism that systematically forms groups, since their falling the given way was a consequence of random chance. So, when searching communities in a data set, one wishes to find them over and above the "communities" that would be present in a random network with the same order (number of vertices) and degree distribution. In the previous chapters, the basis for comparison was a random network of the same order and size (number of ties), in which degree has a Poisson distribution, but here we will take the actual degree distribution, which need not be Poisson and can be scale-free.[2]

Once ties have been distributed over a set of actors, these ties will become channels for gossip, sympathy, mockery, anger, and other emotion and information exchange, and will establish a level of cohesion in that community, whether the ties were initially established randomly, intentionally, or both. Whether you met your partner in the street or through a common friend does not matter any more today; now it is your tie that binds you. So the second problem, of determining cohesion within (and adhesion between) communities, should therefore not be treated statistically.

Although finding communities such that internal density is higher than between communities seems to be an easy job, it is a computationally hard problem because in large graphs there are vastly many possible groups and group overlaps. Jörg Reichardt and Stefan Bornholdt (2006a, with a run-up in 2004) found a general theoretical solution, by representing the problem in a so-called Hamiltonian equation, or Potts spin glass model,[3] for which statistical physics had analytic tools and algorithms at hand (i.e. simulated annealing; Kilpatrick, Gelatt, and Vecci 1983). The overall approach, which most community-finding approaches have in common, is one of optimization, by maximizing "rewards" and minimizing "penalties." Assignments (by the computer) of pairs of (strongly) connected vertices to the same community and unconnected (or weakly connected) vertices to different communities are rewarded. Assignments of pairs of vertices connected by (strong) ties to different communities and unconnected (or weakly connected) pairs to the same community are punished. For example, in Figure 2.3 there is clearly a group on the left hand side and another on the right hand side, further subdivisions left aside, and vertex 7 seems to belong to both. A well-functioning grouping algorithm should enable determination of these two groups by rewarding and punishing itself in the appropriate manner, and should possibly continue with further subdivisions. So far so good, but the major question is how to set the values of the rewards and punishments in order to determine communities well.

A crucial step was to treat this value-setting problem as uncertainty on the part of the researcher, and then to set the values according to a probability distribution (Reichardt and Bornholdt 2006a). This boils down to comparing the actual tie values, from empirical data, with the expected tie values. (Remember that a valued graph and a multigraph can be translated into each other, as was explained in Chapter 2.)[4]

When comparing the actual edge values with the expected values, the *modularity* (Newman and Girvan 2004) of a given assignment of vertices to communities can be computed: the number of edges falling within the communities minus the expected number in its random counterpart with the same degree distribution. Modularity was an important advancement over older methods and became standard in most recent community-finding approaches (e.g. Newman 2006a,b).[5] In the Hamiltonian approach, modularity is a corollary of, and therefore a special case of, a more general and more fundamental theory that underlies it. Searching for further improvement in assigning vertices to communities should stop if the modularity does not further increase, and the algorithm automatically finds the optimum. Notice that there can be different assignments of vertices with the same or very similar modularity values, hinting at group overlaps, which are then to be further evaluated on sociological grounds. The possibility of detecting group overlaps is important because many people are members of different communities at the same time. In practice, however, group overlaps strongly depend on the kind of relationship, thus the data used, for the obvious reason that people at work have different group overlaps from those that the same people have among their friends. A parameter (gamma) makes it possible to set the "coarseness" of community finding to allow for subgroups to be found within larger groups, if the (sub)groups are hierarchically ordered, or to find group overlaps if the groups are non-hierarchical. For example, the Internet community of a Spanish university showed a hierarchical structure of nested sub-communities, that is, of smaller communities being part of larger ones (detected with a different approach from that discussed here, Guimerà et al. 2003). Over a range from two to a hundred group members, the distribution of the number of subcommunities was power-law distributed. Because the order of the network was limited, the power law distribution was truncated for subcommunities larger than 100. For a given data set, the researcher should experiment with several different values of the parameter to check out the results. A default value of 1 yields a neutral result and optimal community detection. Subsequently choosing higher values sets the "grain size" finer and may spot more and smaller subcommunities, if there are any, whereas lower values set the grain size coarser, to search for a smaller number of supercommunities. Last but not least, the Hamiltonian approach can deal with valued arcs as well, not only edges.

If the actual communities are strongly pronounced, and thus divert a great deal from the network's random counterpart by having few inter-community ties and high density within communities, the modularity will be high. If the actual communities are less pronounced, having more between-group ties, community finding becomes more difficult, to the point where they vanish in a sea of random noise and community detection over and above communities that exist randomly is no longer possible. Moreover, for sparse graphs, their randomized equivalents have higher intrinsic modularity than dense random graphs of the same order, and therefore it is more difficult in sparse graphs to find communities that stand out from randomness (Reichardt and Bornholdt 2006b).

Data don't speak, but sometimes they "whisper" (said Gianluca Carnabuci, personal communication). Acknowledging the fundamental limitations of community finding, the sophisticated Hamiltonian approach can detect communities by listening to the whispering of relational data, without any information on social identities or other attributes.[6]

Some researchers look further inside communities at micro patterns, and ask if certain kinds of triads or other patterns occur more often than can be expected randomly for a given degree distribution. This work has a tradition dating back to the *triad census* by Davis, Holland, and Leinhardt in the 1970s (Davis 1979, reviewed by Wasserman and Faust 1994; see also Skvoretz, Fararo, and Agneessens 2004), and is now called *network motifs* (Milo *et al*. 2002, 2004a; debated by Artzy-Randrup *et al*. 2004 and, in a reply, Milo *et al*. 2004b).

CONFLICT

Triads with special interest are *imbalanced* ones, as Fritz Heider (1946) pointed out first, wherein a friend of ego becomes an enemy of another friend of ego, as in Figure 5.1 top left, or, alternatively, three friends all become enemies of each other, as in Figure 5.1 below left. Notice that in Figure 5.1 the position of ego is arbitrary, and the following holds no matter from whose point of view the network is seen. Positive and negative feelings about others are represented by *signed graphs* that have positive and negative ties, the latter indicated by dotted lines. As notational shorthand we can use a subscript for the number of negative ties, and write Δ_1 and Δ_3 for

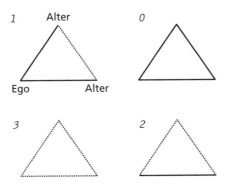

Figure 5.1 *Imbalanced triads on the left, balanced triads on the right, with negative relations as dotted lines.*

the imbalanced triads. In the case of Δ_1, in which two friends of ego are in conflict and the proverb "a friend of a friend is a friend" no longer holds, ego tends to feel distress, whereas in Δ_3 all three persons involved will feel tense. High feelings of distress render these triads imbalanced and instable in the longer run, so there is a chance p that in Δ_1 the initial problem dissolves and everybody becomes friends again, represented by the balanced triad Δ_0, and a chance $1 - p$ that ego chooses sides and together with one friend forms a coalition against the third person, resulting in Δ_2 in Figure 5.1 at the bottom right. In the latter case, "an enemy of a friend is an enemy," which might be less pleasant than generic friendship but is at least stable, according to balance theory. Furthermore, there is a very high chance q, close to or equal to 1, that in Δ_3 two people will team up as a coalition, in this case expressed by the maxim "an enemy of an enemy is a friend", which then also results in the balanced triad Δ_2.

In general, a clique is balanced if every triad within it is balanced. For a triad embedded in a larger clique, flipping sign in the triad, e.g. Δ_1 becoming Δ_2, may unbalance an adjacent triad, e.g. turning Δ_0 into Δ_1, which in turn might lead to a cascade of flipping signs. Antal, Krapivsky, and Redner (2005) captured signed cliques in a Hamiltonian equation (different from the one for community detection), and showed in a computer simulation that, if p is smaller than 0.5, a clique stays in a quasistationary bipolar state, with two subcliques, or coalitions, with only positive ties within, and only negative ties between them. If p is raised to 0.5 or a larger value, the clique under investigation transgresses to a state of generic friendship. Interestingly, the time it takes to reach peace (if $p \geq 0.5$) is much longer than it takes to reach a bipolar balance (if $p < 0.5$). Balance theory is more general than cliques, and has been defined for cycles larger than triads. A cycle is balanced if the multiplication of its signs is positive, and imbalanced if it is negative, which you may want to verify for the triads in Figure 5.1. A graph is balanced if and only if all its cycles are balanced; the concept of balance is meaningless for graphs without cycles.

Dorwin Cartwright and Frank Harary (1956: 286) proved that all signed graphs can be partitioned into two subgraphs with all positive ties within the subgraphs, and all negative ties between them, if and only if they have reached a balanced state. In the extreme case where all signs are positive, the initial graph is recovered without splitting into two.[7]

Balance theory can also be seen as an approach to community detection when conflict plays a prominent role. Balance theory holds for those situations where negative ties do not dissolve, and is well applicable to actors in situations where they cannot escape having contact with one another, such as countries in international relations (Moore 1979) or colleagues in a team. In other situations, actors in conflict may be related to third parties that intervene and end the conflict, or are indifferent to conflicts such that the flipping of signs comes to a halt, or conflicting parties dissolve their social relationship once it turns sour. For example, if in a cycle of four all four ties are negative, it is considered balanced in theory although it seems highly implausible that such a cycle would last. We know that the number of people involved in conflicts, as indicated by strikers (Biggs 2005) or casualties of war (L. F. Richardson 1948) or of terrorist attacks (Clauset, Young, and Gleditsch 2007), is power-law distributed, which means that most conflicts are dampened locally before they escalate to a large population, or lack the "energy" to contaminate communities at larger social distances. Balance theory should take into account that for larger networks the flipping chances will be more heterogeneously distributed, especially for bridges in contrast to embedded ties, whereas current models have only one value of p and no chance of dissolving negative ties. Still, balance theory is a relevant, clear, testable, and parsimonious approach to conflicts in small networks, and is well integrated with sociological and anthropological theory (Davis 1963). It is to be hoped that it will be generalized to larger networks (e.g. Radicchi *et al.* 2007), so that we can better understand under which conditions conflicts escalate or dampen out.

NETWORK STUDIES OF COMMUNITIES

By means of Hamiltonian equations and triad census, we can determine communities and their motifs and (im)balance technically. Often we also want a sociologically rich account, including culture and geography.[8] Examples of community studies from a network perspective include Elizabeth Bott's (1955) work on families, which can be seen as the most elementary communities, Claude Fischer's extensive study in California (1982), the work of Edward Laumann (an overview, 2006; Laumann *et al.* 1989), and of Barry Wellman and his colleagues, who studied a Toronto neighborhood for several decades (e.g. Wellman and Wortley 1990). Wellman (2001) also studied communities on the Internet from its early days onward; see also Holme, Edling and Liljeros (2004). Sociology as a scientific collaboration network by itself was mapped out and analyzed by James Moody (2004). Cutting-edge longitudinal research on kin-based groups in Turkey was conducted by Douglas White and Ulla Johansen (2005), which has a more general relevance because kinship is the most basic social relationship among humans. Another anthropological example is a study of village communities in Thailand (Entwisle *et al.* 2007), and several anthropological studies are reviewed by Schweizer (1997). In a study of a mobile telephone communication network, Granovetter's hypothesis was confirmed that strong ties are within clusters, and that bridges across clusters tend to be weak ties (Onnela *et al.* 2007). Mobilization for trade unions in Sweden was examined by Peter Hedström (1994), and the related subject of *social movements* is reviewed by Della Porta and Diani (2006), which provides many references to the network literature thereof. A case study of particular interest is the Paris commune in 1871, by Roger Gould (1991), who also studied collective violence in Corsica (Gould 1999). Finally, there are imagined communities as well, since people tend to have strong emotions – positive and negative – about others whom they have never met (Anderson 1991). Obviously, communities are not static units, because people have children, migrate between communities, and eventually die. Within and across communities, patterns of ties change because of tie formation and decay, by transitivity, shared or broken affiliations, preferences for particular individuals, and by conflicts and force. Dynamic network models that take several of these factors into account tend to be complex. Still relatively simple and very readable is Palla, Barabási, and Vicsek (2007).

SOCIAL COHESION

Now that communities can be detected, we ask what their cohesion is. At an elementary level, of protection against predators, people can cohere as animals in herds do, simultaneously trying to stay close to others and avoiding collision if possible (Couzin 2007). Rather than a network of social relations there is a network of (geographic) proximities. We can observe this herding behavior in groups of tourists, especially if they do not (yet) know each other well. When they cross a street, following a guide in front who does not see a car coming, the last ones prefer not to be separated from the group, thereby taking considerable risk being hit by a car, as I observe regularly on my way to work. Herd cohesion is apparently a stronger determinant of behavior than risk avoidance. It can have dramatic consequences in panicking crowds when people trample each other or violently squeeze themselves through one exit, collectively failing to notice another exit (for a mathematical model of panic, see Helbing, Farkas, and Vicsek 2000). Herd cohesion is appreciated and cultivated by military leaders, who train their soldiers to march in well-ordered lattice formations to intimidate their enemies. In a less disciplined way, street gangs also use this intimidating effect of cohesion. People feel safer together in a group than as solitary individuals, and collectively they can generate emotional energy (Durkheim 1912; Collins 2004). Groups of tourists therefore become a great deal noisier than they would dare to be at home. Herd cohesion can work as a simple but sophisticated group decision mechanism as well, producing "leadership" as a consequence of information differences between individuals without information transfer (Couzin *et al.* 2005), enabling groups of animals to find food without the guidance that groups of tourists have.

Yet humans can achieve a great deal more than finding food or wandering about in foreign cities. They build these cities collectively, as well as our highly complex society. If we collectively are frightened or celebrate we are set back to herd behavior, but if we stick to our senses we can achieve substantially more than herds can. What then is the structure of advanced social cohesion among humans? The best answer to this question so far was given by the anthropologist Douglas (not to be confused with Harrison) White and his associates, around the turn of the millennium. Their writings have a scope and depth seldom seen in sociology and anthropology (Wolfe 2006), and whether it's Turkish nomads (White and Johansen 2005) or biotechnology (Powell *et al.* 2005), you name it and they've analyzed it, better than anyone before them did.

Douglas White and Frank Harary (2001) start out their foundational paper with a caveat. Cohesion can be looked upon in a general sense, then often called solidarity, which also incorporates social norms, leaders' charisma, and identification with a group, i.e. group loyalty (*asabiya*, as Ibn Khaldoun described in the fourteenth century; Ahmed 2005). In a narrower sense, cohesion denotes social relations that hold a group together. Therefore the network approach, dealing with the *relational* component of cohesion, doesn't fully cover the concept, missing out the *ideational* component. For example, welfare states can be seen as institutionalized solidarity (e.g. Gelissen 2000), but a welfare state is more than a network among civilians and also incorporates the institutions (e.g. laws) that mold network ties by generating expectations in individuals.

Following upon the discussion in Chapter 2, we presume we have binary data on reciprocal relations in a community, represented as edges, but the approach can be generalized to valued edges in case tie strength matters (see White and Harary 2001: 333). The content of the edges considered is supposed to be mostly positive, not primarily antagonistic or competitive. In actuality, humans often have ambivalent, i.e. at the same time positive and negative, feelings towards others, in particular if ties are strong (Smelser 1998), but one may argue that in most cases one mode dominates over the other, so that positive ties can be selected without too much hassle, as in balance theory. Then "a group is cohesive to the extent that its members possess connections to others within the group, ones that hold it together," thus the group is "resistant to being pulled apart by removal of its members" (White and Harary 2001: 308, 309). By looking at where the group is at its weakest, they subsequently sharpen the straightforward proposition to the minimum number of actors who, if removed from the group, would disconnect it in parts or yield a trivial network consisting of a single vertex.

At the same time, cohesion can be approached from a different angle, by arguing that, in cohesive groups, actors are connected by multiple paths. Multiple paths yield *redundancy* of information being passed through multiple channels. Information arriving through one channel, say on how to behave in certain situations, can be confirmed and reconfirmed through other channels, making it more convincing and more legitimate. Furthermore, if there is error in transfer, and information is distorted by noise along one path, it can be corrected through other paths. Redundancy is crucial to hold a group of humans or an organization together, makes it robust, and facilitates the emergence and maintenance of group norms, coordinated action, social learning, and passing on of traditions.

For redundancy, paths must not overlap. If, say, three paths have one noise-producing edge in common, the actors connected by these paths would be (approximately) as vulnerable to noise as if they had a single path incorporating that malfunctioning edge. Should independent paths therefore be edge-independent? Look again at Figure 2.3, and choose an arbitrary actor in the left hand group and another one in the right hand group. There are multiple edge-independent paths connecting these two actors but, no matter how many of these paths there are, they all depend on the single actor (7) in the middle of the group. So in fact edge-independency is not yet good enough: paths should be vertex-independent. Vertex independency guarantees complete independency of paths, thus redundancy. Within a group, some pairs of actors may be connected by more independent paths than other pairs of actors, and cohesive paths can be distributed inhomogeneously in a community. However, the cohesion of the entire group is determined by the *minimum* number of vertex-independent paths connecting any pair in the group. This minimum number of vertex-independent paths is called the group's *K-connectivity*. Bear in mind that "connectivity" is used by others in different meanings, for instance as density, which are to be distinguished from K-connectivity. Here, capital K is used to mark the difference from degree, denoted by lower-case k.

We now have two explications of cohesion: the minimum number of vertex-independent paths connecting pairs of actors in a group, and the minimum number of actors who, if removed from the group, would disconnect it. By means of a deep mathematical result from graph theory (Menger's theorem, see Harary 1969: 47), it follows logically that these two meanings are equivalent. Using this theorem, White and Harary define social cohesion simply as K-connectivity, capturing both meanings of cohesion in one stroke. K-connectivity is not the same as density and, in relatively sparse networks, a reasonable level of cohesion can still be maintained by the presence of redundant paths. In power law networks, random removal of nodes has the highest chance of hitting vertices with low degree, which hardly affects the network's robustness; if on the other hand a hub is removed, the impact on cohesion is severe (Albert, Jeong, and Barabási 2000).

In the spirit of redundancy, White and his colleagues argue that K-connectivity must be at least *2* to establish any level of cohesion at all. The network in Figure 2.3 is a component (no isolates) but has no cohesion to write home about. The group on the right hand side is a *bi-component* (each pair of vertices connected by at least two independent paths) that harbors a 3-component (vertices 7, 8, 11, 14) wherein everybody is related by three independent paths. In general, a *K*-component has K-connectivity. In social networks it is often the case that groups of higher connectivity are embedded in larger groups of lower connectivity (Moody and White 2003), such as cliquish families in sparser neighborhoods. The "depth" of an actor's embedding is defined as his or her *nestedness*, the number of K-connectivity "layers" one has to pass from the surface level of the actor's community to reach the connectivity level where the actor resides. Mind that the nestedness of an actor need not be equivalent with the K-connectivity of the group (s)he is nested in, because one could for example jump from a 2-connected community level straight into a 6-connected clique, which then counts as only one step for nestedness. Notice furthermore that nestedness has a specific definition in the context of social cohesion, whereas many others use the notion with somewhat different meanings in different contexts. For firms nested in a business community, Moody and White (2003) found that, the deeper two firms are nested in the same community, the more similar their political behavior will be. This result modifies Conyon and Muldoon's (2006) small world analysis (Chapter 3 above), by pointing out that, even though on average (looking at local clustering and average geodesic) collusion doesn't exist, it can exist locally.

Redundancy has a cost of tie maintenance and has diminishing marginal returns, but high levels of K-connectivity are not at all necessary for cohesion to be maintained. Even for large networks (near) optimal levels of cohesion are feasible, since they require only low levels of density. For individuals and a given level of cohesion, the costs of cohesion in terms of tie maintenance per individual do not increase with the number of vertices in the network (D. White forthcoming; White and Harary 2001). To see this graphically in an example, look again at Figure 3.2a. There we can add ever more vertices to the lattice network, one at a time. If we do so, each vertex keeps the same number of ties (four), while the cohesion stays at the same level ($K = 4$). Although White and Harary admit that, for trust to be established and maintained, short path distances are important, they also claim that the kinds of information that enhance cohesion hardly decay with path distance. Given the small world experiments and the attrition of information over long paths, however, it seems that cohesive forces at longer average path lengths are weaker, even though multiple paths function as amplifiers of signals. Furthermore, one may doubt if people at long social distances identify with each other as easily as with people at short distances (with the possible exception of kinship ties, White and Johansen 2005). Maybe a distance measure is needed (i.e. average path length, see Friedkin 1983: 55) to complement the K-connectivity measure. More research is needed to sort this out. Certainly, the K-connectivity measure works well for relatively smaller networks.

Coleman (1988)[9] showed that children's dropout rates at school are lower in communities where cohesion is stronger, and Moody and White (2003) found that children's feeling of being attached to their school strongly relates with how deeply they are nested in the school's network. Being nested in a community is relevant for social support, for a sense of belonging and for well-being in general.[10] On top of a cohesive network structure, strong ties are more conductive to support than weak ties (e.g., Wellman and Wortley 1990: 566). Social support, in turn, decreases stress in humans and other primates (Sapolsky 2005), and increases infant survival (Silk 2007; Silk, Alberts, and Altmann 2003). Not all consequences of cohesion are positive, though, because the same ties that hold a group together also enable groups to collectively harm other groups and individuals on much larger scales than incoherent groups are capable of (De Swaan 2007; Horowitz 2001). Furthermore, people who are locally nested without complementary connections to other communities tend to be more narrow-minded and to have less innovative ideas (Burt 2004).

In Chapter 2 we wanted to measure the cohesion of a larger community, which may consist of multiple (sub)communities. Our initial difficulties have now been solved, and with K-connectivity we have the conceptual means to determine the cohesion of an entire network and of all its communities within it. Alternatively, communities can be detected by using K-connectivity as a grouping principle directly (Moody and White 2003). Then the communities marked need not be the same as the ones detected by the Hamiltonian approach, except when communities strongly depart from randomness and are internally dense. By using these two approaches in a complementary way, one can first by the Hamiltonian approach determine communities without making any assumption on the content and function of ties, and subsequently look to see if more strongly cohesive groups are nested within less cohesive groups, as well as cohesive group overlaps that the Hamiltonian approach would not mark.

COOPERATION AND COHESION

So far, we have dealt with cohesion in a relational sense, leaving out the ideational content of the ties, but how much do we know about cohesion in a more general sense? And why does cohesion exist in the first place, when establishing and maintaining ties cost time and effort that people could use directly for themselves? To address cohesion in a more general sense, we must broaden our perspective and concede that humans and their communities can ultimately be understood only from an evolutionary point of view that incorporates culture and biology (Parsons 1964; Richerson and Boyd 2005; Massey 2002).

Until now, we have assumed that people are somehow motivated to maintain social ties and to behave cooperatively with others. Indeed, humans, chimpanzees, and some other species are able to *reciprocate* (Trivers 1971), although non-humans' reciprocity is mostly limited to kin, e.g. parents and their offspring or among siblings.

In fact, the degree of genetic relatedness is an accurate predictor of reciprocity in numerous species (Hamilton 1964). Moreover, intelligent animals, in particular chimpanzees and humans, are able to assess for which tasks cooperation is necessary and to estimate associated costs and benefits, to remember who cooperated or defected previously, and to choose the best collaborative partners (Melis, Hare, and Tomasello 2006; Silk 2007), enabling sophisticated reciprocity (Brosnan and de Waal 2002).[11] Reciprocated cooperation yields increased activation of a certain brain area (striatum) and ongoing reciprocation increases trust, whereas non-reciprocity produces a negative emotional state (Sanfey 2007). However, assessing that reciprocity can occur and entails a positive brain response is not the same as explaining *why* cooperation occurs, in particular for larger groups among non-kin. It is in fact a major scientific problem to explain why people cooperate at all (Henrich 2003, 2006). The argument is simple. If ego makes an effort to cooperate with alter, ego incurs a cost that in many cases will be larger than ego's expected benefit from cooperation (Nowak 2006). Without further provisions, such as institutions or an intervening third party, alter might happily receive ego's cooperative effort without returning the favor. Therefore, cooperation between animals in general is rare, and if it occurs it is mostly between kin, who have an interest in the reproduction of their own genes or of genes related as closely as possible as the next best option. Cooperation among non-kin on a very large scale exists only among humans, which is far more puzzling than cooperation in families or in dyads where ego and alter may have some control over each other.[12] Facing multiple alters, ego has the following dilemma. Ego may realize that if the alters make their efforts and incur their cost, ego can forgo his or her contribution, while a common goal, e.g. collecting or making a resource, will be (largely) achieved without ego's effort. Moreover, the larger the group, the easier it is for ego to shirk, but scale advantages of large groups are necessary to achieve large common goods. For ego, however, it doesn't even matter to what extent (s)he will share in the common good because (s)he bears no costs in the first place, and any share is better than nothing. Therefore selfishness seems always best. However, if ego reasons that way, alters will reason similarly, but, if everybody reasons that way, no collective action is possible (Olson 1965).[13] Even if cooperation suits everybody's interests, without further arrangements the temptation to selfishness will be irresistible. This *dilemma of cooperation* is a general problem that also holds for the maintenance of social relations, and for the same reason. For example, if in a friendship ego is the only one who maintains the friendship, alter benefits from ego's effort without reciprocating. The dilemma of cooperation is also known as the dilemma of collective action. However, the latter expression suggests that there is an initially given collective, which can go into action to achieve a collective goal. But collectives and their goals may emerge in the course of cooperative action, as welfare states did (De Swaan 1988), and therefore the notion of the dilemma of cooperation seems to be more general and appropriate.

An enlightening way to think about the dilemma of cooperation is offered by evolutionary game theory, showing with mathematical precision how the benefits for an individual depend on the relative abundance of cooperators in a given population (Nowak 2006); a population can be any group or community, as we have discussed. One way a game is defined is by the payoffs that actors receive for their efforts.[14] In general, if there is a portion of defectors in the population, no matter how small, then without an additional mechanism supporting cooperation the cost–benefit ratio of defectors will be lower than of cooperators, and defectors will have higher "fitness" (or payoff, or whatever measure of "success") and be favored by selection (Nowak 2006). Therefore no cooperation will exist in the longer run.

One of the most widely studied games is the prisoner's dilemma, which models the dilemma of cooperation. In this game, one of the best strategies given the two options "cooperate" or "defect" (i.e. not-cooperate or compete) is sticking to a pattern *win–stay, lose–shift* (Nowak and Sigmund 1993): ego starts with cooperation, and repeats his previous move (either cooperate or defect) if his cost–benefit ratio is fine for him; if not he swaps. By the way, this strategy was used by chimpanzees in an experimental setting (Melis, Hare, and Tomasello 2006). Win–stay, lose–shift can outperform the widely known strategy *tit-for-tat*, which initially was thought to be the best (Axelrod and Hamilton 1981) but fails if there is noise. Noise means that sometimes cooperation is misinterpreted as defection. However, win–stay, lose–shift loses against all-defect, and in general there exists no winning strategy in the presence of arbitrary other strategies (Boyd and Lorberbaum 1987), which would leave human cooperation, especially on a large scale or for a long time, unexplained. Another problem of the standard prisoner's dilemma is that the players receive their information about each other's behavior at exactly the same time after each round, which seems a rather restrictive constraint; if they don't there tends to be a chaotic pattern featuring cascades of cooperation and defection (Huberman and Glance 1993). Moreover, not all social situations are prisoners' dilemmas (Gelman 2006; Clutton-Brock 2002). Last but not least, in actuality there are more options than either all-out defection or full-blown cooperation, which then cannot be modeled as binary choices between cooperate and defect. There are "light" forms of cooperation, such as market exchange, as well as cooperation at intermediate intensity, involving goodwill and trust (Richardson 1972; see also Chapter 7). Our discussion does not hinge on prisoners' dilemmas, though, and cooperation can be studied in numerous different games.

In a variety of public goods games, cooperation turns out to be enhanced by actors' desiring a favorable *reputation* as cooperator, ensuring that others are willing to cooperate with them and avoiding deterring others by a bad reputation (Nowak and Sigmund 2005). At the same time, ego will prefer to cooperate with alters that have a good rather than a bad reputation for previous cooperative efforts (Panchanathan and Boyd 2004; Raub and Weesie 1990). Reputations can be seen as heuristic shortcuts to complete histories about alters' past behavior, and they disseminate in the form of gossip (Gluckman 1963; Sommerfeld *et al.* 2007). It turns out that, when people have the feeling that they are being observed by others, their brains react immediately and cause them to become more cooperative, anticipating reputation effects (Milinski and Rockenbach 2007; see also Goffman's "front stage", 1959). Reputation fosters cooperation, but it does not by itself sustain cooperation under all conditions, and its influence fades if groups become larger, direct observation becomes more difficult, and people find leeway to strategically manipulate their own reputation and those of others (e.g. Goffman 1959).

Cooperation can also be increased by the threat of *punishment* of defectors. Depending on the context, punishment can be inflicting feelings of guilt, or imposing loss of money, status, or reputation (gossip can be a punishment by itself), and it does not have to be physical. In well-socialized individuals, (anticipation of) criticism will already cause sufficiently strong (anticipation of) feelings of guilt for them to do their cooperative best. A punisher can sometimes be an alter who criticizes ego directly; otherwise a punisher can be a *third party* who intervenes in a conflict between alter and ego (Krackhardt and Kilduff 2002, building on the work of Simmel [1890, 1908] 1950). A third party can also intervene in a conflict between an individual and the group, e.g. if the individual shirks in contributing to a collective goal. Furthermore, a third party can foster appeasement after conflict, which is important to re-establish cooperation after a temporary disruption. Peacemaking has a biological component and exists also among chimpanzees (De Waal 2000). Numerous experimental and field studies have shown the importance of punishment for raising levels of cooperation.[15] In an experiment on a group of monkeys in captivity, a small number of high-status monkeys fulfilled policing tasks by making interventions into dyadic conflicts. This prevented the group from falling apart into small clusters, which happened when these policing monkeys were removed (Flack *et al.* 2006; Flack, de Waal and Krakauer 2005). Also for humans, a minority of punishers suffices to engender cooperation in a group of selfish individuals (Fehr and Fischbacher 2003). This result is consistent with social life outside laboratory experiments, in which, to reduce crime in Chicago neighborhoods, a willingness to intervene (as third party) appears to be necessary (Sampson, Raudenbush, and Earls 1997).

Experiments with humans have shown that in particular the conjoint effect of reputation *and* punishment is highly conductive to cooperation (Rockenbach and Milinski 2006). Moreover, reputation reduces considerably the need for punishment. This is important because, among other reasons, in case of punishment the costs of cooperation are shifted to the punishers, who in their turn have no (immediate) benefit from punishing. From a strictly economic standpoint they should therefore not punish, and therefore it is better to explain cooperation with as little as possible recourse to punishment. For the remainder of the costs of punishment, insights from biology help us out. A defecting alter causes a negative emotional reaction in a punisher, visible in a brain scan, who then acts out following a brain reaction and not a cost calculation (Fehr and Gächter 2002; Bowles and Gintis 2002). Punishing yields an expectation of a positive feeling in the punisher's brain, which can also be observed in a brain scan, and coincides surprisingly with the feeling of rewarding a cooperator (Quervain *et al.* 2004). Thus revenge is sweet (Knutson 2004) – sweeter for men than for women! (Singer *et al.* 2006) – hence the residual costs of punishing to be explained are smaller than economists initially thought.

Furthermore, human brains are sensitive to *unfairness* (Sanfey *et al.* 2003; Knoch *et al.* 2006), in contrast to chimpanzees' (Jensen, Call, and Tomasello 2007), and people tend to reject unfair offers even if this is against their economic interest (Fehr and Fischbacher 2003; Glimcher and Rustichini 2004). Finally, parts of primate brains are specialized to figure out what other individuals think, i.e. they can *mentalize* (Zimmer 2003), and what others feel emotionally, i.e. they can *empathize* (Singer and Fehr 2005).[16] Individuals can mentalize and empathize on the basis of body language, but obviously both capabilities can be developed and used at a far more advanced level if a shared language is available. Earlier we have mentioned other biological components of social life, i.e. reciprocity (Sanfey 2007), trust (Damasio 2005), peacemaking after conflict (De Waal 2000), and anticipation of reputation effects through awareness of being monitored (Milinski and Rockenbach 2007). These social abilities were discussed by social scientists long ago (e.g. mentalizing as role taking, Mead 1934; empathy as sympathy, Smith 1986; monitoring and being monitored, Goffman 1963; reciprocity and trust in exchange relations, Blau 1964; punishment, Durkheim 1895; fairness in collective action, Gould 1993), but their evolutionary context and biological mechanisms have recently become far clearer.

We now know in greater detail how and to what extent our pro-social abilities, including our language ability (Hauser, Chomsky, and Fitch 2002; Diamond and Bellwood 2003), foster cooperation, and why humans have exceptionally large brains to deal with their complex social lives (Dunbar and Schultz 2007). Obviously, for potential social abilities to function well, individuals have to have a childhood conducive to the development of these abilities through interactions with adults and peers. The combination of potential pro-sociality and *socialization* (Simmel [1890, 1908] 1950) leads to a heterogeneous population in a range from completely selfish individuals to highly altruistic ones (Fehr and Fischbacher 2003). Whereas some people are utterly egocentric and others always cooperate, most are somewhere in between these two extremes and their behavior strongly depends on the social situation (Fehr and Fischbacher 2004).

The implication seems to be that, for social cohesion to exist among a heterogeneous group of individuals, not only is the number of vertex-independent paths important, to disseminate gossip, but so are the punishments that can be delivered through these paths. One can also reason the other way around. If in a larger group cooperation is to be established in the longer run, then for any cooperation-enhancing game strategy a cohesive network structure is necessary to make it work.[17] For networks with higher K-connectivity, there are more potential third parties available to intervene, and there is higher redundancy of information about reputations. Support for this argument comes from an experimental study, in which it turned out that, for subjects, the credibility of gossip they heard strongly increased if it came from more different sources, not if it was repeated by the same source (Hess and Hagen 2006). Another support for this argument is the wide occurrence of transitivity, which from an evolutionary point of view means that ego more easily trusts alter and expects from alter a more pro-social stance towards ego if a third person has an intermediary position between them, net of assortativeness. Also a large community in which many people do not interact with each other directly can nevertheless be sustained efficiently, because the number of edges necessary to maintain a given level of cohesion increases only linearly with the number of vertices (D. White and Harary 2001: 336). If more people join the network, tie maintenance costs per individual for keeping cohesion at a given level hardly increase.

A network of social relations distinguishes advanced social cohesion from herd cohesion, which might be strong but in which cooperation is hardly enhanced. A crucial property of a cohesive network is its *stability*, such as repeated interactions and long-term reputations are in games (Fehr and Fischbacher 2003). For stable expectations to develop, social relations must be relatively enduring with respect to actions, e.g. alternating moves of cooperation and defection, otherwise reputation and punishment cannot function out of the laboratory. Incidental defection does not disrupt well-established ties, and is often interpreted as error rather than intentional harm, whereas defection does threaten new or weak ties. This is important because someone who punishes a defector might receive some aggression in return. If short-term actions, e.g. punishment or defection, would normally result in tie decay, all minor disagreements would end up in disbanding the relationship, which is not at all true empirically. Tie decay does occur, though, and, for the system of punishment and reputation to be robust against decay, multiple independent paths are important for the diffusion of norms and gossip to continue, as captured by the notion of K-connectivity. Stable redundant interaction patterns also foster indirect exchange, of i giving to j in exchange for something received from k, which in turn further increases solidarity (Lévi-Strauss [1949] 1969). Cohesion extends punishment even beyond the community network and protects insiders against troublemaking outsiders, when community members come to defend fellow community members against norm-violating outsiders. In a large empirical study of Chicago neighborhoods, Sampson, Morenoff, and Earls (1999) found that residential stability was a crucial factor for collective efficacy. Obviously, it would be a caricature to say that only in static networks can cooperation occur, since we know that in Chicago people move in and out, as they do everywhere else. The point is that, for cooperation to be maintained at the community level, the network as a whole must be relatively more stable than patterns of individual actions. By combining reputation and punishment in a cohesive network structure, and having a biological basis for pro-sociality, cooperation can thus be explained (or almost, see below),[18] as well as its stability in larger communities where many people do not interact directly. Or on the basis of the same concepts, we can also predict when cooperation will fail. Once cooperation can be established at various scales, people can specialize, reap efficiency benefits, and cooperate with differently specialized others to obtain resources large and small, which are basic requirements for our complex society.

Establishing cooperation implies neither that cooperation is equally enjoyable for all cooperators nor that cooperation is immune to strategic manipulation. Gossip is not always true and sometimes is unfairly damaging (Elias and Scotson 1965), as punishments can be as well, and third parties may have a personal interest in decreasing (or increasing) trust between ego and alter (Burt and Knez 1995; Sommerfeld *et al.* 2007). Counter-intuitively, ego's reputation may spread *less* well in (too) highly cohesive networks, because people in very dense networks are under stronger pressure to conform and to "echo" others' predisposition towards ego, rather than stating their true opinion (Burt 2001; Zuckerman 2003). Yet communities with high levels of cooperation have an advantage over communities in which cooperation fails, even if not all community members enjoy cooperating (Richerson and Boyd 2005). However, outside the laboratory where most of the experiments were run, networks can be too sparse and social or geographic distances too large to monitor defection sufficiently for sanctions to be imposed effectively. For example, ego and alter might develop a strong cooperative tie and then succeed in covering up each other's negligence of group interest (Flache and Macy 1996). More importantly, we might have explained *why* people cooperate – to avoid costs and to get payoffs – but these people would hardly know by themselves *how* to cooperate and what to do if they had only game theory at their disposal. For example, after a disaster takes place, many people volunteer to help, even risking their own lives because of strong empathy with the victims. Most of the volunteers are clueless what to do and how to organize themselves, however, in sharp contrast to professional helpers. In both lay and professional groups there is enough willingness to cooperate, but it is skills and accumulated knowledge that distinguish the professionals from the volunteers.

CULTURE AND EVOLUTION

To explain how people cooperate and find out what to do, we have to look at their culture. Peter Richerson and Robert Boyd made major contributions to evolutionary theory, and we will follow their treatment of culture, which they define as follows. "Culture is information capable of affecting individuals' behavior that they acquire from other[s] through teaching, imitation, and other forms of social transmission" (Richerson and Boyd 2005: 5).[19] In contrast to popular wisdom, culture does not have to come in discrete gene-like replicable bits for an evolutionary approach to apply (Richerson and Boyd 2005: 6). Human culture is much more complex than

53

that of apes, which in turn is more complex than that of other animals (Whiten 2005; Whiten *et al*. 1999; de Waal 2005; van Schaik *et al*. 2003). It incorporates institutions – sanctioned "rules of the game" (North 1990: 3) – symbols and their interpretations, languages, and shared knowledge, beliefs, values, and tastes.[20] Notice that their definition does *not* imply that all humans in a community equally share or value all information in their culture, as some sociological definitions would have it. Groups or communities with a distinct (sub)culture can be (parts of) organizations, clans, ethnic groups, social classes, and nations.

To illustrate what cultural evolution and the pertaining key concepts mean, let us start with a simple example, of a soccer tournament in which one team can win (which for evolutionary processes in general is not true). Each team has a different strategy as well as different players with various talents, providing *variation* of strategies and skills. Competition between the teams causes *selection*, in this case of one winning team that has the best package of skills and strategy. In the example, competitive selection works at the group level, at least during the matches. A badly skilled or shirking player in the winning team benefits from the collective team effort and is not individually selected away (yet). After each match, strategies are thought through and new ones are developed for a next match, changing the pool of strategic variants. Ideas for these strategies partly spill over from earlier tournaments and can be transferred to subsequent tournaments, so there is an *accumulation of knowledge*. Not only strategies vary and are being selected, at the team level, but also individual players vary and are being selected; after a match players can be swapped. However, selection at the individual level is in this example caused by conscious decisions, not by competition directly, although there is some interdependence. At both individual and group level, there can, in principle, be multiple forces of selection at work. A very important evolutionary force, which organizers of tournaments take great pains to avoid, is the natural environment. Suppose that some teams play very well in snow conditions and others badly: then, if it snows, environmental conditions would strongly determine the selective outcome of the tournament. Organizers therefore prefer to play in good climates or in stadiums with closed roofs, removing the environment from the equation, so to speak.

In general, evolutionary processes are characterized by *variation* (of genes, strategies, or cultures) and *selection* (Nowak 2006). There should be some continuity in reproduction, or replication, of the variants as well, although not necessarily replication of genes or other information carriers that outlive individuals. Culture is carried on in human memories, and some cultural phenomena such as religion, languages, and ethnic traditions do indeed change slowly with respect to human lifespan (Cavalli-Sforza *et al*. 1982). However, evolution also works on faster-changing cultural phenomena that change and are transmitted *within* the lifespan of individuals, for example strategies in games (Richerson and Boyd 2005). Furthermore, evolution works at *multiple levels* at the same time, and there is selection both of groups and of individuals within groups. If two groups compete for survival, the group with higher levels of cooperation and better knowledge about the social and natural environment has better chances. A popular misunderstanding is that evolution would produce optimally adapted entities, which is rarely the case. People have both useful and hazardous ideas but, if on average their ideas are good enough and no bad idea kills them, they can survive, and a group with on average better knowledge can outcompete another group in the same social or natural environment. In the remainder we will use an evolutionary approach to better comprehend the interplay of communities and culture.

Institutions point out what is not allowed and what is obliged, as well as what sanctions are appropriate and how conflicts should be handled and resolved. Culture thus helps to increase cooperation in communities, along with teaching people how to cooperate. Institutions vary considerably across communities (Henrich *et al.* 2006), depending on how strongly a community is dependent on market transactions with non-community members, and on what scale cooperation is necessary to achieve collective goals (Henrich *et al.* 2001). Humans are culturally socialized in their families, neighborhoods, at schools, and at work (Simmel 1910; Mead 1934). Most children internalize a portion of the norms and values they learn, and then feel guilty if they violate these norms. Anticipation of guilt is an effective mechanism of norm maintenance, although rarely sufficient by itself. In modern states, a large portion of norms is institutionalized in laws and, if a state is mostly non-corrupt, its inhabitants can trust their police and court for intervention in conflicts. Trusted institutions, or representatives thereof, in turn further increase cooperation among non-kin. In an experiment, people could choose between membership of a community with an institution for financially punishing non-contributing to a collective goal, a sum of money that was equally redistributed, and a community without this institution. Most people initially chose the non-punishment community. Migrating between the two communities was allowed. Once people realized that in the community with punishment the remuneration was considerably higher, on account of high cooperation that was virtually absent in the community without punishment, almost everybody moved over (Gürerk, Irlenbusch, and Rockenbach 2006). The migrated changed their behavior and increased both their contributing and punishing acts, even though they had some costs associated with punishing. Over the relatively short time span of the experiment, the subjects already became socialized, although the experimental culture was very simple. In the final rounds, a threat rather than actual punishment was often enough to keep cooperation at a high level. This experiment thus showed socialization and selection (of one institution out of two) at the group level.

Culture tends to be complex and is costly for individuals because they need time and effort to learn and master it, but it has an adaptive advantage. A culture enables a group to adapt to a large variety of environments, because individuals can benefit from the accumulated experience of other people over multiple generations, without having to find out everything by their own trial and error. "We let the population-level process of cultural evolution do the heavy lifting of our 'learning' for us" (Richerson and Boyd 2005: 131). If only a few group members learn first hand, for example by experiencing which fruits are edible and which are poisonous, or by inventing a new tool, all other group members who can get access to this information can benefit without having to discover or invent by themselves. In fact most people combine some trial-and-error learning with a large amount of social learning. "An entity *learns* if, through its processing of information, the range of its potential behaviours is changed" (Huber 1991: 89, italics added). Notice that this definition does *not* imply that learning has to be conscious, that under all circumstances actual behavior is changed, or that learning is always adaptive – sometimes it isn't. In changing environments, culture enables groups to adapt much quicker than they could by genes alone. "When lots of imitation is mixed with a little bit of individual learning, *populations* can adapt in ways that outreach the abilities of any individual" (Richerson and Boyd 2005: 13, italics in original).[21] Most people are hardly aware how much they are indebted to others for their knowledge. It was perhaps this unawareness that the fiction writer Jorge Luís Borges had in mind when he depicted the world Tlön, where plagiarism does not exist and all works are attributed to one anonymous atemporal author. Obviously, this author is all of us together, and the collective result is our accumulated culture that we mostly take for granted. Finally, culture also influences, although does not fully determine, with whom people prefer to connect themselves and how social relations are shaped and maintained, or, said briefly, what people expect from each other.

Culture is much more flexible than genes and can change in multiple ways. New knowledge can be introduced into a community by discovery and invention, called "guided *variation*" (Richerson and Boyd 2005: 116, italics added). Also if an idea that is copied from another community, or learned from the cultural repertoire of the focal community, is subsequently transformed into a new idea or application, cultural variation increases in a guided manner. An example is incremental improvement of a technology, or an application of a technology for which it was not designed initially. A new idea or application can subsequently diffuse through network ties or by proximity. For relatively simple information that can be easily copied, physical proximity of role models is enough and social relations are superfluous. Remember that also visual contact can be represented as a tie (Chapter 2), even though this is rarely done in network studies. However, transferring knowledge often requires social ties (Cross *et al*. 2001), and for complex, partly tacit, knowledge not just weak ties but strong ones (Hansen 1999), especially if it is to be transferred across community boundaries and there is not much common knowledge (Reagans and McEvily 2003). Furthermore, to imitate or copy successfully, the ability to mentalize helps considerably (Richerson and Boyd 2005: 136), and "the evolution of language would have been impossible without it" (Zimmer 2003).

Culture can diffuse by (at least) four different forces of transmission. First, an individual can be motivated to copy or transmit certain information because of its apparent relevance or quality, e.g. to avoid a danger, possibly weighed by an estimated effort to acquire or transmit the information. This is called *content-based transmission*. Learning a foreign language can be very beneficial but for adults it takes years of intense effort, and therefore most people stop after learning only a few. If the relevance or quality of information is uncertain, people tend to copy information from, or imitate the behavior of, others with high prestige for success, or with high status; this is called *model-based transmission*.[22] Under uncertainty, "determining *who* is successful is much easier than to determine *how* to be a success" (Richerson and Boyd 2005: 124, italics in original; see also Girard's mimetic desire, 1961). Notice that the cause of success that led to alter's prestige or status might be unrelated to the trait that ego attempts to imitate. For example, in Europe from the Renaissance onwards, the bourgeoisie imitated the etiquette of the aristocracy, who in turn stayed in the symbolic lead by continual refinement of their manners (Elias 1939).[23] Although table manners such as eating with a fork are by themselves unrelated to success, they became self-fulfilling. Modern societies that have schools and universities have their specialists – teachers – for choosing under uncertainty what knowledge is important for students to learn, and for transmitting it to them. As the example shows, power can play a role in transmission, for better or for worse. The example also shows that transmission of culture can be organized and institutionalized.

As an alternative to imitating role models or to learn from teachers, people may copy from other people with whom they easily identify, i.e. who are perceived as *similar* to themselves, e.g. from the same age, ethnicity, religion, social class, or peer group. In line with the notion of assortative mating, we might introduce the notion *assortative transmission* ("homophily," Rogers 2003: 19, 305). Copying similar people can make sense if these similar others, e.g. colleagues at work, are more experienced in a given (social) environment, or are more willing to share their experience with similar others, in contrast to possibly inaccessible high-status alters. Assortative transmission can also impede adaptation, for example when tourists copy each others' misunderstandings of the countries they visit, rather than copying the natives. Then the outgroup information, although easily available, is not considered legitimate by the ingroup, for the wrong reasons.

As a fourth alternative to gathering information, next to content, role model, or similarity, people can simply conform to the majority, for example when they want to catch up with a dress code or the language in a new environment, or any other code with positive externalities.[24] This is called *frequency-based transmission*. If a majority adopts a custom, e.g. uses cell phones, people who do not comply may come under increasing pressure, e.g. being ostracized from a part of social life, and consequently almost everybody adopts the custom in the end. These four alternative ways of transmission are not exclusive. In an experimental study, for two groups of chimpanzees, each group had one high-status chimpanzee who was taught a food-collecting technique, different in each group (Whiten, Horner and De Waal 2005).

The other chimpanzees copied the food-collecting technique from their high-status chimpanzee who mastered the technique, because it was generally understood that imitation would provide access to food (i.e. the quality of the technique, not only the status of the role model). Chimpanzees who mastered both techniques and were later introduced to either group followed the majority in that group. There were a couple of chimpanzees, apparently with strong individual characters, who did not follow the majority. In addition to self-imposed conformity, a leader or a majority may exert pressure towards conformity and sanction deviance (Henrich and Gil-White 2001). Notice that in many cases humans are hardly aware of the influence of the majority or of high-status individuals on them. For example, people in Western countries tend to believe that they have strongly individual tastes, whereas it has been pointed out experimentally that the influence of the majority on individual taste is stronger (Salganik, Dodds, and Watts 2006).

Information once introduced in a community can be transmitted by one, or a combination, of the above forces, each with a specific bias, and are therefore called "non-random forces of cultural transmission and change" (Richerson and Boyd 2005). The overall result of transmission biases is that, at the end of the day, cultures are more homogeneous within than across communities, a very important point to which we will return in the next two chapters. In other words, there is a one-to-one correspondence between (sub)cultures and (sub)communities.[25] Along with biased forces there are random forces of transmission, such as misremembering, miscopying, or mistransferring information, as well as cultural drift by demographic processes, e.g. people with a certain skill leaving or entering a community. Random forces and cultural drift can either increase variation, e.g. by introducing a new cultural variant, or contribute to selection, e.g. by the disappearance of an older generation that mastered a language no longer spoken.

Evolutionarily speaking, cultural variants compete for cognitive resources, such as attention and practice, leading to *selection* of certain variants by the non-random forces discussed above. Selection pressure will be stronger if the cultural variants affect more aspects of people's lives (Richerson and Boyd 2005: 74), and therefore there is more competition between languages than between songs, of which there can exist a large variety with relatively low selection pressure. Biased cultural selection is based on the scarcity of cognitive resources of the culture bearers, and has to be distinguished from natural, or environmental, selection, which is (largely) independent of their cognition and desires. For example, a shop owner may imitate a successful competitor in selecting products for selling with discount, while the consumers from the socio-economic environment act as a force of "natural" selection on the population of shops and their products.

Since the forces of cultural evolution work through ties and proximity, they can in principle be studied from a network perspective (Cavalli-Sforza and Feldman 1981: 57–62; see also Grabowski and Kosiński 2006; Strang and Soule 1998; Buskens and Yamaguchi 1999).[26] The field of cultural evolution has not yet been integrated with social networks, but there is a body of work on the diffusion of information through networks that is perfectly suitable for this integration (overview, Valente 2005; review of literature, Rogers 2003). In modern societies, mass media can also play an important role in the diffusion of information, sometimes more important than networks of social ties, if the information is simple enough relative to the prior knowledge of the recipients (Van den Bulte and Lilien 2001; Andrews and Biggs 2006). In general, some knowledge, such as technology, is transmitted at a different speed and through different channels from other knowledge, e.g. languages, which makes the overall picture of cultural diffusion rather complex. Network dynamics on the one hand and public sources of information, such as the Web and television, on the other hand yet further complicate the picture. Certainly, to comprehend societies and their evolution we will have to study both networks *and* culture.

It is important to realize that the same selection mechanisms that make culture adaptive can also make it *maladaptive*. People are highly receptive to others' ideas, including false ideas, in particular because testing everything people hear from others is not feasible. To find cues for quality of ideas they look at high-status individuals and at the majority (of their group), but both can be wrong, and people can learn to hate innocent others that they have never met, or they can collectively appoint arbitrary scapegoats. Still entertaining is Voltaire's auto-da-fé in his novel *Candide*; female genital mutilation (Almroth *et al.* 2005), in sharp contrast, is a very sad example of a harmful collective idea. Another example of generally shared falsehood is national character. In a comparative study of 49 cultures, it turned out that people's assessment of their national character was reliable, i.e. generally shared by a national population, although it did not at all correlate with national character as measured with psychological instruments – that also showed that variation across cultures is much smaller than people make each other believe (Terracciano *et al.* 2005). People sharing a nationality can strongly identify with and cooperate with each other, but at the same time they are susceptible to false information about themselves and about others, which leads to disidentification with, scapegoating of, and unreasonable fear of others – discrimination – and sometimes to intense hatred and collective violence (De Swaan 2007; for a network study of Nazis, see Seibel and Raab 2003).[27] Humans' high ability to cooperate on a large scale can render collective violence massively destructive, in comparison with small-scale killing among chimpanzees, who have far smaller networks of cooperation. Currently it is not clear why people collectively develop false ideas about others, which in turn lead to increasing fear and hatred, because true knowledge seems to have a competitive advantage, while irrational fear and hatred do not. Furthermore, to perceive others, possibly short-run defectors or competitors, either as longer-run enemies or as potential cooperators, is partly a matter of how the participants define the situation (William Thomas and Dorothy Swaine Thomas, in Merton 1968b). If a stranger is received with (socially constructed) animosity, the definition of the situation as conflict has real consequences for alter's behavior, and at the same time increases ego's fear. Unfortunately, fear has a biological component that causes us to escape rather than to examine what we fear, thereby decreasing the chances for correcting the stereotypes that we have created (Öhman 2005; Olsson *et al*. 2005). A friendly – not to be confused with naïve – attitude at the start, based on a different definition of the situation, might in numerous cases win over suspicious alters, thereby avoiding unnecessary and costly conflict. Increasing contact with stereotyped people inverts the vicious circle of disidentification. For knowledge about others and about themselves, people would need a mental "immune system" (Richerson and Boyd 2005: 165), protecting them against bad ideas while accepting healthy ideas. Education can play a role in developing children's moral and critical thinking abilities (Guimond, Begin, and Palmer 1989) but, like the immune system of our body, a mental immune system can't prevent us from becoming "sick" sometimes.

Adaptation to changing environments is a trade-off, not an optimum, and the ability for relatively fast cultural adaptation comes at the expense of being vulnerable to the (myopic) selfishness and false ideas of others (Richerson and Boyd 2005). Even if there are good ideas around, people can be culturally prejudiced against them and refuse to accept them. Adaptation takes time, and developing an excellent adaptation takes an enormous amount of time, during which the world might have changed, requiring yet another adaptation. Culture is a mixed bag, and its benefits with respect to genes are mainly in its relative flexibility. "Culture is built for speed, not for comfort" (Richerson and Boyd 2005).

In sum, without culture, people would be able to cooperate only in small groups and in limited ways. With culture, they can cooperate in a great many different ways and in large groups of non-kin. The interplay of biology and socialization leads to an unequal distribution of pro-sociality, with some regular norm violators, some altruists who always cooperate, and in between these extremes a majority that is socialized to cooperate if there is institutionalized punishment and reputation, on top of rewards from cooperation. Of such institutions there is a large variety across different communities, and in general there must also be a cohesive social network that stabilizes expectations to make institutions work. Furthermore, institutions in particular and culture in general tend to be more homogeneous within than across (sub)communities. Culture not only facilitates cooperation, but also makes it possible to benefit from the accumulated experience of many people over multiple generations, and to know far better than uncultured individuals how to cooperate and how to make a living.

SUGGESTED BACKGROUND READING

Social cohesion with examples, Moody and White (2003); community detection for courageous readers, Reichardt and Bornholdt (2006b); a case study on communities of bidders (i.e. market segments) on eBay, Reichardt and Bornholdt (2007); for culture and cooperation from an evolutionary point of view, Richerson and

Boyd (2005); the combined effect of reputation and punishment, Rockenbach and Milinski (2006); the effect of alter's and third party monitoring of ego, Milinski and Rockenbach (2007); gossip, Sommerfeld *et al.* (2007).

EXERCISE 5.1

Get the Zachary karate club data from the Web (http://vlado.fmf.uni-lj.si/pub/net-works/data/Ucinet/UciData.htm) and turn them into a working file (see Chapter 8). Notice that, for the adjacency matrix of the valued graph, you need the lower half of the matrix that you will find on the website. In the network, based on data that Zachary (1977) collected, there are two antagonistic groups, one around actor 1 and the other account actor 34. Try to spot them with the computer; knowing from Zachary's ethnography that there must be two groups, use the argument spins=2 in the spinglass.community command, or "number of spins" in the graphical user interface, even though the modularity will be lower than if, by default, the number of communities is set free. The correct solution can be found in Newman and Girvan (2004) and various places on the Web. Furthermore, analyze the social cohesion of this network.

Chapter 6

Social inequality
Prestige, power, brokerage, and roles

Complex societies are characterized by multiple, partly overlapping communities with a network topology that makes it possible for individuals to reap benefits such as social support, resources, protection, access to better jobs, relevant information, and, last but certainly not least, possibilities of influencing other people – power. Since people's positions in a given network differ, the benefits they can get through their social relations are unequally distributed. Furthermore, positional effects on benefits differ for each kind of benefit. For example, a network position conducive to strategic information is not exactly the same as a network position that yields power, and social network theory has different centrality measures specifically targeted to each of these two benefits.

In the literature, network benefits and their associated network topologies are generically called "social capital" (Boissevain 1974: 5; Bourdieu 1980; Lin 2001; Portes 1998; Kadushin 2004). To explain how these benefits are obtained, however, one must have recourse to other concepts, such as cohesion (bonding social capital) to explain social support (Coleman 1988), or various centrality measures to explain wealth, power, or prestige.[1] Without loss of explanatory power from the social capital literature, we may therefore simplify the discourse by leaving out the gobbledygook, and address specific benefits or sources of inequality directly. Social cohesion and its associated benefit of social support we have treated extensively in the previous chapter, and we will not return to it again. In this chapter we will discuss four different network sources of social inequality, each of which in its own way is contingent on network topology: (1) prestige; (2) status, or power; (3) brokerage; and (4) roles.

Obviously, social inequality is not determined by networks only, and benefits from a network position are enhanced by individual "capital, skill, and industriousness [. . .], along with luck and privilege" (Geertz 1978). Also the broader socio-economic context is important (e.g. Alderson and Nielsen 2002). Finally, culture has an influence on socio-economic inequality, but it seems that the influence of networks is stronger (Erickson 1996).

PRESTIGE AND POWER

Individuals have their skills and talents by which they can establish an advantage over others. But individual differences do not account for the large socio-economic differences we observe in society. In contrast to what one might expect, it's not individual cunning in the first place that increases inequality, although it certainly plays a role; paradoxically perhaps, it's humans' pro-sociality instead. Because people are dependent on others for information of all sorts, they judge others for what they think they are worth as role models, cooperators, or sources of information, trying to assess their potential quality or talent. Imitating role models saves individual learning costs (Chapter 5; Henrich and Gil-White 2001), but appointing role models engenders inequality independently of the role models' efforts to achieve a superior position.

Roger Gould (2002) explained how relatively small personal differences can turn into large social differences. Since rationality is bounded and searching reliable information about alters is costly, people look for cues about alters' quality (Henrich and Gil-White 2001). In other words, people try to find information about alters through the opinions of others about them, for which there should be a community (or a website) where people can get information about others' deferences. Notice that the set of alters that ego judges and is being judged by tends to be larger than his or her ego network proper, and that these ties are asymmetric. For example, a presidential candidate knows only a fraction of all voters, most of whom are beyond the candidate's ego network but have their judgments about the candidates nevertheless. In this, perhaps extreme, case, deference is highly asymmetric. But this is not all there is to it. When people defer to alters, they tend to feel hurt by alters who do not at all approve of ego; even a president can't get away with insulting his voters, and had better express gratitude to them. This universal, though unequal, desire for recognition sets a limit to asymmetry of deference. After all, liking someone a great deal and not being liked back is unpleasant for most people, and they may interpret the asymmetry as a sign of arrogance. People find it less of a problem if the situation is reversed, though, and they don't worry if their alters give nicer compliments than they reciprocate. "In sum, individuals face a trade-off between attaching themselves to *desirable* alters and attaching themselves to *available* alters" (Gould 2002: 1150, italics in the original), i.e. alters willing to reciprocate deference to a satisfying degree. If asymmetry is not painful, as when voting for a president, there is only preferential attachment to the most desirable alters, whereas, if asymmetry is highly painful, people will reciprocate deference in dyads or small cliquish groups in which relations are almost perfectly symmetric. In Gould's model (which produces a Nash equilibrium), the relative weight of asymmetry can be set to match any social situation.

Under a wide setting of parameters, and supported by empirical evidence, Gould showed that social influence *enhances* individual differences; in other words, that differences in merit are socially overstated by the cumulative effect of socially mediated judgments. Notice that this happens without anyone trying to deceive. However, if asymmetry is highly painful, socially mediated quality judgments will understate true quality. Another result of Gould's model is that it is easier for small groups to be egalitarian than for large groups. In a different context, of musical tastes, an experimental study showed that when social influence increased as well (i.e. ego's knowledge about alters' tastes), the difference between the best and the worst songs increased (Salganik, Dodds, and Watts 2006), similar to increasing differences in prestige in Gould's model. The experiment also showed that, except for the very best and the worst songs, increasing social influence made the overall outcome increasingly unpredictable, a result that does not follow from Gould's model, but that might also be true for prestige.

Gould's model explains how prestige orderings, thus social inequality, can emerge, and complements the evolutionary theory of culture that explains why prestigious people are influential. Sport stars, for example, can be influential role models for the clothes they wear, which marketing agencies have well noticed. Different kinds of prestige are attributed to different kinds of performances and, in general, prestige in one domain does not spill over to another domain. As my colleague Gábor Péli said, "Would you go to a violin concert performed by the world body building champion?" Differentiated societies thus have multiple rank orders of prestige wherein differently prestigious individuals can be role models for different things.

Being influential does necessarily imply being powerful. Power was defined by the classical sociologist Max Weber as having the opportunity to influence other people, possibly against their interests.[2] A powerful ego thus must have ties to alters, direct or indirect, to exert influence sufficiently strong to go against their interests, whereas, for prestige, alters choose an ego to be influenced by – believing it will be in their interest – and not necessarily in a direct social relationship. Someone who has prestige without power lacks the force to obligate alters (Henrich and Gil-White 2001). Obviously, people can have both power and prestige at the same time, and there is a grey zone of strategic impression management (Goffman 1959) as well. If ego has power over alter their tie (or path) is asymmetric, but in most cases somewhat reciprocal as an unequal exchange (Cook and Emerson 1978), e.g. of gratitude for a vote, or signs of humility when being commanded by a superior. In organizations, for example, managers provide inducements (i.e. remuneration) in exchange for contributions by employees (Chester Barnard, reviewed by March and Simon [1958] 1993) and, since contributions must be larger than inducements for the organization to exist, the relation is asymmetric although reciprocal.

In most cases, power implies social status and status implies power, and in the network literature the two concepts are often applied interchangeably. We will interchange power and status in the remainder, but always keep them analytically apart from prestige, acknowledging that empirically they can blur. This distinction exists as prestige versus dominance in anthropology, where they are seen as two different types of status (Henrich and Gil-White 2001). Notice that reputation is not the same as status, and someone can at the same time have a high status for being powerful and have a bad reputation for being an unreliable cooperator. In the previous chapter we have dealt with reputation for cooperation, but people can have reputations for many different kinds of performance, e.g. cooking or making jokes. Reputation can therefore overlap with prestige, but is not to be confused with power. Power can be based on skill, weapons, or capital, and individual sources of power are augmented by social relations, although differently from prestige, as we will see.

Among humans, and even among chimpanzees, it's not necessarily the strongest who has the highest rank but the one who is best related and can form a coalition (de Waal 2000). Seen in the simplest way, someone's relational power, or status, depends on the friends (s)he has; in network terminology, power is indicated by degree. However, if ego is related to alters with power, such as company directors who themselves are related to powerful alters, ego has more power than if his or her friends were unemployed drug addicts, who in their turn tend to hang out with other unemployed drug addicts. Not only the number but also the status, or power, of one's friends counts. Similarly, in cultures where kinship is important, kinship can be a source of status, for those who are married to an important person, or have a position in a tree of famous ancestors. Power and status can thus derive from longer paths, e.g. from ancestors without a direct tie but with a path to ego, although the effect of their status, or power, rubbing off on ego fades out with longer path lengths. In general, ego's power, or status, comes not just from having many alters, but from having many powerful alters; they are important because they in their turn are related to powerful alters, and so on and so forth.[3] Relational power is recursive.

From an evolutionary point of view, both status and prestige are forces of cultural transmission and selection (Chapter 5; Henrich and Gil-White 2001). Furthermore, high-status actors can enhance cooperation by taking a mediating role, punishing norm violators more effectively and efficiently than if everybody were involved in interventions (Flack, de Waal, and Krakauer 2005, consonant with the effect of network *centralization*,[4] Marwell, Oliver, and Prahl 1988). They can subsequently help to restore peace and agreement between actors in conflict (de Waal 2000).[5] Power is intimately related to conflict, which we have investigated as network imbalance in the previous chapter.

People with high status can, along with or instead of mediating impartially, abuse their network position for their private interests that go against group interest. In Vilfredo Pareto's (1966) phrasing, an elite can, respectively, augment the utility *of* its community or the elite's utility *for* its community. This distinction is culturally embedded and, in all cultures, legitimate power is institutionalized and distinguished from illegitimate power, pointing out who is allowed to exert power over whom, when, and how. Most cultures have various egalitarian mechanisms to curb excesses of power (Boehm 1993). An example of legitimate power in modern societies is authority in an organizational hierarchy, which details rights and obligations for each position in the hierarchy (Weber 1922).[6] If a rank order is not (sufficiently) institutionalized, it will emerge as a cumulative result of interactions between individuals (Chase 1980, 1982), and will be determined by individuals' abilities to manipulate others and to form coalitions (Ridgeway and Diekema 1989). In the longer run there are almost no, if any, completely egalitarian communities, despite ideologies claiming otherwise.

Power or status thus comes from the power or status of the actors that ego is related to, an intuition that was cast in a model by Phillip Bonacich (1987, 2007), based on theoretical work by the psychologist Leo Katz (1953) and on experimental studies conducted by exchange theorists (Cook *et al.* 1983). His power centrality measure generalizes degree, while maintaining that, if nothing else changes, alters with higher degree are more powerful than those with lower degree. It is consistent with exchange theory's notion that, the more dependent ego is on one or few alters, the less power ego has. The model can handle weighted arcs and edges (Bonacich and Lloyd 2001) and negative ties (Bonacich and Lloyd 2004), and by tuning a parameter it can also express a negative effect of positive ties, for example a politician being a close friend of an influential criminal. Apart from tie strengths, the main difference from degree is that longer paths are taken into account, although the effect of more remote alters diminishes with path length to ego.[7] Obviously, the network must be reasonably stable for power to have an effect – in contrast to force, which can be brief – and, the longer the paths of influence, the more stable the network should be. Bonacich's power centrality measure must be applied to networks that are a component, and the result is a rank order of actors in the given network, wherein more than one actor can occupy the same rank position in case their power is equal. In most networks, actors' power has a variance, which means that, if some given actor comes out as having the most overall power in the network, this outcome does not imply that the top actor also has most power over *each* individual in the network. For example, an ego's direct manager can be more influential than a remote director, even though the director is generically more powerful.

Noah Friedkin (1991) developed a family of social influence models, in which ego's opinion is a weighted sum of alters' opinions over some time of influence through a given network.[8] Friedkin inferred power centrality from his influence model under fairly general conditions, which then corresponds to the share of each individual's influence in the overall group outcome. The game theorists Ballester, Calvó-Armengol, and Zenou (2006) related power centrality to the Nash equilibrium outcome of their game and showed, analogously, that individuals contribute to the group in proportion to their power centrality.

Joel Podolny (1993) used Bonacich's power centrality measure in markets with uncertainty, where search costs for information are relatively high. Podolny found that actors use alters' status as a signal for choosing business partners or suppliers, and that higher-status alters are preferred, which is also true for monkeys (Silk 2007). Status is accorded to actors "because of the abstract [network] positions they occupy rather than because of immediately observable behavior" (Gould 2002). High-status actors can demand higher prices and make more profit for the same products that lower-status actors provide – if the high-status actors avoid too many or too strong ties with lower-status actors who would pull them down in the pecking order. As a consequence of avoiding lower-status partners, in turn, actors end up partnering with equals (Podolny 1994), similarly to the trade-off for prestige between available and desirable alters. Market relations are thus at the same time "pipes" that transfer information and goods, and "prisms" that reflect the status and reputation of actors (Podolny 2001).

At a large, e.g. global, scale, power inequality is a matter not only of relations, but also of symbols and institutions that can be understood and interpreted across communities and cultures, such as financial or military power.

To fully comprehend the math of Bonacich's power centrality, one needs to have some background in matrix algebra. In this book we will apply a more user-friendly variation of Bonacich's power centrality, among other reasons because the computer outcomes of this alternative ranking procedure are intuitively much easier to interpret, and because computations can be done on much larger networks. In this simpler measure, ego's status depends on the statuses of his or her alters recursively, as above, but weighted differently. Intuitively it is easiest to understand for arcs, although the measure also works well for edges, both unweighted and positive. If data for arcs are used, their direction should be toward the higher-status person in each dyad, e.g. in the direction of where deference, subordination, or contributions go. If alter has an arc to ego, alter's status contributes to ego's. However, if alter attaches to many others, e.g. by liking many people, alter's tie to ego is not a very exclusive sign of deference and contributes less to ego's status than if alter's tie is a more exclusive attachment. Hence alter's tie to ego is weighted inversely with alter's outdegree. This way of ranking vertices in a network forms the basis of the search engine Google and is called *page rank* (Brin and Page 1998).[9] It can also rank-order people and organizations well and fast. Google uses status as a cue for relevance, and humans often do the same if they need information under uncertainty. To develop an intuition for this measure, it is a useful exercise to create several small networks on the computer and to compute and compare page rank values.

So far, we have looked at only network position as a source of power, but we shall finish our treatment of power by discussing one important attribute that is meshed with networks, *gender*. Ron Burt (1998) studied promotion in a large organization, comparing the networks of men and women while controlling for education, rank, experience, and other possibly relevant effects. It turned out that, to make early promotion, women's networks should differ from men's (who in turn need to broker, see below). Because women are often taken less seriously than men, especially if it comes to high management positions, women face a legitimacy problem. This can be overcome by a social sponsor, who should be a senior manager who is not the woman's direct boss. From a direct boss it is taken for granted that he – it is most likely a man – helps his subordinates, whereas if another sponsor uses his status to foster a woman's prestige, for example by letting her participate in important projects, he has a marked effect on her career chances. Women need to concentrate the time and energy they spend on social relations on the social sponsor, and the distribution of their tie strengths should be a power law with a high exponent – in sharp contrast to men.[10] An implication is that organizations that want women in high positions and want them to stay there rather than leave should provide social sponsors. Except for the fact that women need a sponsor different from their direct boss, Burt's finding is consonant with the more general theory of status that conjectures that a strong tie with a high-status alter will increase ego's status. Ego's status will then increase in the eye of a third person who in turn is positively related to alter, consistent with balance theory (Chapter 5). Martin Kilduff and David Krackhardt (1994) discovered that the third person's perception of a tie has a stronger status effect than the actual tie has.

BROKERAGE

Independently from social support, prestige, and power, people can reap benefits from occupying a strategic position between alters in different (sub)communities and be a *broker* (Boissevain 1966), or gatekeeper. A broker can slow down, speed up, distort, or interrupt information that passes through (Boissevain 1974), and "facilitate transactions between other actors lacking access to or trust in one another" (Marsden 1982: 202). A broker is the third who benefits (Simmel [1890, 1908] 1950), the *entrepreneur* in French, or *de lachende derde* (the laughing third) in Dutch (Burt 1992: 31). If there are conflicting interests between a broker's contacts keeping them from having a direct relation, a broker can (also) be a *mediator* making third party interventions. Control benefits from brokerage to some degree overlap with power, but are often different. We will first flesh out brokerage in general terms and then present an elaborate example to point out what a broker's ego network topology looks like and why a broker's information should be (1) reliable, (2) diverse, and (3) well timed. Finally, brokering influences the broker's reputation, as any social behavior does, which in turn influences future chances of brokerage.

As a point of departure, we repeat that humans are bounded rational rather than omniscient decision-makers (Camerer and Fehr 2006),[11] and consequently their network contacts are screening devices that filter, concentrate, and legitimize information (Boissevain 1968: 549; Burt 1992: 14). To stress the function of ties as transmitters of strategic information, we might substitute the word *axon* (nerve fiber) for tie, which Anatol Rapoport used in the 1950s. This analogy points out that brokerage is a special kind of diffusion, or transmission, whereby the broker holds a gatekeeper position in a diffusion process. Brokers have their axons connected to places where "useful bits of information are likely to air, and provide a reliable flow of information to and from those places" (Burt 1992: 15). For information to be optimally useful to a broker it should first be *reliable*. The shorter the axons are, the more reliable the information will be, as we saw in the small world experiments. It turned out that benefits from contacts beyond direct contacts ("secondhand brokerage") are negligible, and almost all information contributing to brokerage comes from within the ego network (Burt 2007). The redundancy argument of multiple ties does not hold for brokerage, as will be explained below. Second, to match wishes and offerings, or more generally to make different ends meet in complementary ways, ego's information sources must be *diverse*. A hotel may let a room to a tourist, but is less likely to let a room to another hotel in the same city. Hotels on the one hand and tourists on the other hand provide larger diversity than hotels only. A broker's network should thus be a "pulsing swirl of mixed, conflicting demands" (Burt 1992: 33). Within a community, information, goods, and interests are more homogeneous than across communities, and within a subcommunity information is yet more homogeneous than in the larger community, as we discussed in Chapter 5. In other words, the stronger the cohesion of the (sub)community to which ego is related, the more homogeneous the information to which ego is exposed, and the more redundant multiple contacts with that (sub)community are. Whereas redundancy was good for cohesion, it isn't for brokerage. What ego hears in a cohesive network from one contact is perhaps reconfirming but not so much different from what other contacts in the same (sub)community will tell. In the extreme case of ego being nested in a clique, (s)he hears hardly anything that not everybody else knows as well. A maximally dense ego network is therefore maximally constraining with respect to brokerage opportunities. Hence ego should spend time and effort on establishing and maintaining diverse contacts in different (sub)communities, with as few as possible links between them other than through ego. A broker then has access to information in one (sub)community that is "scarce, maldistributed, inefficiently communicated, and intensely valued" in another (sub)community (Geertz 1978). The more different and mutually unconnected (sub)communities ego manages to be related to, the higher the diversity, or heterogeneity, of information (s)he is exposed to, and the more chances (s)he has to notice and materialize beneficial combinations of pieces of information. The value of each piece of information depends on the evolution of the (sub)community it comes from, which although important is left out of the current treatment of brokerage. Third, although reliability and diversity are important they are often not sufficient, and ego's information should also be *well timed*, such that ego gets the news early enough before someone else finds out about and seizes the opportunity (Burt 1992).

In most cases a broker can't do just anything (s)he likes with information received, because his or her network "brings him the unsolicited – favourable and unfavourable – opinion of others regarding his behaviour" (Boissevain 1968: 548). Depending on the institutional embedding of the network and the expectations associated with ego's network position, there might be norms and sanctions for norm-violating behavior. For example, a broker may buy rotten food cheaply but will meet disapproval and sanctions if (s)he sells it in a market, which will also damage the broker's reputation.

Let us pass first through an example, of Hamidou, a wealthy car reseller from Niger, at the car market in Cotonou, in Benin, West Africa (Beuving 2006). Figure 6.1 presents an overview of different parts of the car market in Cotonou. A ship from Europe delivers about 400 second-hand cars, vans, and trucks (Figure 6.1a). The trucks and vans in their turn are filled with computers, televisions, refrigerators, and other items, such as the ventilation propeller that is being carried away (Figure 6.1b), which are sold at the side of the car market. In Figure 6.1c, a group of salesmen interrupts work to pray in the direction of Mecca. In Figure 6.1d, Hamidou leans on one of his cars, and his body language and that of his cousin in the background tell who is more powerful and who is submissive. In the car market, many different ethnic groups are present and about ten languages are spoken. There is no lingua franca.

Ideally for a salesman, his client on the one hand and the importer of the car of the client's interest on the other hand have no language in common, whereas the salesman can communicate with both. Hamidou might be positioned like actor 7 in Figure 2.3 as a member of two communities, where he is the linking pin in between. Alternatively, he is in the community of one of his contact persons and has a local bridge to the other contact, a *local bridge* being a tie between two components if and only if the components are more densely connected within than between (Granovetter 1973: 1365). In Figure 2.2, the left hand side upper and lower subgroups are connected by two local bridges, (5, 21) and (7, 19). Logically speaking, a bridge is a local bridge but not the other way around. A third possibility is that the broker is in neither contact's community but has local bridges to both of them. Whether as a linking pin or by having local bridges, there is in Ron Burt's phrasing a "structural hole" between the client and the importer, and Hamidou controls what information he passes on from one side to the other side of the "hole."

Revisiting the three information advantages, Hamidou is in direct contact with both importer and customer, and the distance to both is 1. Although his alters could cheat, the information he receives is surely more reliable than if there were more intermediaries in between, who would be in control of Hamidou's axons. Furthermore, Hamidou's information is sufficiently diverse to make a profit, because he can match the needs of one contact with offers from the other contact. His diversity of information further increases if he knows more consumers, importers, and market officials. The timing is fine if Hamidou is the first who talks with the customer and there is not too much discrepancy between the moment the customer airs his desire and Hamidou finding an importer who has the desired car available. Otherwise other salesmen competing with Hamidou might get in contact with the customer and act faster. Hamidou's position is also threatened if the customer and the importer have a language in common and meet each other directly – then Hamidou bridges no structural hole any more – or if consumers (or importers) are in mutual contact with each other and learn about alternative opportunities via other salesmen. From the consumers' (or importers') point of view, car salesmen that are accessible at the same time are substitutable, which is a notion used by economists to address competition. It is to Hamidou's advantage not to be played off against his competitors, which the salesmen can collectively achieve by a cohesive structure among themselves (Ingram and Roberts 2000; Burt 1992). At the same time, the more strongly Hamidou's customers are mutually related and exchange information on car sellers, the more redundant his contact with each of them is from Hamidou's point of view, reducing his information diversity and timing advantages, and thereby the benefit he might have had from being in contact with each of them separated from the rest. The same argument holds for car importers having a cohesive structure among each other.[12]

To generalize from the example, if ego were the center of a star network (Figure 6.2), this would be a maximally autonomous position, e.g. as a manager of otherwise unconnected employees each performing a different task in a different part of the company, or as a linking pin between different (sub)communities connected only through ego. For control advantages, brokerage thus overlaps with power, although (in most cases) it differs in its requirements for reliability, timing, and diversity. Brokerage and power coincide on the advantage of having many contacts, but for different reasons. For brokerage, more contacts yield additional sources of information diversity, whereas for power they yield decreasing dependence on few alters and additional possibilities to influence, for which diversity is less important. For reliability of information, a broker depends on short path distances, but has to avoid trading off timing for redundancy, whereas timing is less urgent for a pure power player. For the latter, reliability of information is an issue, as it is for a broker, but brokerage tends to be more sensitive to unreliability whereas influence can be exerted over longer path distances.

It may seem that maximizing business opportunities though brokerage flies in the face of maximizing social support through nestedness, another network benefit that requires yet another network topology. However, maximal nestedness is neither necessary nor beneficial (Chapter 5), and a reasonable amount of nestedness goes well together with a high level of brokerage. Although simultaneous requirements for bonding and bridging social capital have been presented as a paradox in the social capital literature, actual brokers do not suffer from this theoretical problem. Hamidou is in his cohesive family while simultaneously having many structural holes in his business network. If, in the data, friendship and family ties are used to compute nestedness and distinguished from business relations used to compute brokerage, the problem vanishes also in theory.

A broker needs to establish trust across community cleavages, which is difficult because the intra-community option of third party intervention is absent – otherwise

(a)

(b)

■ **Figure 6.1** *Second-hand car market in Cotonou, Benin. (a) Unloading cars from a ship. (b) Along with cars come electronics, here a ventilation propeller.*

(c)

(d)

(c) Small hangars (paillotes) are for traders to overlook their section of the car park and to talk with business partners. (d) Reseller El Hadj Hamidou and his cousin. Photographs by the author (2002).

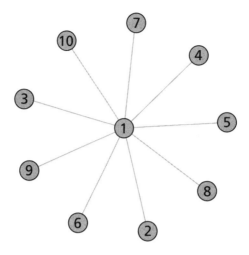

Figure 6.2 *Star network.*

there would not be a structural hole for the broker to bridge. Supra-community institutions can facilitate inter-community trust. In collectivist cultures, such as clans and religious and ethnic groups, exchange is mostly within the community, whereas in individualist cultures, such as Western Europe and the United States, people may or may not have more trust in each other but they have more trust in law-enforcing organizations to fulfill policing tasks if conflict were to arise. Thereby exchange across communities in individualist cultures is facilitated significantly (Greif 1994). In China, the largest collectivist country, bridging a structural hole is seen as "standing on two boats" and is disapproved of if it happens openly (Xiao and Tsui 2007). Therefore brokerage does not yield benefits to Chinese managers, who are supposed to integrate rather than broker, and to increase cohesion and decrease path distances within their organization (Xiao and Tsui 2007). If they by their profession should bridge different departments or organizations, they are supposed to involve other people in the cross-connections and not to have personal benefits only for themselves. In other words, they are supposed to act as non-brokering boundary spanners. The job market in China is strongly regulated by the government and, officially, people are not allowed to search jobs by themselves. Granovetter (1995) showed that in the United States, if people look for a new job, they have the best chances if they transgress the boundaries of their communities, which typically happens by using *weak ties*, whereas strong ties are mostly within communities (Granovetter 1973; see also Ioannides and Datcher Loury 2004). Notice that the weakness of ties is correlated with but is *not* causally related to bridging structural holes. Using weak ties to find a job is possible if trust can be established easily. In China, in contrast, if people want a better job than the government offers to them, they have to make an unauthorized search effort in the labor market, where trust is therefore lacking. To get support for their search, ego must then first establish trust, in a strong tie (*guanxi*) with an intermediary (Bian 1997). The intermediary should have a higher status than ego, and in turn have a strong tie to a high-status alter who has a job to offer. Strong ties and a third party are necessary to establish trust where brokerage by ego is otherwise impossible.

In Western countries also, culture sets limits to brokerage opportunities. Podolny and Baron (1997) discovered that, in organizations, roles are too strongly institutionalized in terms of role expectations and sanctions for structural holes in the formal (i.e. position-related) network to be profitable, whereas bridging structural holes in the network of informal (i.e. friendship-related) network is beneficial. Furthermore, lower-status actors in Western countries need stronger ties than high-status actors to be regarded as trustworthy, in particular when a low-status actor wants a favor, e.g. a job, from the latter, similarly to the job market in China. Consequentially, higher-status actors have more benefit from bridging structural holes – which happens mostly by weak ties – than lower-status actors have (Wegener 1991; Granovetter 1983: 206). Finally, distrust is self-fulfilling, and makes it especially difficult to broker across community or class boundaries. In sum, brokering opportunities are culture and class dependent.

Brokerage is also personality dependent (Kalish and Robins 2006). Bridging structural holes requires an ability to spot them and to move in different social circles, with different norms, idiosyncrasies, dialects, and sometimes languages too (Hayek 1945). Brokers have to mentalize and empathize with alters from different backgrounds, sense their tacit knowledge, and stage credible performances in different social circles. They must be able to handle conflicting expectations in different communities (Merton 1968b), as they go against the general tendency of assortative mating (homophily). Not everybody who bridges a structural hole has the abilities to exploit it. This is also true for bridging the cleavage between social classes, each with a different subculture. For a high-class individual to benefit from his or her position (s)he needs to have sufficient cultural knowledge of lower classes, including the rules when cultural items, e.g. jokes, are (in)appropriate. "Equipped with vast amounts of high culture alone, a person would be shipwrecked in many social seas" (Erickson 1996: 224). Regular brokers are more competent than average people to notice structural holes and to establish new disassortative contacts (Janicik and Larrick 2005). Their ability is also important for them because local bridges between (sub)communities are mostly weak ties, which are much more volatile than strong ties (Burt 2002), making brokerage opportunities rapidly fall by the wayside. At the same time, ego's strong ties have a higher chance of transitivity, which in its turn causes ego's brokering position to disappear after some time. Hence brokers have to be able to establish new ties more often than others, living among the vicissitude of weak ties.

Brokerage not only provides individual benefits but also yields several benefits for the communities involved. First, brokers are the interfaces of communities and increase overall social cohesion. Second, they provide goods from other (sub)communities that people could not obtain otherwise, or only at a higher cost. Third, they are crucially important for cultural innovations of all sorts. With the exception of elementary observations, such as "this hurts," new ideas are novel recombinations of existing ideas and applications (Poincaré 1902; Weitzman 1996, 1998; Diamond 1997), hybridized in a process of knowledge brokerage (Burt 2004).[13] As we have discussed, if ego has a brokering position connecting (sub)communities, ego is exposed to a greater diversity of ideas (Burt 2004), since ideas are more heterogeneous across (sub)communities than within, and thus has a higher chance of creating novelty. For the individual knowledge broker, searching something new is a form of play, with connotations of competition, risk, and prestige (Huizinga [1938] 1964). A knowledge broker can benefit from the diversity of sources also in another way, by expressing his or her own idea to various social contacts, and by receiving a higher diversity of feedback to further increase the quality of that idea (Mizruchi and Stearns 2001). Thus, if ego learns about ideas or applications at different ends of his or her network, which have previously not been combined with each other, (s)he is in a position to recombine them in new ways, as Edison invented the light bulb by combining his knowledge of electricity and candles. "The creative spark on which serendipity depends, in short, is to see bridges where others see holes" (Burt 2004: 351).[14] Innovations and discoveries can subsequently diffuse though society by the mechanisms of transmission we discussed in the previous chapter.

Ron Burt (1992) captured the control, timing, diversity, and reliability arguments in a model of structural autonomy versus *constraint*, the latter being the opposite of the former. He, and many others, tested his model on data on individuals, teams, business companies, and industrial sectors. By now we know that his model holds at different levels of aggregation (person, team, department, organization, industry, country) and in multiple contexts. In Burt's model, an actor is more autonomous if (s)he has more contacts and if these contacts are less related to each other directly, and are related indirectly only through the focal actor. The technicalities are explained in the appendix to this chapter.

Unfortunately, there is one problem with Burt's model. In the example of Hamidou, his clients and importer should be connected only through Hamidou, not through other salesmen, otherwise Hamidou loses his strategic advantage. If there is a competing salesman who has no tie with Hamidou and connects to the same importer(s) and client(s), thus becoming a substitute for Hamidou from his alter's point of view, Burt's model will not take this into account.

There exists another brokerage measure that solves this problem, called betweenness centrality. However, it deals only with binary data, directed or undirected, or it simplifies data on weighted ties to binary ties and then washes away any distinction between strong(er) and weak(er) ties. Depending on the research problem and the data at hand, this might be a shortcoming. Betweenness centrality was invented in computer science as a measure of "rush in a graph" (Anthonisse 1971), and it was introduced in sociology under its current name by Linton Freeman (1977). This measure also captures ego's gatekeeper position and the advantages of having access to information that is (1) reliable, (2) diverse, and (3) well timed. It focuses on paths that pass through ego from here to there, and the most reliable ones are the shortest paths, which this centrality measure selects from all possible paths. However, it allows paths to be longer than direct contacts with ego, which can be problematic for reasons discussed earlier. Within organizations or branches of industry where this measure is most often used (e.g. Krackhardt 1990), average path lengths tend to be fairly short. Then strong attrition over longer distances will not happen and there is less threat to the validity of betweenness centrality. In general we might conjecture that, for actors with the same betweenness, those who have on average shorter distances to their alters are better positioned. Our conjecture can be made precise by using the measure of *closeness centrality* (Freeman 1979), which is defined as the reciprocal of the mean length of all geodesics to and from ego (and, for arcs, direction matters). Obviously, shorter paths are also more likely to yield timing advantages. From the small world experiments we know that information can follow paths that are longer than the shortest and sometimes in less time, but, in large numbers, longer paths are slower than shorter paths.

Betweenness centrality of ego is defined straightforwardly as follows. Take the ratio of the number (not the length!) of shortest paths from a person a through ego to another person b, and the number of *all* shortest paths from a to b including paths that do *not* go through ego. Then sum this ratio for all a and b in the network, for as long as ego is not one of them, which yields ego's betweenness centrality. If there are arcs rather than edges, paths from a to b can differ from paths in the opposite direction (if they exist at all). The value of betweenness is higher if there are more shortest paths through ego, reflecting the advantage of information diversity, and is lower if ego's gatekeeper advantage is challenged by alternative paths of equal length from a to b not passing through ego. If a path from a to b through a competing alter were longer, then according to the shortest path argument it would not count; if it were shorter, the path through ego would not count according to the same argument; therefore the comparisons are always of paths of equal length. For betweenness centrality, the same data can be used as for Burt's brokerage, e.g. on professional, business, exchange, or informal work relations, as well as more abstract information transfer networks, provided that the ties are non-negative. However, since valued ties cannot be used, a reasonable threshold should be chosen.

Betweenness centrality

Betweenness centrality, B_i of i, is defined as the sum of the ratios of the number (not the length!) of shortest paths from j through i to k, g_{kij}, and all shortest paths from j to k, $g_{k,j}$, the latter including paths that do not go through i:

$$B_i = \Sigma\Sigma_{k<j}\, g_{kij}/g_{k,j} \text{ and } k \neq i \neq j \qquad\qquad (6.1)$$

Actors k and j can be anywhere in the same component and are not confined to i's ego network. The double summation is necessary to systematically graze all geodesics where ego sits astride,[15] one summation for the columns of Table 6.1, and one for the column totals. For the betweenness centrality of F in Figure 6.3, for example, we go about computing as follows. F itself is not allowed as vertex in one of the shortest paths through F, so we first delete F's column and row. Each cell in the table indicates a possible shortest path through F, starting with the path from A to B, but only the cells in bold indicate where there is indeed a shortest path through F, for example the path from A through F to G. Along with this path, there are two more paths from A to G of equal length, and we divide the number of paths through F (one) by all paths (three), indicated in the pertaining cell. We repeat the same routine for each cell and add up all intermediate results, and F's betweenness equals 8.33.

In the table we can also see what the maximum value of betweenness can be, analogous to density (Chapter 2). For density, the maximum number of arcs was the number of rows times the number of columns minus the diagonal. In Table 6.1 we removed a row and a column of the focal vertex, therefore the maximum number of shortest paths through a focal actor equals $(n-2)(n-1)$. If there are only edges, as in Figure 6.3, the maximum is half of this number. We may thus normalize betweenness to values between 0 and 1 by dividing by the maximum possible. Notice that, for networks smaller than 3, dividing betweenness by the maximum is not possible. Georg Simmel ([1890, 1908] 1950) legitimizes our limitation to components of order 3 or larger, as he argued a century ago and ahead of his time that the triad should be the smallest unit for sociological analyses. His argument is that a triad offers the strategic possibilities that are also found in larger groups, such as coalition making, brokering, and mediating conflict, which are absent in the dyad.

For measuring brokerage, betweenness has several advantages over autonomy, and several disadvantages as well. Betweenness treats correctly ego's competitors that have no ties to ego (and are structurally equivalent, see below). Furthermore, betweenness is simpler and therefore intuitively easier to grasp. A disadvantage of betweenness is that for some actors it can turn out rather high values due to long

■ **Table 6.1** *Computation of betweenness centrality of F*

AB	BC	CD	DE	EG	GH	HI	IJ
AC	BD	CE	DG	EH	GI	HJ	
AD	BE	CG ½	DH ½	EI	GJ		
AE	BG	CH 1	DI ½	EJ			
AG 1/3	BH	CI 1	DJ ½				
AH 1	BI	CJ 1					
AI 1	BJ						
AJ 1							

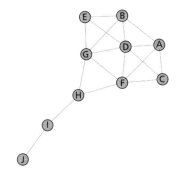

■ **Figure 6.3** *Kite network in which vertices with highest degree (D), closeness (F, G), and betweenness centrality (H) differ from each other (adapted from Krackhardt 1990).*

geodesics that in actuality are irrelevant on account of attrition of information. If only ego-network data are used, this problem disappears, but then betweenness's advantage of correctly handling (structurally equivalent) competitors disappears as well. Autonomy is more straightforward in its treatment of reliability of information by cutting off all paths to ego longer than 1, which hardly matter for brokerage anyway (Burt 2007). Perhaps most importantly, autonomy can handle differences in tie strength, and is therefore arguably the best measure for valued networks.[16]

ROLES

We have encountered brokerage roles and role models, as well as gender, which in most societies induces gender-related roles. In complex societies, both people and organizations have roles, possibly multiple roles in multiplex networks. Roles entail inequality both "horizontally," as specialization, and "vertically" in terms of status. People's roles can be based on gender, age, or education, and organizational roles in a market depend on their products, which have all received plenty of attention in the literature. Here we will focus on roles induced by network positions. Let us for simplicity assume that actors have uniquely one role each, and later generalize to the possibility that actors can play multiple roles. Suppose we do research on a market chain where shops (S, in Figure 6.4) purchase from suppliers (M) and sell to consumers (C). The shops in this market chain example are in a certain social position in their relations to suppliers and consumers, and in their position they fulfill a certain role in the market through their purchasing and selling behavior associated with that role, which possibly includes rivalry with other shops. Also suppliers and the consumers have their network positions and associated roles. Actors in a role, e.g. shops, are therefore regarded as substitutable from the point of view of actors in other groups, and equivalence of roles indicates competition between actors.

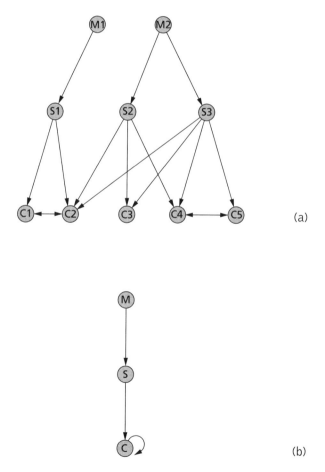

(a)

(b)

■ **Figure 6.4** *(a) Network of suppliers (M), shops (S), and consumers (C). (b) Reduced graph of the three pertaining roles.*

Given these three roles in the example, one could partition the actors into three pertinent groups, producing a so-called reduced graph (as in Figure 6.4b). Notice that the group of consumers, forming a single vertex in the reduced graph, has a reflexive tie to itself, since (some) consumers are mutually related. There are ties of trade between suppliers, shops, and consumers, but competing shops may not be socially or economically connected with each other directly, as in Figure 6.4a, and not all consumers talk to each other. When assigning vertices to roles, then, the grouping principle of maximizing in-group ties, like for community detection, will not yield a result that we want, and another grouping principle is needed, of regular equivalence (D. White and Reitz 1983).[17] Two actors, here shops, are regularly equivalent when they have the same kinds of relations, here purchasing and selling, with other actors who in their turn are regularly equivalent, here the suppliers and customers, respectively. In general, a vertex i is *regularly equivalent* with j if i has a tie with k and j a tie with l, and l and k in turn are regularly equivalent; this should then hold for all relations and for all ties of i and j. The definition is recursive but not circular. A special case of regular equivalence occurs when i and j have ties to exactly the same vertices, which is called *structural equivalence* (Lorrain and H. White 1971; conceptual explication, Borgatti and Everett 1992). For example, in Isabel Allende's novel *Eva Luna* there are two structurally equivalent sisters who know the same people and even share their boyfriend. Another example would be a car trader who has the same client(s) and importer(s) as Hamidou, in the example above. These equivalence notions are important because they make it possible to spell out precisely the social structure of (vertical) inequality and (horizontal) differentiation.

Since the 1970s, sociologists have dealt with roles and positions under the header of block models (because of the block patterns in the permuted adjacency matrix, H. White, Boorman, and Breiger 1976). They have contributed to the study of history (Padgett and Ansell 1993), an area to which many believe that quantitative approaches cannot possibly contribute because of the uniqueness of historical phenomena. They have also contributed to the study of international trade and politics, forming a multi network of countries, and partly confirmed and partly modified Wallerstein's world-system, featuring a partitioning of countries into central, semi-peripheral, and peripheral positions (Smith and D. White 1992; Van Rossem 1996).[18] In traditional block models, the assignment of vertices to groups (blocks) is done by a technique called hierarchical clustering, which sometimes misses actual groups or creates non-existent groups, and has no indication of significance. Furthermore, actors may have multiple roles, e.g. a firm that is a shop and at the same time a supplier for other shops, and the notion of regular equivalence then becomes a straitjacket rather than a solution. Jörg Reichardt and Douglas White (2007) solved these problems from first principles, and represented the role detection problem in a Hamiltonian equation, similar to the Hamiltonian equation for community detection. Their approach can detect roles fast and well, handle noise in the data, take overlapping roles into account, and help to judge whether the principle of regular equivalence (dealt with as regular similarity) or of structural equivalence yields a better block model. The Hamiltonian approach to block modeling thus generalizes the notion of regular equivalence and is superior to hierarchical clustering-based block models. On the basis of the fundamental principle of entropy (Ball 2004), a variety of problems such as community detection, structural balance, block modeling, and core–periphery detection, which used to be treated separately in the literature, can now be solved within the same Hamiltonian framework, which is a truly great achievement.

In this chapter we have seen that differences between individuals' skills and talent are amplified by network topology, resulting in social inequality well beyond individual merit. To conclude that inequality is unfair across the board would miss the point that people in beneficial positions can also bring advantages to others, and for each case one should therefore first examine in detail the utility *of* the community and *for* the community before reaching a verdict. We have distinguished four network sources of inequality: prestige, power, brokerage, and the roles that people have, which in turn are also institutionalized to various degrees beyond actual networks. Last but not least, we have presented techniques to analyze power and brokerage precisely, while the math for prestige and roles can be found in the literature.

SUGGESTED BACKGROUND READING

Prestige, Gould (2002); power and status, Bonacich (2007); structural autonomy, Burt (2004); betweenness centrality, Krackhardt (1990); a mind-boggling network study on Renaissance Italy, Padgett and Ansell (1993); for an account of personal experiences in a variety of social settings, Tolstoy's novel *War and Peace* is arguably the best source.

EXERCISE 6.1

In Figure 6.5, compute by hand betweenness centrality of F, and check if you get the same results as the computer (by first making a file, etc.).

EXERCISE 6.2

In the small networks in Figure 6.6, in which arrowheads have been deleted for clarity, compute constraint *à la* Burt of persons N, B, A, E, H, K, Q; do this by hand (see Appendix), and check if you get the same results as the computer. All arcs have value 1 except the following three arcs:

E → F	0.5
F → E	0.5
K → J	2

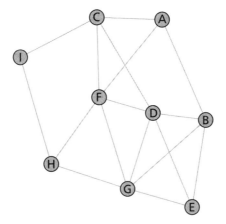

■ *Figure 6.5* Exercise 6.1.

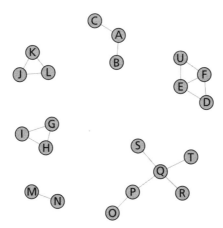

■ *Figure 6.6* Exercise 6.2.

APPENDIX: BROKERAGE

Here we compute brokerage *à la* Burt (1992). We first need a data set with valued arcs or edges, preferably a complete network, e.g. of everybody working in an organization (Burt 2004), or all organizations in a market, or else of a sample of focal actors and at least 25 alters in each of their ego networks. The data collection should result in all focal actors having the same number of alters, unless an actor really has fewer than 25 alters, because the measure for brokerage is not normalized for comparing ego networks of different sizes. Data on any exchange, professional, or work relation can be used, as well as abstract information-transfer relations without face-to-face social contact, provided that the arcs or edges have positive values. At

83 ■

the level of teams or organizations, one can for example establish a tie value out of the number of projects or activities two organizations do together in a given time interval, possibly also taking the number of people involved into account, as a proportion of all staff.

Negative ties, or ties that represent mainly emotional content, won't do for brokerage.

First, the arc or edge values have to be transformed into proportional tie values, motivated by the intuition that somebody who spends little time and attention (or other resources) on each of many contacts is more autonomous and therefore less constrained than somebody who spends all his or her time and energy on just a handful of close friends. We take one focal individual i at a time, with a set of alters constituting his or her ego network N_i; z_{ix} and z_{xi} are the values of the arcs from and to i, respectively; $x \in N_i$ (x being an index for i's direct contacts), and $x \neq i$ (unless reflexive ties from ego to him- or herself play a role, which in most studies is not the case).

The constraint measure below is based on weighted ties of i, and each tie value is put in proportion to the sum total of all tie values of i. Tacitly it is assumed that an arc into the direction of ego is constraining ego nevertheless, even though it is alter who spends his or her time and energy on maintaining it; ego will presumably spend a little time listening to some of what alter has to say, which is not unreasonable because the ties in this context are to some extent about exchange of strategically valuable information. In any case, the assumption is explicit in the equation below, and the sum of i's arcs in both directions is $\Sigma_x (z_{ix} + z_{xi})$, and, accordingly, the share of one single tie between i and j in all ties of i is:

$$p_{ij} = (z_{ij} + z_{ji})/\Sigma_x (z_{ix} + z_{xi}) \qquad (6.2)$$

Hence, for each actor, $\Sigma\, p_{ij} = 1$. For a different contact person q of i we will have to compute p_{iq}, which goes the same way, and we can continue to compute all p values from the data on tie values. For an undirected network, Equation 6.2 simplifies to $p_{ij} = z_{ij}/\Sigma_x z_{ix}$, as you may want to check for yourself. Notice that even in this case, $p_{ij} \neq p_{ji}$, thus symmetric ties lead to asymmetric proportional ties. If this is not clear again at the star network of Figure 6.1, assume that all ties have value 1 and are undirected, and compute proportional tie strength for the central actor and for one of his or her contacts.

On the basis of the definition of proportional tie strength one could establish a very simple measure of constraint, which only captures the aspect of lacking many different contacts, by first squaring ego's proportional tie values,[19] and then summing them to an overall constraint measure C_i:

$$c_{ij} = p_{ij}^{2} \text{ and } j \in N_i \qquad (6.3)$$

$$C_i = \Sigma_j c_{ij} \tag{6.4}$$

If ego spends all his or her attention on one person, his or her constraint equals 1, and the more (s)he spreads her attention over an increasingly larger number of people, the closer ego's constraint approaches 0 (as in Figure 6.1). Clearly this is not good enough for a measure of constraint, because it doesn't distinguish star networks on the one hand (wherein the central actor has minimal constraint) and networks with high local clustering on the other hand (wherein ego is highly constrained). Therefore Equation 6.3 must be extended with a term expressing the constraint-increasing effect of ego's contact persons being in mutual contact with each other. This is modeled by looking for each $j \in N_i$ if there are alters $q \in N_i$ (and $q \neq j$) who in their turn are related to j. For example in Hamidou's ego network, if there is a triad wherein Hamidou, abbreviated as h, has contact with a client c, and with a car importer j, Hamidou is more constrained in his relation with the importer if (1) the client and the importer have a stronger relation with each other, making Hamidou a more superfluous person in their mutual transaction (larger value of p_{cj}), or if (2) this particular client is relatively more important to Hamidou (larger p_{hc}), or both. In the model these constraints on i can be expressed by multiplying the proportional tie between Hamidou and the client and the tie between the client and the importer, $p_{hc}p_{cj}$. If there are multiple clients, possibly varying in importance to Hamidou and the time he spends on them, or if there are multiple indirect paths from Hamidou via other contacts q to the importer that must be taken into account, this can be achieved by adding all indirect paths, $\Sigma_q p_{hq}p_{qj}$. Contact persons q can be anyone constraining Hamidou, be it clients, harbor officials, importers, or other people. To capture the effect of all indirect paths on i's constraint, and generalizing the example by substituting an abstract index i for Hamidou, Equation 6.3 is to be replaced by

$$c_{ij} = (p_{ij} + \Sigma_q p_{iq} p_{qj})^2 \tag{6.5}$$

Equation 6.5 says that for a given alter j there is a sum of *all* other contacts q of i and the indirect paths via them that constrain i with respect to j; if there is no tie connecting q and j, then $p_{qj} = 0$ and i is unconstrained. In other words, there is no transitivity and i has a "structural hole." To compute Equation 6.5, the values of p_{qj} are also to be computed, but that goes exactly like p_{ij} in Equation 6.2, although now from q's point of view – it is the tie between q and j – thus with q's index $z \in N_q$ and $q \neq j \neq z$:

$$p_{qj} = (z_{qj} + z_{jq})/\Sigma_z (z_{qz} + z_{zq}) \tag{6.6}$$

Overall constraint of ego is still expressed by Equation 6.4, but now with c_{ij} as defined by 6.5, and after computing for all contact persons j of i a value of c_{ij}, these intermediate results are summed, $C_i = \Sigma_j c_{ij}$. To get used to these equations and to develop an intuition for them, it is best to work with them and to go carefully through the exercises, and then to compare the hand-computed results with what one would intuitively expect, and to compare them with the computer output.

The *structural autonomy* A_i of ego is higher if constraint is lower, with the greatest social capital benefits at low levels of constraint (Burt 1992). Parameters $\alpha > 0, \beta > 0$ can relate the model to empirical data about success, e.g. profit:

$$A_i = \alpha \ C_i^{-\beta} \qquad\qquad (6.7)$$

Some authors – not Burt himself – thought they could more simply say $A_i = 1 - C_i$ instead, believing that constraint cannot exceed 1. Apparently it has passed unnoticed that in a triad constraint can exceed 1 (it can go up to 2), and one wonders what negative autonomy would mean. No big deal, since a linear transformation can easily solve this minor issue. What is worse is that the distribution of autonomy (assuming $A_i = 1 - C_i$) fits Burt's and other data less well, and therefore it is Equation 6.7 that we need instead. Autonomy is not to be computed for dyads and isolates, since the results are non-monotonic and counter-intuitive. This is not a problem because the very idea of brokerage is that there is an actor in between at least two others.

Chapter 7

Organizations as networks

Organizations are an extension of "natural" community life, gradually more purposeful and designed more consciously. Examples are firms, hospitals, governmental agencies, universities, churches, armies, labor unions, voluntary associations, prisons, political parties, sport clubs, schools, and criminal organizations, to mention just a few. An *organization* can be regarded as a special purpose community,[1] and can likewise be defined as a network – a component, to be precise – of people spending part of their time in working and in power relations to each other, with relations extending to the socio-economic *environment* of the organization. Obviously, both internal and external relations are fleshed out culturally. Following up on our community detection approach (Chapter 5), organizational boundaries tend to be fuzzy, since individuals can be members of multiple organizations or communities, and can have ties to other organizations.

To approach organizations as multiplex networks is a well-established tradition in sociology (e.g. Nohria and Eccles 1992; Brass 1984), dating back to Bavelas (1950). Whereas other approaches focus on resources, interests, skills, or decisions, the network perspective points out more precisely where resources come from, where they go to, and how they get there. Individual interests, decisions and skills are perceived as being related to those of others in the organizational network. The network perspective thus provides a unifying framework that can integrate insights from numerous other approaches without Procrustean stretching or squeezing (e.g. Knoke 2001). For example in the case of decision making, another approach to social action (March and Simon [1958] 1993; Cyert and March [1963] 1992), the network approach can contribute the structure of decision interdependencies, diffusion of information and decision rules, congestion of information, and possible conflicts of interest in the network.

This chapter applies insights from previous chapters to the domain of organizations, and is more practically oriented towards organizational problems, in contrast to the previous chapters, which presented general theory, while keeping in mind that "nothing is as practical as good theory" (Lewin 1945).[2] We will argue that organizing is a matter of both tinkering and design, but also that organizations are always more than their planned counterparts, that they ingest and use a great deal of knowledge – culture – from their environments, and that they have a dynamics of their own (Simon 1996: 185; Alon 2003).

Modern organizations were preceded by military and religious forms of organization, and more recently by the governing bodies of national states. They emerged in the wake of the industrial revolution in a rationalizing society in Europe and the United States, with intensified competition between business companies on the one hand and between national states on the other hand (DiMaggio and Powell 1983; Chandler 1992). Rationalizing societies are characterized by (1) an increasing importance of science and technology; consequently, (2) an increasing belief in the ability to control one's fate, true or false; and (3) institutional pressures on actors to account for their actions and decisions (Weber 1922). General education and literacy are part and parcel of this development, and the role of knowledge in production increases progressively. In numerous areas, knowledge has become more important than energy and other resources (Stinchcombe 1965; Mokyr 2002). As a spillover from science, technology, and literacy, modern organizations and the requirements for their staff have become more a matter of conscious design and social engineering than of tradition, but are always strongly influenced by the social "technology" available at the time of their founding (Stinchcombe 1965: 153). In general, values of "natural" cultures have a strong influence on the values in the cultures of the pertaining organizations (Hofstede 1980), whereas practices, in contrast, are more strongly correlated with the field or industry the organization is in (Hofstede *et al.* 1990).[3] Through Western influence, modern organizational forms spread across the world, where they were hybridized with local culture and forms of organization, for example older forms of administration in China that emulated modern factories. From the onset of the industrial revolution, organizations progressively incorporated commercial, teaching, health care, administrative, cultural, and political activities from society (Coleman 1974). Many of these activities were previously conducted in families or local communities, whereas others, such as sports and tourism, were initially eccentric activities for a handful of wealthy individuals before they got into the hands of organizations that turned them into large industries. Yet other activities were non-existent a century ago, such as e-commerce. In parallel with these developments, an increasing number of people became employees of organizations, which "vacuumed up a good part of what we have always thought of as society, and made organizations, once a part of society, into a surrogate of society" (Perrow 1991: 726, cited in Scott and Davis 2007). All these people had to work under an increasing time-discipline, in comparison with others not working in modern organizations (Tilly and Tilly 1998; Merton 1947). With the exception of a few Western countries, family enterprises remain numerous today, especially among small organizations, which in the West as well are often family run. While the number, diversity, and global dispersion of modern organizations increased considerably – although during the last few decades their average size has decreased – they gained a growing influence on society worldwide and on each other, often at the expense of individuals' influence on their own lives (Coleman 1974). Our global society of organizations can thus be conceptualized as an ultra-network relating a manifold of inter-organizational fields that in their turn consist of organizations and individuals.

WORK, MOTIVATION, AND MODULARITY

To achieve organizational goals, organizations' members must first of all cooperate. Because (the threat of) punishment fosters cooperation in simple experimental situations (Chapter 5), one might think that cooperation can be organized by a system of rewards, punishments, and supervision. As a matter of fact, an influential school, Taylor's scientific management, is based on this idea. Call centers are a recent form of Tayloristic organization. However, high levels of control are experienced by employees as coercion and distrust, and lead to soldiering (by which Taylor meant evading work) rather than solving it, as Taylor (1911) hoped, and to apathy and relatively low performance as well (Braverman 1974). Tayloristic optimization of efficiency is largely a "side-show" (H. White 1992: 182) in a managerial struggle for control. In response, the employees stage their own "show of cooperation as the situational performance through which conflicting interests are tacitly managed" (Collins 2004: 21). Scientific management divides planning, to be done by managers only, and task execution of mostly simple tasks, to be done by subordinates, thereby degrading the latter's skills (Form 1987). Everyone who has worked in a call center knows that sometimes departing from the prescribed questionnaire would improve communication with clients, but the workers are forced to read out exactly what they see on their computer screen. Although efficiency is important, and at Taylor's time his method indeed improved it, many putative efficiency-enhancing interventions, including contemporary ones, are unrelated to organizational performance, but are sustained by modern society, which expects a display of rationality and legitimizes ceremonial conformity to its prevailing norms (Meyer and Rowan 1977).

A competing school, human relations (Handel 2003: 77–84), found on the basis of experiments in a factory that, rather than cooperation at some basic level to avoid punishment or to receive remuneration, employees work much better and harder if they are actively engaged with, or *committed* to, their work (Pfeffer 2007).[4] Commitment is only possible if people find their work meaningful and if their work and social contacts at work fulfill their broader emotional and social desires (McGregor 1960). Interesting work and interactions with colleagues on the basis of sympathy are intrinsically satisfying (Lawler and Yoon 1996), and reciprocal interactions among colleagues reduce stress (Sapolsky 2005).[5] Commitment is hindered by mindless repetitive tasks and excessive managerial control, which Taylor thought would optimize efficiency. Commitment can be enhanced by (1) letting members co-decide how to do their work and with whom they collaborate; (2) providing a satisfactorily large variety of tasks (Herzberg 1968);[6] (3) a commitment-enhancing organizational culture, e.g. with practices and values inspired by human resource management (Pfeffer 1997: 169–173) modulated by the local culture; and (4) managers who are committed to their employees by sufficiently communicating with them (Perrow 1986: 80), and by providing training and job security (Pfeffer 2007). Uninterested management, in contrast, does not increase commitment among workers.[7] Remember that humans have pro-social abilities (Chapter 5), and therefore employees generally don't need to be bossed around to be cooperative – unless managers or owners of the organization are unfair to them in the first place (Pfeffer 2007; Fliessbach et al. 2007), rules mismatch practice, or the work to be done is unpleasant or dangerous. On the job training is normally largely sufficient to socialize people in the culture of the organization, and to teach them what they need to know about it, its norms and practices included (Kunda 1992).

Interestingly, not only control but also commitment is non-monotonic, and drawn in a graph both have a "humped" relation with performance. Commitment is optimal when people are in a state of "flow," a feeling of energized focus and involvement (Csikszentmihalyi 1990). If commitment becomes too high, people become overly conformist, uncreative, resistant to change, and more easily tempted into corporate crime (Whyte 1956; Randall 1987). Furthermore, too strong commitment to a course of action leads to discrediting negative information that could be vital to learn from experience, and to denial of failure. Failure, however, "is an important social invention. [It] is the social recognition and construction of breakdowns which offers a fresh start. Failure thus permits and stipulates a sharp ending to what seemed locked-in by social pressure" (H. White 1992: 12). Not for the highly committed, though. High commitment typically involves costs, but "sunk costs . . . are not sunk psychologically" (Staw and Ross 1989: 217), leading to stronger denial of mistakes and an escalation of commitment (Arrow 1974: 28–29). From a network point of view, we may expect that too high commitment is to be found in highly cohesive departments with insufficient local bridges to the rest of the organization and to the environment. In these cases, increasing external control can bring commitment down to healthier levels. To keep organizations healthy and well functioning thus requires maintaining a delicate balance between too low and too high commitment.

A network of social ties among colleagues beyond strictly work-related contacts creates not only commitment but also a "radar" for searching and selecting information, which overcomes individual bounds of rationality (March and Simon [1958] 1993). Furthermore, redundancy of ties decreases noise and makes it possible to correct errors, and short path distances increase responsiveness and minimize delays. If social ties are so good, it might seem that in the best organization everybody has ties with everybody else and the social structure is maximally supporting, resilient, and robust – a clique. We have seen that highly cohesive and closed structures entail an escalation of commitment, however, so a clique would not be best. But there is another problem. Since the number of ties increases quadratically with the number of staff, in larger organizations people would end up communicating day and night, and no work would ever get done. Although technological innovations, e.g. email replacing letters, can help to push forward inherent size limits, soon a point is reached beyond which increasing network size leads to decreasing returns (Mattick and Gagen 2005). Yet another problem of highly dense organizations is that they are inflexible and therefore unresponsive to changes in the socio-economic environment. Resilience and robustness enhance stability rather than adaptability, for which some flexibility is necessary. The trade-off between adaptability and stability is a central problem in evolutionary theory (Ehrlich and Levin 2005), and is equally central for organizations (March and Simon 1958).

Is there a way to reconcile flexibility on the one hand with robustness and resilience on the other hand? Let us begin with an example, a hotel incorporating a restaurant. The restaurant and the hotel are interdependent because they mutually enhance overall profit from partially the same customers. At the same time they are *loosely coupled* (Weick 1976) in the sense that the hotel's occupancy doesn't affect the restaurant's functioning in the short run. Even if the hotel is empty, the restaurant can still attract clients from the neighborhood, and if the restaurant is empty the hotel can let rooms. In the hotel, if rooms are cleaned too late or not properly, rooms cannot be let and clients will complain, and the negative effect is immediate. There is no way to keep the two kinds of work apart so that dirty rooms would leave the hotel unharmed. If nobody from the cleaning staff shows up, the hotel has an immediate problem, whereas the restaurant closing down would have only a minor short-run effect on the hotel. Therefore the cleaning staff is *tightly coupled* with the reception (although less the other way around).

In general, if there are several parts of an organization that fulfill different functions, or the same function in parallel (e.g. multiple production units in a factory), and the functions are loosely coupled, the organization can be decomposed into units, or modules (Simon 1962). Tightly coupled tasks are to be put together within a unit of the organization, whereas tasks that do not relate to each other immediately are to be put in different units.[8] As a matter of fact, the concept of modularity of organizations coincides perfectly with modularity of communities (Chapter 5). In actuality, on top of work relations, people might become friends across organizational units and mix gossip with work-related information, or, in contrast, fail to collaborate where according to plan they should. Actual modularity will always differ from design, sometimes improving upon it, sometimes not. Units too much insulated from the rest of the organization tend to develop stronger group identification and weaker identification with the remainder organization; hence they establish stronger distinctions between insiders and outsiders, and stereotype the latter (see Elias and Scotson 1965). Having more inter-unit social exchange than strictly necessary from a functional point of view enhances overall cohesion and reduces misunderstandings and conflicts. On top of joint projects, cohesion can be increased by migrating employees once every now and then between units, which can also diffuse organizational culture (Argote *et al*. 2000; Argote and Ingram 2000).

In a modular organization, a failure in one unit can be contained and wreaks no havoc in other units, and social or technical innovations can be tested within modules while the remainder organization is insulated against disruptions, at least in the short run. For example, if cooperation in one department fails, for whatever reason, cooperation within other departments can, in principle, continue. In product design, which is, or at least should be, modular as well, a distinction is made between innovation of individual modules on the one hand, and of the architecture (i.e. the overall structure) on the other hand, the latter being far more disruptive (Henderson and Clark 1990). Notice that the modules of a product or service in most cases do not, and do not have to, match one-to-one with the organizational modules, as hotel reception and cleaning can be better coordinated within the same department. Within each module in an organization, the number of work relations is not excessively high, and search and coordination through these relations is well within the bounds of individual rationality. Experiments have shown that a power law distribution of ties impedes coordination, while a distribution of work relations in which everybody has on average the same number of ties (e.g. Poisson or Gaussian) combined with short path distances improves coordination, indicated by a substantial reduction of the time needed to complete collective tasks (Kearns, Suri, and Montfort 2006).[9] With modularity, flexibility is increased because the organization can add, restructure, or delete modules, or change some interfaces between modules, without having to disrupt large portions of the organization. Therefore the organization is also sufficiently robust and resilient, which, for example for multi-unit enterprises, was shown in a historical analysis by Alfred Chandler (1992). Flexibility is gained at the expense of coordination across modules; thus there is a balance to be found. A typical example of malfunctioning is a sales department and a production unit being insufficiently aware of each other, resulting in dissatisfied clients. Tightening the interface between two departments, for example by increasing the frequency of meetings, would improve coordination but at the same time decrease flexibility and efficiency, whereas loosening the interface would make the departments unresponsive to each other and overshoot the goal of adaptation. When flexibility is too high, an organization might be able to "fly" – briefly – but will readily fly apart (Hedberg, Nystrom, and Starbuck 1976), a point that is often overlooked. To maintain coordination among multiple modules, some degree of centralized decision making is necessary (Simon 1962), for example by establishing standards of output or a protocol of information transfer. Centralization can thus be institutionalized and does not need to be authoritarian (Sanchez and Mahoney 1996), although some authority will often be necessary in practice.

Herbert Simon (1962) argued that modules stand in a hierarchical structure. For example, teams are parts of larger units, such as departments or business units, which in turn are part of an organization, of which several can be part of a holding company. A *hierarchy* is an *ordering* relation[10] that is visually often represented as an upside down *tree* with a "top," or "root," element, and from the top there is exactly one path to each element in a finite number of steps. A hierarchy can therefore be represented as a network.[11] In the example, the ordering relation is on the subsets of the holding company, and the top element is the entire holding company; an element in a hierarchy can be a set by itself. Hierarchy in the abstract does not imply authority as in the hierarchy of command. Hierarchies are extremely widespread, e.g. one can parse a sentence hierarchically, write a paper in paragraphs and put them in sections ultimately united by the overall problem, or search progressively more specifically in a directory. Likewise, computer programs are composed from functional modules, and human bodies from organs and limbs. In the trivial case, a hierarchy has only one level, a "flat" hierarchy, for instance collaborating firms in a field. Herbert Simon argued that, for fitness in general, organizations and other complex systems should be modular, by which he meant both hierarchical and with centralized coordination.[12] Not surprisingly, modularity is a core issue in biology and computer science (Hartwell *et al.* 1999), and biological networks with a hierarchical structure of modules seem to be almost universal (Oltvai and Barabási 2002; Ravasz and Barabási 2003). An example from cognition is "chunking" of pieces of information that belong together (Gobet *et al.* 2001), e.g. a series of actions chunked into one routine action, which yields considerable adaptive advantage over brains that can't chunk. If modularity is insufficiently achieved in an organization, adverse outcomes can be severe. Nuclear reactors and chemical plants cannot be built sufficiently modularly for functional reasons. There, a local error can disrupt the entire system, with disastrous consequences (Perrow 1984). Finding a suitable modularity is feasible in many cases, although possibly difficult (Ethiraj and Levinthal 2004), whereas finding optimal modularity beyond the simplest cases is very difficult. It depends on the technology used, the environment the module must be adapted to, and other factors. It usually takes multiple generations of a product or of an organizational design before a satisfactory modularity settles down, until an environmental shock – e.g. an innovation – obliterates the previous design and tinkering starts anew (Schumpeter 1942). Still, a modular organization is the best design known to date and has both stability and flexibility without giving in performance, and is searchable as well (Adamic and Adar 2005).

COGNITION AND CULTURE

As communities have cultures, so do organizations (Hofstede 1980; Hofstede *et al.* 1990). In the organizational literature, a focus on culture is recent, and owing to this historical coincidence culture has often been treated as a residual category, of everything that was not already dealt with by well-established theories at the time. There was a strong emphasis on (tacit) values and symbolic practices, and on socialization and commitment (e.g. Kunda 1992). Here we will incorporate all of that, but stick to our treatment of culture in Chapter 5, where it was defined more broadly as "information capable of affecting individuals' behavior that they acquire from other[s] through teaching, imitation, and other forms of social transmission" (Richerson and Boyd 2005). The focus on information directs us towards information search and learning. Indeed, most of what organizations can do results from (1) learning by its individual members (trial and error; training; education; discovering abstract regularities; invention), and (2) absorbing new members with new knowledge into the network that these people form (Simon [1945] 1997). We may add a variation to the second item, of learning by transferring members across units within the same organization. Although learning has an individual cognitive dimension, "Individual learning in organizations is very much a social, not a solitary, phenomenon" (Simon 1991: 125), and most learning happens in networks (Chapter 5). Therefore most of what organizations learn falls within our definition of culture and matches our network approach quite well. Organizational culture makes it possible for both individuals and organizations to benefit from accumulated experience of many people over multiple generations, in and outside the organization (but see March, Sproull, and Tamuz 1991 on when such experience is lacking). Technology is a case in point, of knowledge that draws from generations of research and applications and is crucially important for organizations. Not only technological knowledge but also knowledge about how to deal with employees (e.g. human relations management) and institutional expertise (e.g. lawyers) are vital for organizational performance.

Individual – but not isolated – members and organizations specialize in certain activities, which with time and effort leads to enhanced mastery, or dexterity, of those activities and of the knowledge used (Smith 1986). Mastery also helps to select, judge, and apply knowledge from the environment (Simonton 2000), an aspect of mastery called *absorptive capacity* (Cohen and Levinthal 1990).[13] Absorptive capacity, or prior experience, lowers considerably the transfer costs of the pertaining knowledge (Teece 1977), e.g. an organization specialized in medical research has lower costs for searching, selecting, and using new medical knowledge than a car repair shop would have. We may conjecture that a reasonable level of social cohesion will have a positive effect on mastery, both for individuals nested in a cohesive network and for cohesive organizations or units.[14] For well-circumscribed repetitive tasks, e.g. building a series of ships or aircraft of the same type, the number of hours used to complete them decreases with the number of units produced, along a so-called *learning curve* (Argote and Epple 1990).[15] While employees get used to each other and improve their coordination, they develop their individual skills in response to their collective effort. Consequently, labor costs decrease at a decreasing rate, with the largest decrease for the first couple of units produced, and

leveling off after a large number of units. This collective exploitation and refinement of knowledge marks the development of organizational *routines* – smoothly
coordinated sets of actions, analogous to individual skills (Nelson and Winter 1982;
Cohen and Bacdayan 1994; Gersick and Hackman 1990). Decisions once mastered
as routine can proceed largely unconsciously, freeing individual minds for making further improvements or for other concerns. As a consequence, routines are
based at least in part on tacit knowledge – can you fully explicate the grammar(s)
of your mother tongue(s)? Consequently, routines cannot be imitated quickly by
competitors lacking direct access to this tacit knowledge. Routines do not imply
that tasks are repeated each time exactly as the previous time. On the contrary,
routines make possible smooth and fast corrections of (small) errors and alternative
courses of action towards the same end (Sidney Winter, personal communication).
Routines enable organizations to produce reliably, accurately, and relatively fast and
efficiently. For routines and their learning curves, there is a small negative effect of
organizational forgetting, if turnover is high (low turnover has no negative effect), or
if the time in between subsequent production units is very long (Thompson 2007).
Non-repetitive tasks, e.g. customized services, are less routine than repetitive tasks;
learning takes place but not along a learning curve. For firms competing with each
other, those firms with superior routines are favored by selection, while innovation causes variation, which now brings us to evolution at the organizational level
(Nelson and Winter 1982, 2002).[16]

From an evolutionary perspective, routines embody the tension between stability and adaptability. Although routines enable an organization to exploit current
skills and knowledge, and to reap economies of scale along the learning curve,
they lock in the organization on a *path-dependent* trajectory, in which current skills,
knowledge, and technology strongly determine tomorrow's (David 1985; Arthur
1989).[17] The same routines that make an organization efficient and effective also
make it inert, at least in the short run (Hannan and Freeman 1984). Most organizations compare feedback from past performance with their aspirations, which in
turn are partly based on their (mostly local) peers' performances, and if they are
satisfied, and performance equals or is above aspirations, they may get stuck in a
competence trap and stay as they are (Greve 2003). However, if the environment
changes, e.g. consumer preferences or dominant technology, or if the organization
wants to stay ahead of developments in its environment, it has to explore new possibilities and search for new knowledge. Performance below aspirations can trigger
a change of learning strategy (Greve 2003; Cyert and March [1963] 1992). The
trade-off between stability and adaptability now comes in the form of *exploitation*
versus *exploration*, respectively (March 1991). Certainly, exploitation and incremental refinement of current routines is more efficient, but if the organization misaligns
itself to its environment, it has to take its chances and try the cognitively more
demanding and therefore more risky and less efficient strategy of exploration. New
knowledge consists of hybridizations of existing knowledge and applications that

have previously not been combined with each other (Chapter 6), at least not by the focal organization. A new product, for example, is "either a new combination of components or a new relationship between previously combined components" (Fleming 2001). To get new knowledge, an organization has to imitate other organizations that it perceives as successful, or it has to innovate, but organizations more often borrow than invent (March and Simon [1958] 1993: 188). The ease of adoption of external ideas varies with the complexity of the pertaining knowledge (Kogut and Zander 1992) and its trialability and observability (Rogers 2003).

With appropriate data that represent arcs from the focal organization to its knowledge sources – other actors or their publications or artifacts as search targets – exploration can be modeled network-wise as brokerage[18] (Hargadon 2002; Burt 2004; Chapter 6 above). Knowledge borrowing and brokering tend to be more successful if the organization has a prior developed absorptive capacity ("memory") to which new ideas relate more easily (Sutton and Hargadon 1997), just like individuals. Serendipity exists but, as Louis Pasteur said, "chance favours the prepared mind." Absorptive capacity thus makes possible a spillover of current knowledge to new knowledge within the organization; in other words, exploitation can to some degree have economies of scope, along with economies of scale. Therefore exploration is in most cases not just adopting external ideas, but combining external ideas with previously developed internal knowledge. In the knowledge network, an actor re-using its own ideas gets a reflexive arc (a loop pointing to the actor itself). The more of its ideas an actor re-uses, the more self-exploiting it is, on a continuum between exploration and exploitation (Carnabuci 2005; Carnabuci and Bruggeman 2007a).[19] The more exploratory, or brokering, it is, the more heterogeneous is its pool of ideas.

Exploration has very little or none of exploitation's efficiency advantages. Furthermore, exploring organizations grapple with uncertainty, and are more vulnerable to powerful organizations (Pfeffer and Salancik 1978), and to fads and fashions that sometimes bring useless knowledge or impair the adoption of useful knowledge (Abrahamson 1991; Staw and Epstein 2000; Sorge and van Witteloostuijn 2004). Finally, striving for innovation all the time leads to superficial knowledge and underdeveloped routines (March 2005). An innovation should therefore be followed up by a phase of specialization in the newly acquired knowledge, which means that the new idea is progressively integrated with current knowledge, refined, and exploited, until its productive potential runs dry (Carnabuci and Bruggeman 2007a). Since unchanging environments don't exist any more, organizations should oscillate between phases of exploitation and exploration to stay aligned with their changing environments.[20] Alternatively, they can have different parts of the organization focus on either exploration or exploitation, as universities do research and teaching in parallel in different "modules," mostly by the same staff but at different times. However, educational programs too need to be refreshed, albeit at a slower pace than research findings, and, in general, permanent exploitation is from a bygone age.

Ideas taken from sources that in turn are strong knowledge generators have higher potential for ego than ideas from sources with low levels of knowledge generation (Carnabuci 2005). For example, ideas from a highly productive top university tend to be more useful for generating new knowledge than ideas from a less productive and lower-quality university. In short, knowledge growth is *autocorrelated*, a statistical approach to cultural transmission and reproduction (Chapter 5). To assess the influence of autocorrelation in networks, researchers (Leenders 2002; Doreian 1989; Dow *et al*. 1984) use models that have their origin in spatial models – things developing close by tend to be more influential than developments far away. Spatial autocorrelation is even true for such abstract things as the growth of technological knowledge (Jaffe, Trajtenberg and Henderson 1993; Henderson, Jaffe, and Trajtenberg 2005; Singh 2005), and inventors pay closer attention to inventions in their own region and more easily adopt local ideas than (possibly relevant) ideas from elsewhere. Another example of knowledge autocorrelation, both social and spatial, is philosophy, and philosophers are more creative, as indicated by their impact on colleagues, if they let their own ideas be influenced by other creative philosophers (Collins 2000). Finally, there is strong temporal autocorrelation of an actor's knowledge growth, and past inventiveness is an accurate predictor of current and future inventiveness. Along with strongly positive effects of autocorrelation on knowledge growth, there is a smaller positive effect of knowledge brokerage – if alternated with specialization – and a small but significantly negative effect of knowledge competition (Podolny, Stuart, and Hannan 1996; Carnabuci and Bruggeman 2007b). As to the latter, if many organizations tap ideas from the same sources, the ideas generated on the basis of these sources tend to be more similar and therefore less novel than if only few organizations crowd the niche.

It was already known that truly breakthrough inventions are mostly done by small teams, or sometimes individuals, and are subsequently exploited by large firms that make cumulative incremental improvements, and then make much more profit (Baumol 2004). On the basis of longitudinal network studies we now know that, for the production of technological and scientific knowledge in general, teams have become progressively more important, and their results have become increasingly better than those of individual scholars and engineers (Guimerà *et al*. 2005; Wuchty, Jones, and Uzzi 2007). A team brokers knowledge at the aggregate level by pooling diverse specialists. By staying small (fewer than ten), their coordination costs remain within bounds. Team members initially stimulate each other and cross-fertilize ideas, but if they keep working together for too long they exhaust the potential for path-breaking new ideas, as their pool of ideas homogenizes. To continue knowledge production at a high level, a new team has to be composed, against progressively higher inertia of longer-lasting collaborative ties (Ramasco and Morris 2006). A new team should consist partly of novices and partly of experts, and the experts should previously not have worked together, thereby maximizing potential cross-fertilizations (Guimerà *et al*. 2005). The collective output of all

97

teams working in research and technology – in papers and patents – forms a large body of codified and publicly accessible knowledge that does not deplete with usage (Arrow 1962; Mokyr 2002), even though the transfer of this knowledge can be costly (Teece 1977). Codification of knowledge reduces ambiguity, and it facilitates transfer, storage, search, and interpretation. Therefore the stock of public knowledge is a key resource in the knowledge-based economy (Mokyr 2002), together with its education systems and supporting institutions.

Along with technological knowledge, societies accumulate institutional knowledge in their culture. Even preliterate societies do so, although their knowledge is less generally accessible and passes mostly by word of mouth (Diamond 2001). In modern organizations, some of the institutional knowledge from society is used as part of their organizational design and coded in *formal rules*. This did not happen overnight. Initially, and centuries before the industrial revolution, individuals in organizations became regarded as independent from the positions they occupied. Also organization's *property* became separate from their owners' and from other member's property (Coleman 1974). Thereby organizations became individual-independent, also their life span became undetermined, and organizations became acknowledged as legal actors on their own (Coleman 1974; Greif 1994: 941). One of the consequences of this independence is that, if people make a career move, they lose the formal ties of their former position, whereas they can bring with them a great deal of their informal ties, which have a higher "portability" (Podolny and Baron 1997: 677).

Incumbents in an organization often gave, and sometimes still give, positions to friends or family, simply because humans have a strong tendency to reciprocate, or because an incumbent notices a strategic advantage in employing a well-trusted candidate. Our pro-social nature evolved over more than 150,000 years on the savanna by living in small groups, not during the last century in modern organizations. However, during the industrial revolution, nepotism got too much in the way of the new ideals of effectiveness (i.e. reliability and accuracy) and efficiency, and meanwhile new institutions had been developed to deal with it. Members of organizations were to be assigned to positions on the basis of their formal *qualifications*, i.e. diplomas of education and attested experience (Weber 1922). The importance of education has increased progressively ever since, especially in knowledge-intensive sectors of the economy. Being a relative or a friend of someone in the organization, or having personal charisma, was no longer good enough, although rarely completely ruled out (Perrow 1986: 7). Some modern organizations searching for staff ask their employees if they know competent candidates, who then obviously are friends, which may sometimes lead to good candidates.[21] Furthermore, formal rules specify the *positions* in the organization and the rights and obligations pertaining to these positions (Weber 1922). These positions are in a hierarchical *authority* structure. Positions and their obligations and rights structure individuals' behavior into *roles*, e.g. a manager or a secretary, not so much by prescribing specific behavior, but mostly by prescribing decision premises that role-takers should take into account (Simon 1991). "Each of the roles in an organization presumes the appropriate enactment of the other roles that surround it and interact with it. Thus, the organization is a role *system*" (Simon 1991: 127, italics in the original; see also Chapter 6 above). Roles help members and outsiders to develop stable expectations about others' behavior, thereby reducing complexity and uncertainty (Luhmann 1964). Behind the working consensus of front stage role behavior, there is of course a world of backstage ambivalence, jokes, gossip, and role distancing (Blau 1964; Luhmann 1964; Kunda 1992).

On top of job qualifications, task execution also became to some degree rationalized and prescribed by rules, depending on the degree to which tasks can be explicated. Complex services are also partly routine[22] but their rules, with many exceptions, are mostly tacit. Other tasks are simpler and can be better explicated. Once owners of organizations realized that *standardization* made possible vast economies of scale, they standardized inputs, working procedures, and outputs wherever they could, which in many cases also facilitated coordination. Where the best results of standardization were achieved, e.g. the protocol for data transfer on the Internet or on mobile phones, it was least noticed. With modern technology, the step from standardization to automation (a machine is a set of materialized rules) is small and, in parts of the world, machines have taken over many tasks that were done by humans in the past, and got new tasks as well.

Finally, modern societies require organizations to be accountable for their decisions, for which organizations have to produce *documents*. All modern organizations have positions with rights and obligations; requirements for occupants of these positions; roles; routines; expectancies about results and the making thereof; and a separation of individual and organizational property (Weber 1922). If much of this is coded in formal rules, and the hierarchy of positions is tall, the organization is called a *bureaucracy*, or "mechanic" organization, whereas organizations that have less strict, less outspoken, and more informal rules and authority are called "organic" (Burns and Stalker 1961). The differences are gradual and the two ideal types span a continuum on which actual organizations stand. Some organizations prescribe a large amount of paperwork documenting important decisions made, which is often seen as a hallmark of bureaucracy. In modern societies, part of bureaucracy is "outsourced" in laws and other institutions that demand obedience to rules and the production of documents, which also hold for organizations that have an organic structure. Even rock bands have accountants, and often other bureaucratic features as well. Bureaucracy is most famous for its failures, which inspired Franz Kafka to write his novel *The Trial*, and Orson Welles to make a movie of it. Indeed, if organizations have rules that appear senseless or harmful to employees, their commitment will be impaired. Ill-crafted or outdated rules, even those that were intended to increase efficiency and effectiveness, distort communication across hierarchical levels and with clients, handle exceptions badly, and can engender vicious circles of frustration among employees and clients alike, followed by yet more rules in managerial attempts to curb decreasing performance (Merton 1940). Shortcomings of the rules are often misperceived and, if a problem at hand mismatches the organizational frame of reference as set by the rules, the structural causes of the problem often remain in a twilight zone, and the blame is put on individuals or on bad morale (Luhmann 1964). Suboptimal behavior tends to become daily routine (Crozier 1963), until the organization is out-competed by another one, disbands, or is taken over, which for governmental organizations may take a very long time.

Despite its dark side (Vaughan 1999), the bureaucratic organizational form was a major innovation, which by making organizations independent from their members created considerable flexibility in societal development (Coleman 1974: 24–25). Organizations became corporate actors, "flexible units, which could be born and die, expand and contract, move into new arenas of action, and engage in market transactions, . . . through which technological developments could bring about social change" (Coleman 1974: 28). Organizations without rules are not viable and are more vulnerable to corruption than bureaucracy. Rather than throwing bureaucracy by the board, Arthur Stinchcombe (2001) argues that designers of organizations should strive for *effective rules* that (1) in their abstraction and generality still accurately match and indicate the cases they are intended for; (2) are communicable, i.e. transparent and sufficiently parsimonious; and, most importantly, (3) can be modified on the basis of feedback on their consequences, e.g. when mismatching a world that has changed. Notice that these requirements are altogether very similar to our requirements for scientific knowledge mentioned in the first chapter. Apparently, there exist general properties of useful knowledge, be it scientific or institutional. Finally, some authority is necessary to legitimize the rules, their interpretations, and their consequences (Stinchcombe 2001), as well as most new ideas in general, we might add. This authority can sometimes be abstract, e.g. some written source with high status, seemingly independent of any person, but authority ultimately depends on people, real or imagined.[23] The formal organization – if it works – is not the opposite of the informal organization, as many people tend to believe, but a refined version of it (Stinchcombe 2001: 3), like a well-crafted mathematical model of an intuitive conception.

Changing organizational rules, or culture in general, is very difficult without employees' commitment, which in turn will depend on their perception of the benefit of, and effort associated with, learning something new and giving up something old. Culture, even seemingly boring bureaucratic rules, can provide meaning and orientation to some, who might not be willing to give up these rules easily (Luhmann 1964). The introduction of new members as role models can break though old routines, provided that the new role models are protected against group pressure from incumbents, for example by introducing a larger number of novices at once, with a new technology and new ways of conduct to deal with it.

POWER AND AUTHORITY

A salient commonality of humans and other social animals is their establishment of rank orders (Chapter 6), with status pertaining to the level in the order, expressed in (body) language and possessions. Even dogs and chimpanzees recognize differences in authority among humans, and one doesn't need a trained ethnographer to draw the organizational chart. In modern organizations, this rank order has evolved into a formal *authority* relation that is institutionalized on bureaucratic principles (Weber 1922), even in organizations that proclaim themselves non-bureaucratic; culture is partly subconscious and sometimes self-contradictory, here in the form of ideology versus practice. The amount of power someone has depends on the level of his or her position in the hierarchy, which is the path distance from the top to the position in question. As said earlier, holding a position in a modern organization is to be based on qualifications or merit, not on nepotism, (family) tradition, or charisma (Weber 1922); briefly, the right person is supposed to be at the right place. Formal authority is an instance of hierarchy, in the vernacular of organizations labeled "the" hierarchy. In the literature, hierarchies are often called "vertical" social structures and are juxtaposed to informal "horizontal" relations, but one should realize that, in organizations, social relations are mostly a mixture of authority, sympathy, and other intentions and emotions, and all relations are part of the multiplex network making up the organization. There is nothing intrinsically horizontal or vertical about social relations, and graphs of authority relations can be rotated at any angle without changing the relation. In Figure 7.1, dark thick lines depict an authority relation wherein the top manager is vertex 1, and light thin lines are work relations

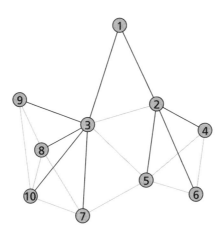

Figure 7.1 *Formal authority (dark and thick) among organizational members who also have informal work relations (light and thin); the top manager is vertex 1 and the hierarchical level of each other member is the path distance in the authority relation to the top.*

beyond the subordinate relation. Holding a position in a hierarchy of authority is a prime source of power in organizations, and for most people more important than a brokering position in the network of informal work relations such as friendship and advice (Krackhardt 1990; Krackhardt and Hanson 1993). The right to make and change rules that influence everybody else makes managers especially powerful.[24]

Ideally, the hierarchy of authority is congruent with the hierarchy of modules, with each based on a different kind of relationship, e.g. in Figure 7.1, where actors 3, 7, 8, 9, and 10 are in one department and actors 2, 4, 5, and 6 are in another. The positions in the hierarchy of modules stand in the subset relation, whereas positions in the hierarchy of authority stand in the subordinate relation, where "x being subordinate to y" is equivalent with "y has authority over x." If employees are subordinate to multiple bosses at the same time, they might receive conflicting orders, leading to ambiguous obligations and to conflict. To prevent this from happening, unity of command is required (Fayol [1916] 1949), which is the reason why authority in organizations must be a hierarchy (and not, say, a lattice), which indeed most organizations are.[25] To settle disputes between two or more subordinates in a hierarchy, there is always a person "up" in the authority tree where their branches meet (their least upper bound), who is then responsible for resolving the conflict (third party intervention, Chapters 5 and 6), even though that person may be neither the cause of the conflict nor aware of it. This is an evolutionary reason why most organizations have unity of command. To avoid confusion of command from the top level, if there is a board of directors wherein all people share the same position at the top, they must speak to the outside world as if one (corporate) actor.

In general, conflicts in organizations are rare (1 to 8 percent of ties are negative, and then mostly asymmetric; Giuseppe Labianca, personal communication). Their impact, however, is much stronger than that of positive ties (Labianca and Brass 2006; Labianca, Brass, and Gray 1998). People who are more similar tend to feel more attracted to each other but also have a higher chance of conflict; conflicts between men and women are much rarer than among men, and people with similar levels of education have a higher chance of conflict (Völker and Flap 2007). The strongest factors of influence on conflict are at the organizational level, in particular uncertainty about the future, unfair management, and high competition between employees (Völker and Flap 2007).

Organizations where authority is strongly rule-based are mechanic. A mechanic (i.e., bureaucratic) organization is efficient in relatively stable environments (Burns and Stalker 1961; Radner 1992). However, efficiency is not the only criterion of performance; for organizations to be viable, they must also be robust, even if that is less efficient. To survive in more "turbulent" environments, which are more complex and uncertain for organizational decision-makers, organizations must process more information, which lays an excessive burden on the top positions in a hierarchy (Dodds, Watts, and Sabel 2003). Organizations must then be doubly robust, first in protecting individuals from information overload, and second in protecting the overall organization from overloaded (or otherwise malfunctioning) individuals. Dodds, Watts, and Sabel showed by computer simulations comparing multiple organizational forms that extending the authority relations with "horizontal" and "oblique" work relations between members at lower ranks in the hierarchy – Fayol's "gang planks" (grey lines in Figure 7.1) – increases robustness considerably, even a small amount of such ties. These non-authoritarian connected employees can coordinate their work and adapt their tasks without continually relying on higher management decisions. There is a complementary result from another series of computer simulations on power-law distributed networks, wherein the hubs, which tend to have the highest betweenness centrality, are the first vertices to suffer information overload, and their mutual ties are the first that will get congested. Counter-intuitively, if a small fraction of the most congested ties is removed, other, less burdened, ties (partly gang planks) have to take over, which increases overall transmission efficiency (Zhang, Wang, and Li 2007). A gang plank is a two-edged sword that reduces managerial information load on the one hand and increases the organization's information-processing capacity on the other hand. Notice that (horizontal or oblique) work relations beyond the subordinate relation are, or at least should be, implemented in a well-designed modular organization, including those that cross-cut organizational modules.

Organizations that strongly rely on gang planks tend to have less rigid subordinate relations and rules, less pronounced division of labor, and more decentralized decision making. These are organic organizations, on the continuum that has mechanic organizations at its other end, which in turn are characterized by strict rules and division of labor, and centralized decision making in a strongly articulated hierarchy (Burns and Stalker 1961). The best organizational structure thus depends on the environment, to which it should be aligned. Different units of an organization may face different environments, and a mechanic car manufacturer, for example, will have an organic research and development team (Lawrence and Lorsch 1967). Furthermore, as national culture influences organizational culture, in countries with more power distance, i.e. strong authority, this will resonate in their organizations (Hofstede 1980). In principle, modular systems can self-organize without authority (Gordon 2007) and, in organic organizations, a certain degree of self-organization creates more commitment than the authoritarian mode of conduct in mechanic organizations does. Again, the culture in the environment will make a difference (Hofstede 1994). Although highly intensive control frustrates rather than motivates the majority of workers in most cultures, a small minority of notorious non-cooperators (Chapter 5), in contrast, does need frequent managerial control to stay in line.

In authoritarian organizations, there are obviously power differences, but even in egalitarian organizations, if they are not very small, power inequality emerges without deliberate effort. In larger organizations, if members don't want to spend all day in discussion to reach decisions democratically, they can democratically choose representatives as their (temporary) leaders. These chosen leaders, in turn, will create or apply at least some rules to make the organization function well, they will specialize by accumulating leadership experience, and they will develop and use a network matching their position (Michels [1915] 1962). Consequently, power differences will increase, which Robert Michels called the iron law of oligarchy.[26] It is then very difficult for leaders not to (partly) pursue their own interests that differ from the common interest. Lipset, Trow, and Coleman (1956) discovered that informal networks, not part of the hierarchy, and legitimate opposition can counter the iron law, if there is no strong external threat to organizational survival.

Authority pursued too strongly is a problem for several other reasons as well. Henri Fayol, and many others after him, pointed out that, if left unattended, people in authoritarian organizations tend to eschew responsibility while striving for more power, which readily leads to dysfunctional organizations. Furthermore, humans have a moral sense (Haidt 2007) and expect rewards from cooperative efforts to be shared, otherwise the deprived feel frustrated. To legitimize increasingly large differences in authority and associated income beyond individual talent or contribution, leaders invoke ideology (Bendix 1956), which however is never truly convincing in the long run, and at some point leads to moral outrage (Bebchuck and Fried 2006; Boehm 1993). Finally, authority has adverse consequences for personal health: people in lower ranks have far higher chances of getting "cardiovascular, respiratory, rheumatoid, and psychiatric diseases" and have higher "mortality from all causes" (Sapolsky 2005: 648; Salgado 1993). The exercise of authority should thus be limited for multiple reasons, which was already known in China more than 2000 years ago.

> The best rulers are scarcely known by their subjects;
> The next best are loved and praised;
> The next are feared;
> The next despised:
> They have no faith in their people,
> And their people become unfaithful to them.
>
> When the best rulers achieve their purpose
> Their subjects claim the achievement as their own.
>
> Lao Tzu

Unfortunately, managers feel more often attracted to a military analogy to organizing, and prefer to read Sun Tzu's *Art of War* instead, whereas, in many cases, long-term benefits from cooperation are much higher than from authority, control, and coercion.

ENVIRONMENTS AS FIELDS

Organizational *environments* are crucially important for organizations' survival chances, and consist to an important extent of other organizations. Over the economy as a whole, organizational size (for almost any measure of size, Ijiri and Simon 1977) is power-law distributed (Axtell 2001), which implies that most organizations are small. Also growth rates are power-law distributed; while most firms stick closely to their current size, some grow or shrink substantially (Stanley *et al.* 1996). Social network analysis sees organizations being nested in fields, following the institutional approach to organizations (DiMaggio and Powell 1983). An example is the field of biotechnology, featuring six kinds of organizations, each involved in a different kind of activity: biotech firms, government institutes, public research organizations, pharmaceutical corporations, financers, and suppliers of laboratory equipment (Powell *et al.* 2005; Powell, Koput and Smith-Doerr 1996).[27] The cooperative relations among these organizations are of four kinds: financial, collaboration on research and development, licensing production, and commercialization. Notice that collaborators can at the same time be competitors for consumers or skilled employees. Other examples of fields are the telephone industry, where companies are nowadays related by roaming contracts (historical, Barnett and Carroll 1987); apparel, where firms are in production chains (Uzzi 1996, 1997); and the subfield of the heavy electrical equipment industry, in which organizations make illegal collusive agreements (Baker and Faulkner 1993). Organizations often have people specially employed to maintain external relations in their fields, so-called boundary spanners. They transform information from another organization into a form compatible with the "code" of their own unit, and the other way around.

In general, a *field* is a community of organizations and individuals sharing a certain culture – norms, beliefs, practices, and a reputation system (D. White *et al.* 2004; Bourdieu and Wacquant 1992; Constant 1980). A field can encompass multiple (sub)populations or branches of industry, as the biotech example shows. Fields have no clear boundaries but can be detected with a Hamiltonian approach (Chapter 5), which would also point out community overlaps and subfields. Within a field-spanning network, organizations are dense spots rather than units with distinct boundaries (Davis and Marquis 2005). Through inter-organizational ties, organizations exchange information, materials, skilled labor, and other resources. Large companies are also part of a network of interlocking directorates across fields, as we discussed in Chapter 3. The field network can help its participants to pool resources and access new niches, and it redistributes uncertainties and revenues, although often unequally (Granovetter 2005b; Gulati and Gargiulo 1999). Because in the longer run business relationships tend to develop aspects of friendship and trust, subsequent cooperation can be established much faster than in arms length market relations, and requires less monitoring (Uzzi 1997). Contributions to partners are made with a longer time perspective than arms length market transactions, with "voice rather than exit" (Podolny and Page 1998), and mostly in a "spirit of goodwill" (Ronald Dore, cited in Podolny and Page 1998). A cohesive network and shared institutions foster the diffusion of information through the field. Part of the information spread within a field is about the participants, enabling organizations to choose and sometimes to avoid potential partners (Powell *et al.* 2005: 1180). We may here remember a result from evolutionary theory, which tells us that reputation combined with possibilities for sanctions enhances cooperation considerably (Chapter 5). Also geographic proximity increases cooperation (Powell *et al.* 2005).

Both geographic and network proximity can sometimes entail conflicts, as for individuals within organizations. Furthermore, not all information exchange increases adaptation; "ties that bind could also blind" (Knoke 2001). As mentioned before, networks that are too cohesive foster escalation of commitment and become inflexible and impede innovation, and cohesion has an optimum between low and high values. For the field of Broadway musicals, Brian Uzzi and Jarrett Spiro (2005) showed that the performance of creative teams is highest at intermediate field levels of cohesion, when there are plenty of structural holes that can be bridged on the one hand, and enough paths to transmit information on the other hand. At very low levels of cohesion (which they measured as small-worldliness), the field is hardly institutionalized and information passes insufficiently, whereas at high levels of cohesion there are insufficient structural holes left that can be bridged, and information, although efficiently transmitted, becomes too homogeneous for teams to have a competitive "edge." Organizations positioned in fields can thus broker structural holes, although role expectations, partly cast in laws, set constraints, as for individuals within organizations (Podolny and Baron 1997).

To comprehend the dynamics of an organizational field, Powell, D. White, Koput, and Owen-Smith (2005: 1138) introduced the metaphor of a dance club.[28] Visitors may dance repeatedly with one partner, or in the same group, or change partners or groups regularly. Past choices of partners and styles of dancing leave a trace, affecting both skills and partnering opportunities. For salsa music (not Powell and colleagues' example) one can dance Cuban style, Los Angeles style, or mambo on two, which influences partner choice. If turnover is not too high, routines and partner choices feature path dependence. Under bounded rationality and uncertainty, dancers (or firms) look at other dancers (i.e. volume and quality of other firms' products), and use them as a "mirror" in which they see themselves, and to which they adjust their own aspirations and behavior (H. White 1981; Cyert and March [1963] 1992). "A market is an 'act' which can be 'got together' only by a set of producers compatibly arranged on the qualities which consumers see in them" (H. White 1981: 519). For the dancers, newly invented practices may stay within a cohesive group, such as friends knowing each other from the same dance school, or may spread across the entire dance club, like innovations in the economy. High performers receive higher prestige and are more likely to become role models, which we discussed in Chapters 5 and 6. Sometimes the music changes, e.g. from salsa to merengue (symbolizing an institutional change), and then the dancers must change to a different dance, often with different partners.

In biotechnology, ties form and dissolve relatively frequently and easily, whereas in other fields, such as the Korean *chaebol*, ties are enduring and breaking up painful or unfeasible (Hamilton and Biggart 1988). Choosing partners or breaking up with them depends strongly on the field and its institutions, and on status as well (Podolny 1993; Chapter 6 above). In the biotech industry, the degree distribution is (approximately) a power law, but the mechanism is more complicated than simple preferential attachment, because biotech firms have different preferences for different kinds of attachments; they don't just want to link to organizations with many ties (the US National Institutes of Health had the highest degree) because they want different partners for collaboration, financing, commercialization, laboratory equipment, and other needs, not just partners of one kind. In their partner choice they are mostly disassortative. To stay in business, biotech firms need to be exposed to new ideas in their research collaborations, and therefore they have a preference for new research partners (Powell *et al*. 2005: 1177), whereas novelty is not a relevant criterion for their financial, commercial, and equipment partners. Additionally, in a paper appropriately entitled "Dancing with strangers," Joel Baum and his co-authors (2005), building on Cyert and March (1963), demonstrated that Canadian investment banks take more risk (i.e. accept less third party control) in their choice of business partners if their performance is below their aspirations, in turn resulting from comparison with peers of the same size and same specialization. As one might expect (Chapters 3 and 4), large fields such as biotechnology are sparse and locally clustered, have short distances, are searchable, and feature fat tails in their degree distribution.

Along with various forms of cooperation, field dynamics are determined by competition, of structurally equivalent organizations that may not have ties with each other. As for evolutionary processes in general, also in fields it holds that "When an organization faces strong competition, the consequences of making the wrong structural adjustment will be much faster and more severe than when competition is weak" (Barnett and Carroll 1995). The fates of organizations due to competitive pressure, and their niche differentiation to avoid it, have been studied most extensively by organizational ecologists (an overview, Hannan 2005; Carroll 1985; Barnett 1997). William Barnett and Morten Hansen (1996) contributed by showing that a complete absence of competition is no good either, because organizations then doze off in their (in)competence trap, whereas modest levels of competition keep them alert and better performing, as in sport and anywhere else. Finally, organizations can absorb other organizations by merger and acquisition. Jeffrey Pfeffer and Gerald Salancik (1978) argued that, in dyadic relations, an organization is more likely to absorb its partner the more control the latter has over resources critical to the focal organization, and the fewer alternatives are available (see also Casciaro and Piskorski 2005).

107

DYNAMIC CAPABILITIES

To get resources, an organization must dance in complex patterns with partners in its environment. In order to survive it must also be efficient and effective to a certain degree, as well as accountable to those who ask questions, and it must maintain a dynamic balance between flexibility and robustness. To address these issues, we may summarize this chapter in a theory of four dynamic capabilities of organizations, in line with evolutionary theory (Winter 2003), although the four capabilities mentioned here have not yet been stated explicitly in the literature. *Dynamic capabilities* enable an organization to "create, extend, upgrade, protect, and keep relevant the [organization's] unique asset base" (Teece 2007). They are *"collective activities* through which the organization systematically generates and modifies its operating routines in pursuit of improved effectiveness" (Zollo and Winter 2002, emphasis added). The central claim of the dynamic capabilities literature is that organizations with better dynamic capabilities have higher survival chance, or fitness, in environments to which these capabilities are aligned.

At the baseline of all organizational effort, members of an organization must collaborate and be committed to doing so, otherwise not much, if anything, can be achieved collectively. In a similar vein, organizations must collaborate with other actors (stakeholders) in their environment. However, as the world and its actors change, emotional distance must sometimes be taken, at least among some actors in or outside the organization, and some relations have to be terminated. An organization that is capable of alternating longer periods of commitment with brief moments of graceful disengagement has a dynamic capability for *cooperating*. To support this prime capability, the organization should have a modular structure that is robust without becoming rigid. However, modules must sometimes be added, changed, or dissolved, or interfaces between modules changed. Therefore *structuring* also should be a dynamic capability rather than a static one. Third, the organization must be controlled, by subtle authority and effective rules, but some individuals must be controlled more than others, and, in times of crisis or radical change, stronger leadership may be necessary temporarily, if continuing the organization is preferred over disbanding it. A uniform level of authority for everybody at all times is less adaptive in a changing environment than dynamic and versatile ways of *controlling*. Furthermore, when comparing an army with a health care center, it is clear that, in fields and national cultures with high power distance (Hofstede *et al.* 1990), control should be exerted differently than in cultures with low power distance for the organization to be aligned with its environment. Finally, an organization must learn dynamically, and oscillate between exploitation and exploration. During phases of exploitation, it can develop routines that make it efficient and effective, at least for a while. If it changes its routines regularly, it can develop a meta-routine for exploration and for alternating between the two modes of learning. In a broader perspective on learning, we must also incorporate the formal rules of the organization. These rules can be used as they are (institutional exploitation) for as long as they are effective, but rules must sometimes be changed or replaced by new rules if they are no longer effective (institutional exploration). Organizational *learning* in a broad sense relates to the collaborative effort that makes it happen, and comes full circle from cooperating, with which we started.

Organizing is highly complex because, in a changing environment, cooperating, structuring, controlling, and learning must be performed simultaneously and balanced dynamically. Obviously, this is a formidable task, well beyond the capabilities of (isolated) individuals. To accomplish this task, an organization can draw upon its network of skilled members and dance partners that enables it to absorb a vast repertoire of knowledge from its environment, and to develop routines and meta-routines. Paraphrasing Richerson, Collins and Genet (2006), we may conclude that the organizational network makes an organization far more intelligent and adaptive than individuals could ever be on their own.

SUGGESTED BACKGROUND READING

The best book of all, Simon ([1945] 1997), in its fourth edition half a century after the first; fields of organizations, Powell *et al.* (2005); modularity, Simon (1962); creative teams, Guimerà *et al.* (2005); coordination of teams, Kearns, Suri, and Montfort (2006); an overview of organizational theories, both recent and classic, Scott and Davis (2007); a monograph on networks and organizations, Kilduff and Tsai (2003).

EXERCISE 7.1

Ask a firm or a department thereof with about 20–25 employees (not too many more) if you are allowed to collect data, and explain you are a student, the purpose of your research, and last but certainly not least that you will treat the data confidentially and identify people only with a number. Read Krackhardt and Hanson's paper (1993), replicate their research of expertise and trust relations, and compare each of these relations with the formal hierarchy. Analyze centrality, groups, and cohesion, and provide sociological as well as contextual embedding of the concepts you use and of your results. For some hints on data collection, see Chapter 8.

Methods
Data and software

To do empirical network analysis, we need data and software to analyze them. Here we will provide some general guidelines for data collection and then revisit most of the network concepts from the previous chapters from a computational point of view.

DATA

In data collection, a main cleavage is between experimental and non-experimental research. Experimental network data are few and far between, although it would certainly be worthwhile to do more experimental research in our field (Kosfeld 2003). The small world experiments (e.g. Dodds, Muhamad, and Watts 2003) are actually field experiments, not as rigorously controlled as laboratory experiments; only exchange theory has a tradition of lab experiments for social networks (e.g. Cook *et al.* 1983). Conducting experiments in Second Life is in its infancy (Bainbridge 2007). For learning how to set up experiments, the (social) psychological literature has the best information. The remainder of this section is about non-experimental data.

If one goes beyond ego networks, the most important decision to make is on the network *boundary* (Laumann, Marsden, and Prensky 1983). Mis-specifying a boundary is a main cause for non-valid results. For example, if somebody bridges structural holes between his or her community and other communities, and the researcher decides to study only the respondent's community and then concludes that the respondent has a low brokerage value, this outcome is invalid and an artifact of a mis-specified boundary. The boundary of the research population should thus be drawn around a (super) community large enough to contain the topologies of interest, be it structural holes, cohesion, or other. Boundaries that are meaningful for, and socially constructed by, the pertaining actors – that is, around ethnic, organizational, or other actual communities, or around given social events or activities (foci) – are usually best, although not always; for example, not for laboratory experiments or for hidden populations. Furthermore, drawing a sample (of vertices or ties) from a population rather than investigating the entire network is dangerous; see Lee, Kim, and Jeong (2006) for how strongly and how capriciously network measures deviate from true scores on the basis of samples; see also Borgatti, Carley, and Krackhardt (2006). For most network measures, one needs (almost) complete network data, not samples.[1] Degree, local clustering, and brokerage, exceptionally, can be computed on the basis of ego-network data, which can be an advantage.

In our digital age, there are numerous data sets available based on electronic media, for instance mobile telephone data (Onnela *et al.* 2007), Web page links, blogs, Web communities, log files of email traffic, and data sets that other researchers have made publicly available on the Web – but then one has to check how these data were collected to assess their validity and reliability. Examples are financial transactions between countries, collaborations between firms, patents, and scientific citations, as well as thousands of other opportunities to be seized. These data sets are excellent training material for analytic skills and can be used as test beds for new network measures and methods.

If no data are readily available on the researcher's subject of study, or if negotiations to get email or telephone data have no result, one has to study social behavior in the wild. For the latter, *ethnographic* research is very well suited (Hammersley and Atkinson 1995). "Human beings follow their sentiments and their interest, but they like to think they follow reason. They also look for – and never fail to find – a theory which, a posteriori, gives a certain colour of logic to their behaviour" (Pareto 1966: 151). Therefore a good rapport between the researcher and the subjects in the field is important to enhance the possibilities to discover not only their reasons for, but also some of the hidden motives and tacit rules of, their behavior, among other means by contrasting reported with observed behavior. Moreover, for many communities, access is possible only if respondents trust the researcher, and the car trade in West Africa (example in Chapter 6) as well as many other social settings can therefore be studied only ethnographically or not at all. Despite the number of books on ethnography, and suggestions made in some of them, hardly any method can be learned in class other than getting inspiration from exemplary research and some classics on the *verstehende* approach (e.g. Schütz 1932, Geertz 1973). In contemporary parlance, *verstehen* means that the researcher mentalizes and emphasizes with the respondents. To do so, an ethnographer must become aware of his or her own influences and projections on respondents' behavior that (s)he attempts to describe (Weber 1949), which Sigmund Freud called countertransference (Devereux 1967). After all, not only for research subjects but also for researchers it holds that "*Le coeur a ses raisons que la raison ne connaît point*," as Pascal said (the heart has its reasons of which the reason is unaware). An ethnographer has to have a certain talent and an ability to establish social contacts – networking – with people from different (sub)cultures to see underlying rules and preferences through actual behavior. Both talent and ability need time to develop rather than piles of books to study.

Communities in Western countries can often be accessed through surveys, which is clearly more efficient than ethnography, but has other difficulties (Bernard *et al.* 1984; Bernard, Kilworth and Sailer 1982). People tend to forget weak and ephemeral ties (Brewer 2000), misinterpret questions (Bailey and Marsden 1999), get readily overburdened with questions (McCarty, Killworth and Rennell 2007), have an egocentrically biased view (Kumbasar, Romney and Batchelder 1994), and conceal or fantasize parts of their social lives (Freeman, Romney and Freeman 1987). For these reasons, developing a good questionnaire is almost an art.

To aid respondent's recollection of possible weak ties, it is best to prepare a *name generator*, a list of all names in a given (sub)community, e.g. an organization, and to ask with whom the respondent is related. If responding to a name generator is set up as a game with monetary rewards for correct answers – alter should then confirm ego's claim on the existence or absence of their tie – validity and reliability are increased considerably (Brañas-Garza, Cobo-Reyes and Jimenez 2006). People receive "different strokes from different folks" (Wellman and Wortley 1990) and, if resources that people can get from their contacts are a focus of study, a *resource generator* can be used (van der Gaag and Snijders 2005), but resources important in one culture are not necessarily seen as relevant in another, making inter-cultural comparison difficult.

To flesh out relationships, for instance about shared activities or exchanges, *name interpreters* are used. A respondent should be asked for each social contact all the information the researcher wants to get about that contact (types of relationships and tie strengths), because associations between different memories about that person will aid the respondent's recollection (Kogovšek and Ferligoj 2005). Then move on to the next social contact with the same series of questions. Obviously, but often overlooked, the language of the questions should be targeted to the (sub) culture of the respondent, preferably to their age group and gender as well, otherwise the questions might be misinterpreted or lower the respondent's motivation to answer further questions. Mentioning specific social activities or exchanges can help respondents (Brewer 2000), bearing cultural differences in mind. For example, British people meet in pubs and Spanish people in parks, and a researcher doing a European comparison should be aware of and use these kinds of cultural cues to elicit valid responses (Meredith Rolfe, personal communication). Also immediate graphical feedback, on a laptop, about the network the respondent is trying to recall can help further recall (McCarty and Govindaramanujam 2005).

The question "How many people do you know in prison?" (Zheng, Salganik, and Gelman 2006) is clear for respondents in all subcultures, and has other advantages perhaps less obvious. Although the mean respondent in the USA knows one person in prison, most people do not know anyone in prison whereas some know many. This overdispersion (i.e. variance exceeding the mean) is indicative of the clustering of the community of prisoners. Asking how many people named Nicole respondents know does not yield overdispersion, because Nicoles are not clustered. On top of clustering, this question complemented by similar questions, e.g. about airline pilots and lawyers, can be used to estimate the number of ego's contacts.

For *tie strength*, one can ask about the future rather than the past, and ask if the respondent believes that after five years (s)he will still be in contact with that alter (Völker and Flap 2007). If the answer is yes, the tie is probably strong; if the answer is no, it isn't. Obviously, for very old or very young people, or people in a war situation, the question is unsuited. Alternatively, a five-point ordinal scale can be used, which is more reliable than other, e.g. binary or eleven-point, scales (Hlebec and Ferligoj 2002).

Using third party informants to tell the researcher about ties between focal actors and their alters creates new biases, because informants fill in the blanks in their memory by using simple but flawed heuristics. For example, if an informant observes i interacting with j and j interacting with k, then by the heuristic of transitivity the informant is likely to believe first that i and k have a social tie as well, and second that all three actors belong to the same group (Freeman 1992). In actuality, both may be false. David Krackhardt (1987) developed a systematic approach to comparing informants, or informants with focal actors. Because of all these pitfalls, before embarking on a network survey it is best to study in far more detail the experiences of experienced researchers. A good start is Marsden's (2005) overview.

Ego-network variables can be used in standard statistical models, along with attributes such as education and age. For studies of entire networks, if the process of interest changes faster than the network, a static approach will do, but, if the network changes faster than the process, a dynamic approach is necessary (Kossinets and Watts 2006). Currently there is no consensus on which dynamic approach is best; one approach is by exponential random graph models (Robins *et al.* 2007), another is Palla, Barabási and Vicsek's (2007). Whatever approach or subject is taken, owing to network interdependencies, network variables tend to be *autocorrelated*. For example, for two persons A and B who work together, the value of A's productivity might be to some degree determined by B's productivity, and a measurement error in B's work has ramifications for the error in A's. When measuring length, in contrast, the value and measurement error of A's length are independent of the value and error of B's. Autocorrelation means that values, errors or both are interdependent, cross-sectional, or temporal (Leenders 2002). Standard regression models hinge on the assumption that data are independent, and therefore ignore the – possibly large – effects of autocorrelation, which leads clearly to falsehood for many network studies if ignored. Roger Leenders (2002) explains what to do. A possible escape from autocorrelation is a sample of ego networks from a population large enough for the chances of ego-network overlap to be negligible.

SOFTWARE: R

We will use the software R, because it's free on the Web; it's open source (so everybody can program in it and for it as well); it can do most of what we need, some of which can't be done by any other program; and it can do statistical analysis as well, in contrast to all other network software. Another free network software is Pajek, which is accompanied by an extensive textbook (de Nooy, Mrvar, and Batagelj 2005). Data files from Pajek can be used in R, and R can export Pajek files, so if one is used to one program one can extend one's options by also using the other. However, Pajek has no functions for advanced community detection, social cohesion, and power, and it can't do statistics.

DOWNLOAD R AND THE IGRAPH PACKAGE

Go to www.r-project.org/, click CRAN, click a mirror site nearby, and choose the system of the computer (Windows, Apple, Linux). Since Windows is the most widely used, this text proceeds from that, but the differences from the other systems are small. After clicking on Windows, click "base," and click the latest version, which at the time of writing was R-2.6.0. It will probably land on the desktop and, after you click on the icon, it will install itself at C:\Program Files\R\R-2.6.0. It will present a series of dialog windows and it's best to accept all default options (for non-expert R users). At this point the base package of R is installed, which itself can do more than SPSS, and in addition to the base package one can import hundreds of packages for special purposes, e.g. for networks, and for many other subjects as well. We will use the *igraph* package, developed by Gábor Csárdi. Click on the R icon and a *console* window will open, with a prompt ">" after which commands can be typed. From the menu, choose "packages" and subsequently "install packages," and select a mirror site in a pop-up window. (A Mac has a different console window, with most of its menu at the top of the screen rather than at the console proper.) Sometimes when a new version of igraph is distributed, however, at some of the mirror sites it's not immediately available, resulting in an error message that igraph is not available; then choose another mirror site. Austria usually works well. Most of the network measures from this book can be handled with igraph; other network measures are in Carter Butts's sna package, and exponential random graph models are in the statnet package (Handcock *et al*. 2003).

For relatively straightforward graphs and the frequently used network measures, the igraph package has a *graphical user interface* (GUI) with a menu that will be explained below. For all other options, no menu is available and commands have to be typed in the R-console, treated further below. Commands may look very user-unfriendly, but they enable the user to do many more things than would be possible with a menu that is inherently limited in its options. In any case, for most network measures discussed in this book a user-friendly menu will do.

The igraph package has a tutorial complementing this book (http://cneurocvs.

rmki.kfki.hu/igraphbook/) and a reference manual (http://cneurocvs.rmki.kfki.hu/ igraph/doc/R/igraph.pdf) for additional functions and for technical details that go beyond the current treatment.

Just when this book went into print, a new version of R came out. For consistency with the remainder, set its working directory to the R folder, by the following menu:

file > change dir

GRAPHICAL USER INTERFACE (GUI)

Click (again) on the R icon. Load igraph into the working session by typing in the console window,

library(igraph)

and hit the enter key (if an *error* message shows up, see footnote).[2]

A separate GUI for igraph – not for the remainder of R – comes directly from a website (check out the igraph Web page mentioned above for updates and other news). Currently, it is at

http://geza.kzoo.edu/~csardi/socnet.R

If this website malfunctions by the time you read this book, then type "Jeroen Bruggeman" in a Web search engine and, wherever I work, on my website I will have this program available. Save it on your computer in the R folder as plain ASCII file – *not* as html – for instance under the name GUI.R. Check that your computer does not on its own account change .R into .R.txt or .R.html. In the R-console window, type the source that R should use to find the GUI:

source("GUI.R")

If that yields a problem, then type the website as source directly:

source("http://geza.kzoo.edu/~csardi/socnet.R")

On the menu of the GUI for igraph (not in any other window), follow the options graph > create > by hand. Now an editor will present itself in the R window, and you will have to choose if you want arcs or edges. Supposing that all vertices are identified with numbers starting from 1, then an arc *from* vertex 1 *to* vertex 2 with *value* 5 can be typed in three subsequent cells in the first row,

1   2   5

and *on a new line* in the same way, e.g. from 2 to 1 a negative arc,

```
2        1        -1
```

Edges have to be typed in only once, e.g.

```
1        2        5
```

A network without *values* takes only two columns in the data file, because then all values equal 1 by default and the third column can be left out. If a binary measure, e.g. betweenness, is computed on a valued graph, the computer will set all values other than 0 to 1, and then compute the result. If this is not what you want, e.g. because a (different) threshold for tie strength would make sense, take this into account when entering the data, or use the more advanced options of full-fledged R.

If all data are in, close the editor window. Now a dialog window will say "creating a graph by hand"; for arcs click "directed" (or leave unmarked for edges) and then click OK.

Names to identify vertices can be used instead of numbers, and the data file with names has the same format as above.

```
Birte      Stefan      5
Stefka     Bianca      3
```

You may combine names and numbers, for example Daniel_2, or Daniel2.

Once the data are typed in, it's safest to *save* them first, graph > export, and then the format option you prefer, which can be as they are typed in (edge list), or as adjacency matrix, or in Pajek format. The most efficient is the edge list option, and easiest to change as well. However, if you've created an undirected network (with edges), then save it as adjacency matrix. To make changes in the data, open the edge list in an editor, e.g. Notepad (or, if Word is used, make absolutely sure the file is saved as plain text in ASCII format), and make the changes wanted. External network data files can be *imported* by the menu options graph > import, and the files may have various extensions such as .txt, .dat, and others that are compatible with R. Imported edge lists will always be interpreted by the GUI as directed, even if they were initially created as undirected, hence undirected graphs should be saved as adjacency matrix, as said above. Finally, in case of multigraphs, the option graph > create > simplify removes multiple ties between the same pair(s) of edges, which would otherwise "confuse" some of the computations.

In the GUI, before drawing or computing anything, *mark* the graph you want to work with on the upper left hand side. After you mark the graph it can be drawn, and the easiest way is draw > simple. Click away the picture, redraw the graph, and notice that, although the network topology is still the same, the places where the lines and dots are drawn are not. To save the result, use the right mouse button and choose metafile if the result is to be used in a Word document, or else postscript. Draw > advanced has additional options to draw or to leave out identity markers of vertices and of ties, to adjust the size of the vertices, and by the "interactive" option to drag vertices by mouse into different positions.

Density, degree, and local clustering (as global transitivity) can be computed by marking the respective options in graph > basic statistics. For degree and average degree, if the file contains arcs the computer will add up indegree and outdegree, so, if you have in mind an undirected graph where two arcs A -> B and B -> A denote a single edge A -- B, then simply take *half* of the value(s) the computer presents. On the right hand side of the GUI, under "Dir" there will be YES or NO for directed and undirected graphs, respectively. Local clustering is unaffected by this difference.

Average path length (i.e. mean geodesic) is under "distances" on the menu; centrality measures are under "centrality"; social cohesion one gets by subgraphs > cohesion > cohesion of all components; and community detection can be done by subgraphs > communities > spinglass algorithm, for which you may take the default options. There are some self-explanatory options for the result of community detection, e.g. to draw the communities in different colors.

Graphs can be created automatically by graph > create > random and then for a random network of order n and size m, with the option "Erdos–Renyi G(n,m)." If you wish, mark "directed," and type the order in "Vertices" and the size in "Edges." For a directed graph you will get m arcs, and for an undirected graph m edges, which doubles density. For a scale-free network choose "Barabasi–Albert," mark "directed" if you wish, type its order in "Vertices" and half of the required mean degree value, $1/2 \langle k \rangle$, in "edges per time step." The network generated will have approximately and not exactly $1/2 \langle k \rangle$ on account of the uncertainty built into the simulation.

This should suffice for most of the network concepts treated in this book. At the time of writing, roles and balanced graphs could not yet be dealt with by igraph, but these options may have been added by the time you read this book. The remainder of the chapter treats the same network concepts using commands, which make it possible to draw fancier graphs, to customize computations, and to blur the boundary between using R and programming in R.

GET A BASIC FEEL FOR R

Everything beyond the options treated above has to be done by commands, and perhaps by some programming. Those readers already familiar with R may skip this general introductory paragraph and go to the igraph specifics below. Click (again) on the R icon for the console window. Now type 2+3*5 and hit enter, and you'll see that R can be used as a calculator. In front of the result it says [1] to indicate the first and in this case only line of the outcome. Spaces may be used, so 2 + 3 * 5 will yield the same result. In case parentheses are used but one is forgotten, e.g. 2 + (3 * 5 and enter, R will return a + sign on a new line. This doesn't mean it wants to add anything; it wants more information from the user, in this case a closing parenthesis. In case something goes wrong or it takes too long, on the menu of the console there is a *stop* button. Try log(10) and log10(10), and notice that, as a default, R takes logarithms on the basis of *e*, and that the user should make it explicit if a logarithm on the basis of 10 is required. If a result makes the user realize that (s)he wanted a slightly different action instead, typing a (long) command again can be avoided by using the upward arrow key: all your previous commands can be retrieved step by step. In the example, go back to 2+3*5, then use the left arrow key, and make a change, e.g. 2+3+5, and hit enter.

Type plot(log10(1:100)) and see what happens. To continue, either close the graphics window or click on the console window. For anything more complicated than this it's better and often necessary to work with *objects* and to assign them a value. Objects have a name, and almost any name can be chosen, but simple and brief mnemonics are always best, and numbers only are forbidden. In the following example, object x gets assigned the value of a computation, here the square root of 4, and the arrow from sqrt(4) to x indicates the assignment:

```
x <- sqrt(4)
```

Typing the other direction will produce the same result:

```
sqrt(4) -> x
```

To see what's behind an object name, x in the example, type the name and enter, and R will reveal what the object name stands for. Using space on either side of "<-" avoids confusion, but R will also do its job without space on either or both sides. When you type capital X an error message will be returned, because R is case sensitive, and x and X are entirely different objects. Now square x and assign the result to capital X, and add a semicolon and the name of the newly created object X:

```
X <- x^2; X
```

The semicolon is read as "and" and then typing an object name, here X, displays the content of the object. To object names can be assigned more than just simple numbers and, to make things more interesting, they can be assigned a social network, or, to be precise, a graph representation thereof. First, the igraph package should be loaded, and it should be loaded in each new R-session when it is needed:

```
library(igraph)
```

As an example of an object that is a network, a clique of five is generated and is called "clique":

```
clique <- graph.full(5)
plot(clique) # plot a graph
```

Comments can be typed after the "#" sign and will be ignored by R.

If the layout is unsatisfying, which it probably is, then add a layout "argument" for improvement:

```
plot(clique, layout = layout.kamada.kawai)
```

R-functions such as plot, sqrt, and many others, have opening and closing parentheses, and in between the user can specify *arguments*, separated by commas, to indicate more specifically what the function should do and on what object(s). Often, the first argument denotes an object, here a graph. However, the *order* of the arguments does not matter. In the example, the second argument layout.kamada.kawai is named after its inventors.

Objects can also be matrices and vectors (and a lot more), and R can do matrix algebra on top of a great many functions already programmed. For instance a vector (i.e. a list) of 50 numbers drawn from a random distribution is generated as follows:

```
a <- rnorm(50); a
```

A general and generally useful command for getting some information about an object, whatever the object is like, is

```
summary(a)
```

It then depends on the kind of object what information is given about it. If after some time a series of objects is created and the user is baffled by the sheer amount of them, the command ls() will list them. If some of them are no longer wanted, for instance x, g, and a, type rm(x,g,a) and the objects mentioned as arguments of the rm function will be thrown away. For throwing everything away, use

```
rm(list = ls())
```

By exception, the removal commands can also be given from the menu on the console. In case you need *help* there are several possibilities. Initially, it is quite

119

useful to work oneself through a tutorial on the Web, e.g. www.math.ilstu.edu/dhkim/Rstuff/Rtutor.html, which also helps to interpret other sources of help, like the not-so-very-easy-to-read manuals at CRAN. In an R-session one can ask for help, for example to take a square root:

```
help.search("square root")
```

or more briefly but not as generally applicably as help.search:

```
?root
```

To *quit* a working session, type q() and R will ask if the workspace image should be saved; answer "no," otherwise the saved workspace image may interfere with subsequent working sessions.

DATA FILE

R can read many different formats, including SPSS, Excel, and others – no Word documents though. Each of these formats requires a special command (see R manual) but for now we will create our data within R, in its proper editor (which looks similar to, but is not exactly the same as the GUI's). The editor to create a data frame (object) named D will show up after the following command:

```
D <- edit(data.frame())
```

In the field of social network analysis, vertices are normally numbered from 1 onwards along the natural numbers (although R permits the user to make life inordinately complicated by using imaginary or other numbers instead). Names can be used, too. Let's presume for the example that the vertices are connected by positive or by negative ties. An arc from vertex 1 to vertex 2 with value −1 is written in three subsequent cells on the first line,

```
1        2        −1
```

and *on a new line* in the same way, e.g.

```
1        3        1
```

and continue until all data are in. In an external editor, such as Notepad, and on a Mac, press the return/enter key after typing the final line. It's unnecessary (although permitted) to list pairs of unrelated vertices (i.e. arc value 0), and it's unnecessary to type arcs into the other direction for an undirected network, since later all arcs can be turned into edges in one stroke by a command. The same story holds if names are used, e.g.

```
name_1      name_2      -1
name_1      name_3       1
```

When the data editor window is closed, the data will be automatically but only temporarily saved in object D; to save the data beyond the R-session:

```
write.table(D, file="D.dat")
```

Now the file D.dat will be saved in the R folder, and from there it can be further edited in Notepad, Crimson, or another editor program outside R.

To import a file from the R folder,

```
D <- read.table("D.dat")
```

Importing an externally created file with a .txt extension goes the same way. In the external editor (Notepad, Crimson, or any other), hit the return key after typing the final line of the data and save the file as an ASCII file, for instance with the name Data.txt in the R folder. In R,

```
Da <- read.table("Data.txt")
```

To make changes to the data with the R-editor,

```
D <- edit(D)
```

If the original is to be kept unchanged, use a different name for each update, e.g. D1 and D2, and remember that these files exist only during the session if they are not explicitly saved by the write.table command, otherwise they will be lost.

Unfortunately, igraph works internally with an *index* that starts at 0 (because it's programmed in C) whereas matrices and vectors in R start at 1. In the future, the internal index will be reprogrammed to establish consistency. For now, and before doing anything else, recode the first two columns of the data matrix by subtracting 1 from each vertex number. A position at row i and column j in a data frame or matrix is denoted $D[i,j]$, and a blank at the first argument $D[\ ,j]$ means for *all* rows, column j. In our case we have columns 1 and 2 (denoted 1:2, which means from 1 to 2), for all rows,

```
B <- D[ ,1:2]-1 # reset index
```

Now everything is set to plot the graph and to do network computations. Remember for each session to load the igraph package first,

```
library(igraph)
```

and turn the data frame B into a *graph object* (by first stating that the object is to be regarded as a matrix and then taking the transpose of it),

```
g <- graph(t(as.matrix(B)))
```

Alternatively, all arcs can be turned into edges:

```
g <- graph(t(as.matrix(B)), directed=FALSE)
```

Either way, if there are tie weights, they must be imported separately from the third column of the data file D:

```
E(g)$weight <- D[,3]
```

If *names* rather than numbers have been used as identity markers in the data file F:

```
g <- graph.data.frame(F)
```

The default is a directed graph. Tie weights form the third column of the data file F as above, with F substituted for D.

If data come in an *adjacency matrix*, save the file as Q.dat in the R folder, and turn it into a graph object:

```
Q <- read.table("Q.dat")
g <- graph.adjacency(as.matrix(Q), weighted=TRUE)
```

If the ties have no weights, then it doesn't matter if weighted=TRUE is left in or out; in doubt if the ties are directed, the following command will tell true or false:

```
is.directed(g)
```

It will also say that the graph is directed if every arc is paired with an arc in the opposite direction, i.e. when there is A -> B and B -> A for every pair of vertices, which in igraph is different from an edge A -- B.

From graph object to matrix,

```
Q <- get.adjacency(g, attr="weight")
```

If the weight attribute argument is left out, all ties receive the value of 1 in the matrix representation.

Importing, saving, and editing data

```
D <- read.table("D.txt") # import file
D <- edit(D) # inspect or edit data
New <- edit(data.frame ()) # create new data
write.table(New, file="D.dat") # don't use .txt
B <- D[ ,1:2]-1 # adjust index of vertices
library(igraph) # load the package for graphs
g <- graph(t(as.matrix(B))) # turn data into graph
g <- graph(t(as.matrix(B)), directed=FALSE) # undirected
n <- graph.data.frame(Name) # names as data
E(g)$weight <- D[,3] # tie weights from third column
```

Turning an *incidence* matrix of people (in the rows) to group affiliations (in the columns) into an adjacency matrix of (overlapping) groups goes as follows. Suppose the initial matrix is an SPSS file, then save it as ASCII file with extension .dat, open it in an external editor to check its contents, and remove commas and other inappropriate signs, e.g. replace ",10" by unquoted .1. Columns and rows not wanted can be deleted after importing it into an R-session:

```
B <- read.table("people.to.group.dat")
```

For example, remove columns 1 to 3:

```
D <- B[ ,-(1:3)]
```

Treat the data frame as a matrix:

```
D <- as.matrix(D)
```

Create an adjacency matrix A of affiliations by affiliations, $A = D^T D$, and set its diagonal to 0:

```
A <- t(D) %*% D; diag(A) <- 0
```

123

Adjacency matrix *A* can be turned into a graph object by the commands treated above, and be further analyzed by the commands treated below.

PLOTTING A GRAPH

This paragraph deals with fancier than basic graphs (see GUI above), if some vertices or ties have properties (e.g. size or color) that make them stand out from the rest. If nothing special is required, the simplest drawing can be had by typing this:

```
plot(as.undirected(g), vertex.label=NA, vertex.size=3, layout=layout.fruchterman.
reingold)
```

Properties of vertices and ties are to be set by using commands that start with V and E, respectively. To set the values of the ties of *g*, by E(g)$weight, the information from the third column of D can now be used:

```
E(g)$weight <- D[,3]
```

Let's depict negative ties in blue and positive in red. Mind the double "==" signs below – absurdly complicated but what can one do about them?

```
E(g)[weight == -1]$color <- "SkyBlue2"

E(g)[weight == 1]$color <- "red"
```

Alternatively, all ties can be painted black:

```
E(g)$color <- "black"
```

To see what colors are possible, also for vertices and for labels, check out colors() and see also the igraph manual.

Plotting, finally, and setting the index back to normal for visual inspection by using vertex.label=V(g)+1 as argument:

```
plot(g, layout=layout.fruchterman.reingold, vertex.label=V(g)+1)
```

The Fruchterman–Reingold algorithm is faster than Kamada–Kawai (see above) and is therefore recommended for very large graphs. Both algorithms yield different layouts (but the same topology) each time they are executed, and repeating a plot a few times may yield a more satisfying result. If the order is so large that labels and arrows obfuscate the graph,

```
plot(as.undirected(g), vertex.label=NA, vertex.size=3
```

and the rest the same as above.

Alternatively, vertices can be made a bit smaller than standard and the labels can be depicted on the side by using the arguments vertex.size=4, label.dist=.5. To get a possibility for manual repositioning of vertices:

```
tkplot(g,
```

and the rest the same as above.

A nice plot option is to draw strong ties thicker than weak ties. First set all ties to thickness 1, and then set the ties equal to or above some threshold, here 2, twice as thick:

```
E(g)$width <- 1

E(g)[weight >= 5]$width <- 2
```

Then the plot function will notice widths automatically; it is not necessary (although permitted) to explicitly use the argument edge.width=E(g)$width.

Save the figure, by clicking the right hand side of the mouse, as postscript if Ghostview is installed, or on Windows as metafile. Finally, if vertices are to carry their names rather than numbers, and the graph is not too large, it is possible to depict them. Either the file was already done (see above) or else a list of names has to be added in the order of their identity numbers. For example Figure 2.2 was created by assigning four *names*, and don't forget the quotes:

```
V(g)$name <- c("Milena", "Andra", "Pachanga", "Ciprian")
```

If later a change is to be made, use the edit command (see above) and, for plotting, put somewhere as arguments within the plot function:

```
vertex.label=V(g)$name, label.dist=1
```

From there on, experiment with the label distance (try label.dist=1.1 to see the difference) to get it exactly right.

If you have a graph g1 and want to use the same layout for a subsequent graph g2 with some ties or vertices added, first plot g1 and then:

```
lay <- layout.fruchterman.reingold(g1)

plot(g2, layout=lay)
```

CENTRALITY MEASURES

To generate *degree*, if direction is to be ignored in a directed graph:

```
d <- degree(as.undirected(g), mode="total")
```

Leaving out as.undirected(g) for a directed graph results in adding up indegree and outdegree. For an undirected graph the result is the same and one can simply use:

```
degree(g)
```

For indegree and outdegree separately, use the argument mode="in" or mode="out" respectively, e.g.

```
di <- degree(g, mode="in")
```

Obviously, degree ignores tie weights.
Sort the result along its values from low to high, not along the index:

```
names(d) <- seq(d); sort(d)
```

This sorting from low to high can be done with any of the centrality measures below.
Structural autonomy is done in terms of *constraint*:

```
C <- constraint(g)
```

To round off numbers to, for instance, two decimals, and at the same time sort the result:

```
names(C) <- seq(C); round(sort(C),2)
```

Notice that rounding can slightly alter the order.
Power centrality measured as "page rank" is defined for positive binary graphs, directed or undirected, and as usual it presupposes that, for the data used, the right choices of threshold and direction have been made.

```
P <- page.rank(g)
```

Closeness centrality ignores weights; mode="in" is for paths from alters to ego and mode="out" is from paths from ego to alters. The function below ignores direction:

```
closeness(g, mode="all")
```

Betweenness centrality for a directed network:
```
B <- betweenness(g, directed = TRUE)
```

and normalized:

```
max <- (vcount(g)-1)*(vcount(g)-2)
```

```
Bn <- B/max
```

Normalized betweenness for undirected networks:

```
Bn <- 2*betweenness(g, directed = FALSE)/max
```

The above functions have additional possibilities, for example computing a centrality measure for only a few specific vertices; see the igraph manual for these other possibilities. The *mean* of whatever measure can be had simply by

```
mean(x)
```

SMALL WORLDS, COHESION, AND COMMUNITIES

To find out the *order* and *size* of a graph g, use the functions vcount and ecount, respectively. Consequently, *density* for a directed network is

```
da <- ecount(g)/(vcount(g)*(vcount(g)-1))
```

and density for an undirected graph is twice the above. Density can be computed simply as follows, which automatically takes direction into account if the graph is directed.[3]

```
de <- graph.density(g)
```

Average geodesic ignores tie weights and direction:

```
L <- average.path.length(g)
```

Local clustering by transitivity (i.e. triangle clustering). Neither the concept nor the program is intended for directed graphs, so just to be sure:

```
T <- transitivity(as.undirected(g))
```

Community detection works for (positively) valued edges and arcs:

```
sp <- spinglass.community(g)$membership
```

The result, sp, then has to be sorted (as the centrality results above). If $membership is left off, the output is less easy to read, but then the modularity value is presented in the results. An additional argument gamma can be added (and gamma=1 is the default value, see Chapter 5) for subgroup detection. The algorithm tries to avoid the trivial solution of putting all vertices in a single group; if there is no escape from it (e.g. a clique), the modularity value will be bad. However, if the network is indeed a clique, it makes sense to detect only one community, and this is what the program will do correctly. The algorithm is very good but may take too long for very large graphs. For those graphs there are less accurate but faster algorithms available; see the igraph manual.

Social cohesion as K-connectivity considers valued ties (even with negative values, so take care!) as non-valued edges.

```
sc <- graph.cohesion(g)
```

To find cohesive subgraphs ("blocks", or subcommunities) and their levels of cohesion, first install the digest package, in the same manner as igraph:

```
library(digest)
```

```
coh <- cohesive.blocks(g)
```

If the graph is relatively small:

```
plot(coh, layout=layout.kamada.kawai, vertex.label=V(g)+1, vertex.size=10)
```

The *nestedness* of a vertex is the level in the hierarchy of its pertaining subgraph, presented at the right hand side of the plot output above; vertices in the top node of the hierarchy, which represents the entire network component, are at level 1 in terms of their nestedness, no matter what the K-connectivity of the network might be. For larger graphs that cannot be meaningfully inspected visually:

```
coh$blocks # subgraphs and their vertices
```

128

```
coh$block.cohesion # K-connectivity of each subgraph
```

The internal igraph index of vertices starts at 0, as will be clear from the numerical output, but in all likelihood the index of your data file starts at 1, so add 1 to every vertex number in the result presented on the screen. From the two numerical outputs, the nestedness of vertices can be inferred.

RANDOM NETWORKS AND POWER LAWS

Generate an undirected random network of order n and size m:

```
g2 <- erdos.renyi.game(n, m, type = "gnm")
```

If it must be directed:

```
g3 <- erdos.renyi.game(n, m, type = "gnm", directed=TRUE)
```

To generate an undirected scale-free network of order n, argument $m = k$ below denotes not size, as in erdos.renyi.game, but half of the mean degree. For example $m = 10$ results in a graph with mean degree 20. A chosen value approximates the mean degree in the outcome, owing to uncertainty built in the simulation.

```
g4 <- barabasi.game(n, m = k, directed=FALSE)
```

If it must be directed:

```
g5 <- barabasi.game(n, m = k) # by default directed=TRUE
```

For additional possibilities to create random networks, e.g. with edge decay, see the igraph manual.

To see what a generated graph looks like, leave out vertex labels and depict vertices quite small, and use the arguments vertex.label=NA, vertex.size=3 in the plot function.

To check out if the degree distribution looks like a *power law*, start out with creating the degree distribution:

```
dd <- degree.distribution(g4)
```

The argument log="xy" in the plot function produces logarithmic x and y axes:

```
plot(dd, xlab="degree", ylab="frequency", log="xy", type="b") # try also
type="l"
```

129

If it does look like a power law, you may be interested to compute the maximum likelihood estimator of the power law exponent (Clauset, Shalizi, and Newman 2007; Newman 2005), i.e. the slope of the fitting line:[4]

```
a <- power.law.fit(dd); summary(a)
```

To see autonomy and betweenness of, say, a scale-free distribution together in one figure, first compute betweenness (directed or undirected) and constraint as above, then choose parameter values, for this example $\beta = 0.5$ (which is within the range of values that Burt found in his empirical studies) and $\alpha = 1$, to define *structural autonomy*:

```
A <- C ^ (-.5)
```

Below, the argument pch and a number yield a particular shape for the dots in the figure (try other numbers or look into the general R manual at the CRAN site).

```
plot(sort(B), pch=16, xlab="rank order", ylab="B, A(red)", main="Centrality")
```

On the next line,

```
points(sort(A), pch=17, col="red")
```

The correlation is

```
cor(A,B, use = "pairwise.complete.obs")
```

More interesting, perhaps, is the correlation of rank order positions:

```
cor(A,B, use = "pairwise.complete.obs", method="spearman")
```

MORE CONVENIENT R-SESSIONS

For elaborate R-sessions much typing can be avoided by writing the commands and functions in an editor, and running them all in one stroke in R. Type a series of them and don't forget to include the loading command(s) of the package(s) needed at the top, and to tell it at the end to write the output to a file. To remember what the commands are supposed to do, write comments after a # sign. Save the file with extension .R, for instance with the name co.R

In R, type source("co.R"), and all commands are executed in the order in which they were put in the command file. A command file can also be taken from a website:

```
source("http://. . ./co.R")
```

After an error, it is not necessary to type again all commands in R. Modify the command file, save it, and run it again. More generally, create for yourself a convenient working space, which along with an R-console window has an editor, with data files and command files, and one or two Web pages with R-tutorials or manuals, since remembering large numbers of R-commands might be hard.

■ *Street in Cotonou, Benin. Photgraph by the author (2002).*

Glossary of network notions

Adjacency matrix Matrix representation of a network, wherein each cell (q_{ij}) at the intersection of row i and column j contains the value of the arc from vertex i to vertex j. For an undirected network, with edges, the matrix is mirror symmetric towards its diagonal, because, for all cells, $q_{ij} = q_{ji}$.

Arc Network representation of an asymmetric social relationship between two actors, depicted as an arrow in the pertaining graph. The direction in which the arc points depends on the definition of the particular social relation, e.g. authority goes in the opposite direction from submission, which are two different ways to depict the same power relation.

Assortative Assortative mating or mixing, also called "homophily," means that ego prefers to establish ties with alters who have some properties in common with ego, for example religion, kinship, ethnicity, status, or degree.

Autocorrelation The term network autocorrelation is used if the value or increment of a property of ego depends on the value or increment of that property of ego's alters, respectively. For example, the productivity and the productivity increase of an employee depend on his or her colleagues' productivity and productivity increase, respectively. The height of an employee, in contrast, is unrelated to the height of her colleagues, and body length is not autocorrelated. Furthermore, the productivity of an employee depends on his or her past productivity, and in general, temporal autocorrelation means that the current value or increment of a variable depends on its past value(s) or increment, respectively. Both network and temporal autocorrelation can, and usually do, contain measurement errors, a third type of autocorrelation.

Balance A concept from balance theory to study conflict and the forming of coalitions. Cycles in signed graphs with an odd number of negative ties are unbalanced, whereas cycles with zero or an even number of negative ties are balanced. A network is balanced if all its cycles are balanced.

Binary graph A network without tie values (other than 1), i.e. a tie between two vertices is either present (denoted 1) or absent (denoted 0).

Betweenness centrality A measure to assess the gatekeeper, or brokerage, advantages of actors. First, take the proportion of geodesics (their number, not their lengths) from vertex A to B passing through ego and all geodesics from A to B, including those not passing through ego. Ego's betweenness centrality, then, is the sum total of these proportions taken over all pairs of actors in the network, ego excluded. Basically, betweenness is for directed and for undirected graphs, not for valued graphs.

Bipartite graph A network with two kinds, or types, of vertices, usually actors on the one hand and their social foci or shared events or locations on the other hand, for example music festivals and their visitors. The aggregate units are connected through the actors they have in common, e.g. visitors to multiple festivals, and the actors might be connected through the foci/organizations/events they jointly participate in, at least if the aggregates are small enough for everybody to meet each other. Data for a bipartite network are put in an incidence matrix, from which through simple matrix algebra both the actor network and the foci network can be obtained (see Breiger 1974).

Block model See **Regular equivalence.**

Bridge and local bridge A bridge is a tie connecting two otherwise unconnected network components (or only indirectly connected via other components). If there is more than one bridge connecting two components, the notion of local bridge should be used instead. Strictly speaking, there can be only one bridge between two components.

Brokerage Ego is in a brokering, or gatekeeper, position if his/her alters have no direct contacts with each other, and no indirect contacts apart from their path via ego (or through paths longer than that, which are irrelevant because of attrition of information). A brokering, or gatekeeper, position is supposed to yield information to ego that is reliable, diverse, and well timed. The two most widely known measures for brokerage are constraint (Burt 1992), used to compute brokerage in terms of structural autonomy, and betweenness centrality. Advantages and disadvantages of each are discussed in the main text.

Centrality When unpacking the notion of centrality, there turn out to be different kinds of centrality indicating different positional advantages. The simplest of all is degree – indegree might be regarded as an elementary indicator of popularity – whereas power centrality is more sophisticated, and also depends on the degree of the alters, and their alters, and so on. Other widely used centrality measures are betweenness, closeness (Freeman 1979), and Burt's (1992) constraint.

Centralization A network with one or few actors having high centrality, and all others having low centrality, is more centralized than a network wherein centrality is evenly distributed. For a given centrality measure, one takes the summed difference between the highest centrality score and all other centrality scores, and then normalizes the result by dividing it by the maximum possible summed difference (Freeman 1979). With the exception of Estrada and Rodríguez-Velázquez's (2005) subgraph centrality, all other centrality measures have their maximum in a star network.

Clique A maximally connected network of minimally three vertices, wherein each vertex has an edge (or an incoming and outgoing arc) to every other vertex in the network.

Closeness centrality Closeness indicates how close ego is on average to all other vertices in the network. In an undirected network, ego's closeness centrality is the reciprocal of the mean length of all geodesics from ego to all other vertices in the network. If the network is directed, geodesics from and to ego are considered separately in the overall mean path lengths, since a path from ego to alter and a path from alter to ego are likely to have different lengths.

Closure A confusing notion to indicate cohesion. In the field of social networks, in contrast to all other fields in sociology, closure does not imply that the network is closed to outsiders. K-connectivity does not have this connotation and is a far more precise approach to cohesion.

Cluster A cluster is a relatively more densely connected subgraph within a larger and sparser graph. A cluster is not precisely defined but is a heuristic notion towards communities and their detection. Local clustering, in contrast, is precisely defined.

Community A group, or cluster, of vertices that is more densely connected internally than externally with other clusters in the network. A clear-cut boundary is not required and, with a Potts spin glass approach from statistical physics, communities can be determined statistically, by comparing actual with expected tie values – modularity for short. A community that stands out gradually from its network environment can thus be detected, and the more pronounced communities are, i.e. the denser within and sparser between, the higher the modularity of the network. Actual communities can overlap, and smaller, more densely connected communities can be hierarchically nested in larger and sparser ones, which can also be examined by the spin glass approach.

Component, K-component, and **giant component** A graph or subgraph without isolated vertices, i.e. from each vertex there is a path to any other vertex in the network, is a component, also called a connected (sub)graph. In a bi-component, each pair of vertices is connected by at least two independent paths, whereas in K-components there are minimally K independent paths connecting each pair of vertices. A giant component is a disconnected subgraph of a yet larger graph if it contains the majority of the vertices of the larger graph.

Connected graph See **component.**

Connectivity Notion used with various meanings by different authors. See **K-connectivity.**

Constraint See **Brokerage.**

Cycle A path with at least two distinct ties that ends at the vertex where it starts.

Degree The number of ties of (or incident with) a vertex. For a directed network, the number of arcs that start or end at the vertex, which can be counted separately as outdegree and indegree, respectively.

Density The actual number of ties in the network divided by the maximum possible number of ties.

Diameter The longest geodesic in a given network.

Directed graph, or **digraph** Network with arcs, and each edge represented by two arcs in opposite directions.

Distance In a network, the distance between vertices A and B is their shortest path length.

Dyad A social bond between two actors, which is represented in a network by one or two arcs or an edge.

Edge Network representation of an (approximately) symmetric social relationship between two actors, depicted as a line in the graph connecting the two pertaining vertices.

Ego network For a given list of actors, an actor that for a moment is at the focus of the researcher's attention is called "ego." Ego's "alters" are those actors with whom ego has ties. An ego network consists of ego, his/her alters, and all ties between these actors. In the end, every actor in a network can be ego, each in his/her turn.

Geodesic Shortest path between two vertices. In small world studies, the mean geodesic of a given network is taken to characterize the average distance of the entire network.

Graph See **network.**

Hierarchy A hierarchy is a partially ordered set (i.e. reflexive, antisymmetric, and transitive) with a "top," or "root," element, and from the top there is exactly one path to each element. Hence a hierarchy is a connected and directed acyclic graph (but not the other way around).

Incidence matrix A matrix representing a bipartite graph, with actors in its rows and social foci (or organizations, or other aggregates of actors) in its columns. A cell (q_{ij}) denotes actor i's (strength or frequency of) affiliation with event (or organization or location) j.

Indegree Number of arcs pointing to a given vertex.

K-connectivity This notion is used for social cohesion, and K equals the minimum number of vertices that, if removed, would make the network fall apart, which by

Menger's theorem is equivalent to the minimum number of vertex-independent paths connecting arbitrary pairs of vertices in the network.

Local clustering Proportion of actual ties between ego's alters and the maximum possible number of ties between ego's alters. It is a variation of the measure for density, with the index set modified, and is usually applied as a mean value of the local clusterings of all ego networks within a larger network. Alternatively, transitivity can be used as a measure for local clustering, with slightly different numeric results but for small world studies qualitatively the same.

Modularity See **Community.**

Multigraph, or **multiplex graph** A network with multiple relations, e.g. financial and friendship, each expressed by its own set of ties.

Neighbors Vertices at path distance 1 from each other.

Nestedness A community has K-connectivity. The community may contain subcommunities with higher levels of connectivity, e.g. a clique of six friends embedded in a school of three-connectivity. The community can then be depicted as a hierarchy, in which the top node is the entire community, branching down into (possibly nested) subcommunities with higher levels of connectivity, e.g. a clique of friends within a class within a year group within a school. The nestedness of a vertex in the community is the level of its pertaining subcommunity in this hierarchy, starting at 1 for the top level of the entire community. Hence nestedness is maximally equal to, but in most cases smaller than, K. The easiest way to see this is to analyze a small and familiar network with the computer, which will depict the hierarchy of nested subcommunities.

Network A network is equivalent to the notion of graph in mathematics. It has a non-empty set of vertices, i.e. nodes, and a (possibly empty) relation defined for these nodes, i.e. a set of ties. Furthermore, ties may have values, and there can be multiple relations.

Organization An organization is a special purpose community, i.e. a K-component wherein people are in authority, working, and informal relations with each other.

Organizational field An organizational field is a community of organizations and individuals sharing a certain culture of norms, beliefs, and practices and a reputation system.

Outdegree Number of arcs starting at a given vertex, pointing at other vertices.

Path Sequence of consecutive edges connecting two vertices in a network. If the network has arcs, paths follow the direction of subsequent arcs, and paths in one direction can be different from paths in the opposite direction.

Path length The number of consecutive ties along a path connecting vertices A and B, and for arcs following the direction of subsequent arcs from A to B. The shortest path from A to B is called a geodesic.

Power Ego's power *à la* Bonacich depends recursively on alters' power. Ego is more powerful if (s)he has more contacts, and if these contacts in turn have more contacts, and so on recursively. The Bonacich power, or status, model makes it possible to incorporate various subtleties, such as tie strength, negative ties, and negative effects of positive ties (e.g. to notorious criminals), and the weakening of power contributions over longer paths. Simpler and intuitively easier to comprehend is the page rank measure for status and power.

Prestige If ego defers to another actor for some quality attributed to her/him, ego will in most cases take into account the judgments of her/his alters about this person, but wants to avoid admiring someone who despises ego. The resulting prestige rank ordering of actors is the overall effect (Nash equilibrium) of all these deliberated and socially influenced deferences (see Gould 2002 for the details).

Power law, or **scale-free distribution** In the context of networks, power laws, also called scale-free or fat tail distributions, are mostly about degree. In a power law distribution, the probability $p(k)$ for a vertex to have degree k is proportional to $k^{-\alpha}$. In most empirical cases, $2 < \alpha < 3$. Tie strength is also power-law distributed, and has many other (non network related) properties. Owing to the costs of tie maintenance, actual networks can be slightly less fat-tailed than power laws, and then feature an exponential cutoff. Ties that require high maintenance, e.g. between best friends, are not power-law distributed.

Preferential attachment For an actor i with degree k, its chance of receiving an additional tie, $p(k)$, is proportionate to its current degree k. This mechanism of proportional growth is also called "the rich get richer," and explains power law distributions of ties.

Regular equivalence A concept used to study social roles. Two actors A and B are regularly equivalent if they have the same relations to other actors who have the same role in turn, i.e. if A has a tie with C and B a tie with D, and C and D in turn are regularly equivalent. This should hold for all ties of A and B, and for all relations if there is more than one. An example is a network with a core and a periphery, in which the core actors interact with each other and with peripheral actors, who in turn do not interact with each other, only with actors in the core. The pertaining adjacency matrix can be permuted such that all core actors are in the upper left corner and the peripheral actors are in the remainder of the matrix. The patterns of 0s and 1s in the permuted matrix look like blocks, and this approach to role detection is therefore called block modeling. One can draw a reduced graph with each group of regularly equivalent vertices as a single vertex, in the example one vertex for the core and one for the periphery; a tie connects the two vertices and the core has a reflexive tie with itself. If in a network vertices A and B have the same social contacts, or approximately so, they are structurally equivalent. Structurally equivalent actors are therefore regular equivalent, but usually not the other way around.

137

Relation In a network, a relation is a set of ordered pairs of vertices, represented by a set of ties connecting the pertaining vertices. The order means that if vertex A is related to vertex B, represented by an arc from A to B, this does not imply that B is also related to A, in other words, an arc in the opposite direction exists only if it is stated explicitly. In undirected networks, wherein related pairs of vertices stand in a symmetric relation, the order does not matter. In multigraphs there are different relations defined on the same set of vertices, e.g. of love and business, each represented by its own set of ties.

Role See **Regular equivalence.**

Searchable networks Networks in which actors can find each other in reasonable time and with feasible effort.

Signed graph Network wherein ties can be negative (denoted −1) or positive (denoted +1) or absent (denoted 0).

Small world A small world is a large and sparse network with a small average geodesic. In most cases, a small world denotes high local clustering as well, although a small average distance is its core feature.

Social capital Social capital is a smorgasbord of network benefits, each with its conductive network topology. All good social capital literature focuses on specific mechanisms that generate specific benefits, and the litmus test for publications in this field is to remove the notion, which leaves good works unharmed, and to see how much explanatory power is left.

Status In networks, status is usually treated as equivalent to power. For conceptual discussions and the distinction with prestige, see Chapter 6.

Structural autonomy See **brokerage.**

Structural equivalence Two actors, or vertices, A and B are structurally equivalent if they have (approximately) the same relations with the same alters, e.g. two businessmen with the same clients. The notion can be used to study competition.

Subgraph A subgraph has all its vertices and ties embedded in a graph of which it is part. Mathematically, every graph is a subgraph of itself.

Tie Network representation of a social relationship between two actors as an arc or an edge, possibly with a tie strength as well.

Tie strength, or tie value The strength, or intensity, of a social relationship, indicated by the value of the pertaining tie. Granovetter (1973) immortalized the distinction between strong and weak ties.

Transitivity If vertex A has a tie with B and B a tie with C, then transitivity is the chance that A has a tie with C. In the context of small world studies, transitivity of an entire network is the proportion of triads (wherein A, B, and C are mutually connected) and the number of triples (wherein at least two out of three ties are present), and is used as a measure of local clustering. Notice that one triad has three triples, and the measure of transitivity takes this fact into account by multiplying the numerator by three.

Triad Three connected vertices, i.e. a clique of three. In the context of triad census, a triad means three vertices with the possible ties among them; even three unconnected vertices count as a triadic state.

Undirected graph Network with edges only, no arcs.

Valued graph Network with tie values that indicate tie strengths.

Vertex Network representation of an actor (person, organization, or country), also called node.

Notes

1 Introduction

1 As Ann Mische and Harrison White put it concisely (1998: 695), "Social action is interaction that induces interpretations and thus builds continuing relations."

2 The paper that inspired my wordplay was 'Network Motifs: Simple Building Blocks of Complex Networks' (Milo *et al.* 2002). Notice that one of the founders of modern social network analysis, Harrison White (2000), said that "The so-called micro–macro gap is an optical illusion of trying to visualize socio-cultural processes through [ill-chosen] natural science framings."

3 http://wordnet.princeton.edu/

4 For so-called dissimilarity measures and their application in multidimensional scaling, social network analysis borrows from linguistics and psychology.

2 Representation and conceptualization

1 One might further distinguish emotional intensity proper from emotional intimacy and from similarity of experiences (*Erlebnisnähe*, Schütz 1932).

2 In formal logic, a *theory* is defined as a set of sentences (i.e. premises and conclusions) in a given language that has rules of inference, and its conclusions are validly inferred from its premises. If and only if a theory is consistent, it can be interpreted in, i.e. applied to, a *model* (van Dalen 2004). Models represent part of reality under investigation, and can be graphs, mathematical models, or statistical approximations of empirical data; there are many other kinds too, such as downsized airplane models for wind tunnel testing. It is important to realize that theory and model are different entities and at different levels: a theory says something *about* a model and, if a model is in a language (e.g. set-theoretic), then its theory is in a meta-language. Analogously, a photo model, representing consumer desires, is different from a text in a fashion magazine describing her. A theory or text can be inconsistent but models cannot be, no matter how paradoxical their behavior might seem, whether photo models or scientific models.

3 For patterns of diffusion over time in this particular network, see Moody (2002).

4 The basis for graph theory, as well as for all other mathematics, is *set theory*, dealing at a foundational level with collections of things, their properties, and their relations (for an introduction see Devlin 2003).

5 For a non-empty set of objects B, and in the simplest case without arc values, a *graph* $G = \langle B, Q \rangle$, and $Q \subseteq B \times B$, and Q and B are disjoint. More generally, a graph with p different relations can be written as a "$p + 3$ tuple," $G = \langle B, v_Q, R, Q_1, \ldots, Q_p \rangle$, wherein a function v_Q maps for

each Q the pertaining arcs on their respective values, or "weights," and R is the set of rational numbers. In practice, negative numbers are rarely used as arc values, since positive relations are far more common and negative relations usually short-lived; a minus sign and a plus sign are used in *signed graphs* in balance theory (Chapter 5). For an easy read on graph theory with sociological examples, see Flament (1963). Harary (1969) has less sociology but more sophisticated theorems.

6   At aggregated levels of countries or organizations, there are sometimes more precise and more robust data available than at the level of individuals, for instance about financial transactions, which warrant the choice for valued arcs.

7   "Trust is a psychological state comprising the intention to accept vulnerability based upon positive expectations of the intentions or behavior of another" (Rousseau *et al.* 1998: 395). Trust is neither a behavior nor a choice, but a psychological condition that can arise in interdependencies under uncertainty.

8   For valued graphs, see Boccaletti *et al.* (2006: 199).

9   For a valued graph, the cells of its adjacency matrix, q_{ij}, will have the pertaining tie values. To count degree, valued graphs should in most cases be turned into binary graphs first; otherwise if somebody has degree k this may mean k acquaintances or one very strong love affair of k intensity or anything in between, and ambiguity slips in. See also Boccaletti *et al.* (2006: 199).

10 There are exceptions, for example firm's investments, which are (partly) in themselves. If there are reflexive ties, then the maximal density values (see box) have to be adjusted accordingly.

11 A hilarious and deliberately bad match of an intuition and its formal model is Northcote Parkinson's (1957) explanation of bureaucratic growth. George Spencer Brown (1957: 1–14) has a wonderfully eccentric view on modeling.

12 For the learning strategy of conjectures, proofs, and refutations by counter-examples, see Imre Lakatos' masterpiece (1976).

3 Small worlds

1   For a translation of a Hungarian passage into English, see Braun (2004).

2   In the literature, transitivity is often but misleadingly called *triadic closure*, suggesting that once a triad is "closed" no further ties could be attached to the pertaining actors, which in general is false.

3   Many non-anthropologists distinguish "developed" from "underdeveloped" or "developing," countries, even though in actuality all countries are developing. The "underdeveloped" are defined in terms of their putative shortcomings, although for different criteria, e.g. cultural traditions, sports, or music, the order of development would be quite different. Sadly, inhabitants of "underdeveloped" countries have adopted the dominant discourse, if only to be seen as candidates for financial aid, while inhabitants of self-proclaimed "developed" countries sometimes may learn *about*, but do not consider learning *from*, poor countries. For a historical account of "the people without history" and the pertaining discourse of supremacy, see Wolfe (1982).

4   After completing this chapter, I noticed that my circular village bears similarity to the "smallest world" of Dorogovtsev and Mendes (2002: 1109). I use my village to illustrate the original Watts model rather than presenting a new case, though, and in Burkina Faso there is no church in the middle of a village, and if there were a religious building it would more likely be a mosque.

5   If the case of arcs, a path from i to j will usually be different from the path(s) from j to i.

6   For valued, or weighted, networks, there exists a measure of weighted clustering (Barrat *et al.* 2004).

7   One might argue that if a person has 1000 contacts, who in their turn have 1000 contacts each, one would reach out to all humans in about three steps, but that is nonsense because of very large overlaps of these contacts due to local clustering.

8 Before industrialization, there were populations that were isolated for quite some time, which thus were for a while out of touch with the rest of humanity (Cavalli-Sforza, Menozzi, and Piazza 1993). Here we assume that the world is one component, i.e. from every human there is a path to every other human, which is valid for modernity. The existence of a giant component in networks in general is not entirely trivial, though (see Newman, Watts, and Strogatz 2002).

9 In the UK, 92 percent of the board interlocks have a single shared director (Conyon and Muldoon 2006).

10 Sociology's subject matter is more general than social relations only, and covers all social interdependencies, including those between actors who do not interact (Elias 1970). As an example, consider small firms competing for the same consumers, without being aware of each other. Bipartite graphs are useful devices to extend the social network approach to represent interdependencies in general.

11 Other small world studies of corporate interlocks using simpler measures without correction are Kogut and Walker (2001) and Davis, Yoo, and Baker (2003); Baum, Shipilov, and Rowley (2003) studied the small world of partnerships between Canadian investment banks.

4 Searching and fat tails

1 The probability of establishing a tie at distance r_{ij} decays with distance, r_{ij}^{-a}, for a given $a \geq 0$.

2 The Web is a socially constructed network, wherein humans establish links between websites. Broder *et al.* (2000) and Kleinberg and Lawrence (2001) studied its structure, Albert, Jeong, and Barabási (1999) its diameter, and Huberman and Adamic (1999) its growth dynamics.

3 Power laws were well known for a long time in physics and complexity studies; for an introductory overview see Goldenfeld and Kadanoff (1999). They had also been encountered in degree distributions of social networks, e.g. by John Scott (personal communication), but before 1999 nobody realized how general they were. In a power law, or scale-free, distribution, the probability $p(k)$ of a vertex to have k ties is proportional to $k^{-\alpha}$ and in most empirical cases $2 < \alpha < 3$.

4 This claim raised some eyebrows: Kentsis (2006) argued that social reality is more complex; a rebuttal by Gama Oliveira and Barabási (2006) basically follows Farquharson's plea (quoted in Chapter 2) for relatively simple but general models.

5 From the Bible: "For unto every one that hath shall be given, and he shall have abundance: but from him that hath not shall be taken away even that which he hath" (Matthew 25: 29).

6 For an actor i with degree k, its chance of receiving an additional tie is proportionate to its current degree, $p(k_i) \sim k_i$.

7 For a power law $x^{-\alpha}$ its counterpart with exponential cutoff is $x^{-\alpha} e^{-\lambda x}$. Its generation can be explained in various ways, e.g. by tempered preferential attachment based on optimization constrained by actors' having only local knowledge (D'Souza *et al.* 2007), and by q-exponentials (D. White *et al.* 2006). General and historical treatments of power laws and their cousins can be found in Newman (2005) and Mitzenmacher (2003).

5 Communities

1 If H and G are graphs, then H is a *subgraph* of G if and only if H has all its vertices and ties in G. Hence every graph is a subgraph of itself.

2 Be aware that in the literature some authors use the notion of size for the number of vertices, but context will avoid confusion.

3 A spin glass was initially meant as a model for magnetic particles; for a simple explanation, see Philip Ball (2004: 347–351).

4 If for a given degree distribution two vertices i and j have the degree of k_i and k_j, respectively, and in the network there are m edges, then the expected number of edges (or edge value) connecting

i and j can be determined by seeing what the chance is that an edge departing from i will connect to j and the other way around. This expected number e_{ij} is proportional to $k_i k_j / 2m$, and can be compared with the actual edge value q_{ij}, which is the basis for computing the modularity of an assignment of vertices to communities.

5   An alternative approach to community detection is the clique percolation method by Palla *et al.* (2005), which works well and fast if communities are dense. It can also detect community overlaps and nested communities, two options it has in common only with the Hamiltonian approach out of many community detection approaches. However, if communities are sparse, as large social communities tend to be, they won't be detected. Hence this clique percolation method is treated here only in a footnote, but check out their mouth-watering software, which can be had from their website.

6   This approach also mounts to a, somewhat technical, definition of *community*, as a set of vertices having the following three properties: (1) every proper subset of a community has a maximum coefficient of adhesion with its complement in the community, compared with the coefficient of adhesion with any other community; (2) the coefficient of cohesion is non-negative for all communities; and (3) the coefficient of adhesion between any two communities is non-positive (Reichardt and Bornholdt 2006b).

7   Davis (1967) generalized balance theory to more than two clusters. For an overview of balance theory, see Wasserman and Faust (1994).

8   Notice that "Climate also affects the structure of the network. Where it is warm, and people spend a large part of their lives in public – on street corners or doorsteps, in squares or shopping – there are obviously many more opportunities to establish and service contacts" (Boissevain 1968: 548).

9   Coleman used the term *closure* to describe locally dense networks, whereas closure is normally used for social exclusion. The connotation of exclusion was not at all intended by Coleman, though, but created a great deal of confusion among some of his readers. An interesting aspect of his work is inter-generational "closure," or solidarity, that is important for welfare states, among many others.

10 If researchers will use K-connectivity to further investigate the consequences of connectivity and nestedness, an interesting puzzle for them is posed by exceptions to the rule. Sometimes people deeply nested in a community manage to disentangle themselves and move to a different one, for example a change of religion, or from gang to police. Although social inequality can play a role in these cases, motivating an "escape" from relative deprivation, it is currently unclear why only a few out of many deprived attempt such escapes.

11 Perception of other beings is biased if the observer feels superior, which can be easily demon-strated in psychological experiments. Japanese scholars had the advantage of relatively unbiased perception of monkeys, in comparison with Western scholars, and it was Kinji Imanishi and other Japanese who pioneered in this field decades before others caught up (de Waal 2003); see Whiten (2005) for a recent overview. A superb single-page antidote to ethnocentrism in general is provided by Sean Nee (2005).

12 Explaining the evolution of cooperation among humans and other animals was regarded as one of the biggest scientific challenges by the editors of *Science* (Pennisi 2005).

13 In some cases, the collective good must be achieved by collective *in*action, e.g. refraining from using a scarce environmental resource when selfish actions to collect it harm other people (Hardin 1968), but the dilemma is qualitatively the same, in both cases dealing with externalities of individual (in)action (Schelling 1978).

14 An easy introduction to game theory and other evolutionary models is McElreath and Boyd (2007). A brief German introduction to game theory with sociological applications is Raub and Buskens (2006), and an overview of rational choice research on social dilemmas is Buskens and Raub (2007). Notice that evolutionary game theory makes no assumptions about the rationality

of actors. Notice furthermore that for pairs of actors in dyadic interactions in a (prisoners' dilemma or other) game, their degree of family relatedness (Hamilton 1964) and the importance of the future, i.e. the chance of continuation of their relationship (Axelrod and Hamilton 1981), can be interpreted as indicators of tie strength in a network interpretation of the situation.

15 If ego, alter, and punisher are not all from the same community, the amount of punishment changes in ways that theory has not yet predicted (Bernhard, Fischbacher, and Fehr 2006).

16 Empathy exists in a primitive way even in mice, which respond to pain in other mice (Miller 2006). Humans are far more helpful than chimpanzees already at a very young age (Warneken and Tomasello 2006), which is very likely related to humans' ability to mentalize. Probably feelings of guilt also are related to empathy (Tangney 1995). There is a cultural effect on empathy, and people in collective cultures are better at it than in individualist cultures (Wu and Keysar 2007). Empathy is a double-edged sword that also makes it possible to deceive others (Zimmer 2003; Singer and Fehr 2005).

17 Gerald Marwell and Pamela Oliver pioneered researching network effects on collective action (e.g. Marwell, Oliver and Prahl 1988; an overview, Oliver and Marwell 2001), but at their time they did not have the concept of K-connectivity at their disposal. As for K-connectivity, notice that the paths through which gossip flows need not be the same as those through which punishments are delivered. Notice furthermore that third party intervention does not need to take place in triads or yet existing ties; someone higher up in a hierarchy can command a subordinate to punish or to intervene, and the punisher does not yet have to have a tie with the norm-violator, e.g. a policeman and a criminal. As mentioned, it was already known that network topology affects cooperation (e.g. in power law networks, Santos and Pacheco 2005), but the relation with K-connectivity and its underlying argument are new. Patrick Doreian *et al.* (1996) hint at a connection between cooperation and balance theory.

18 Here we have pointed out proximate causes of cooperation; a full-fledged evolutionary approach, necessary to explain its ultimate causes, goes beyond the scope of this book.

19 Whereas Richerson and Boyd limit culture to what individuals acquire "from other members of their species," I generalize their definition to permit inter-species transmission. For example, humans tried to imitate birds before they invented fixed-wing airplanes. For their work on culture, Richerson and Boyd refer to the pioneering contributions of Donald T. Campbell (e.g. 1960, 1976), Luigi Luca Cavalli-Sforza (e.g. Cavalli-Sforza *et al.* 1982, Cavalli-Sforza, Menozzi, and Piazza 1993), and of course Charles Darwin (1874). An overview of their mathematical models is Boyd and Richerson (1985); introductory is McElreath and Boyd (2007). In this introduction to social networks, the treatment of cultural evolution must be brief, and important subjects such as gender, religion, and the co-evolution of culture and genes, to mention just a few, are left out.

Cultural *proximity*, or similarity, can be measured through interviews (Hofstede 1980) or text analysis (Carley 1994; Mohr 1996), and subsequently expressed as a network of similarity "ties," and mapped out by multidimensional scaling (Cox and Cox 2001) or investigated by community detection approaches. Since people are highly sensitive to small cultural differences, a logarithmic similarity measure can be used to account for this sensitivity (Adamic and Adar 2003: 222), as a variation of the Jaccard measure.

20 Whereas Richerson and Boyd have a broad conception of information, including ideas and knowledge, the literature distinguishes *information* (symbols or symbolic representations) from *knowledge.* The latter comprises understanding of, expectations associated with, or interpretations of given information, depending on what literature one consults. The distinction closely approximates but is not identical to the distinction between declarative and procedural knowledge.

21 Herbert Simon ([1945] 1997: 97–99; 1990) had a similar and partly complementary argument for why a combination of social and individual *docility* is beneficial. Notice that the optimal balance of individual and social learning depends on the speed of change of the environment; the

more stable the environment, the more people can rely on other people for acquiring already existing knowledge about that environment (Richerson and Boyd 2005).

22 The distinction between content- and model-based transmission is not always sharp. Certainly, seeking information from experts, either for the quality of their knowledge, or for their prestige, or a mixture of both, is an important mechanism of knowledge transfer in modern organizations (Borgatti and Cross 2003).

23 Elias's work is much richer and interesting than could possibly be told here, and also deals with internalization of norms as self-control of socially disapproved impulses, among many others.

24 Positive externalities exist when the value of a code (e.g. Internet protocol, industrial standard, language) increases with the number of users of that code. Even if positive externalities exist, humans may for various reasons stick to their tradition, e.g. because of high switching costs, biased judgment, group loyalty, or a desire to distinguish themselves from others.

25 Along with community-specific cultural variants, there are also inter-community cultures, as communities often evolve into a hierarchical structure of subcommunities; for example, the European countries with their country-specific laws and regional languages in the European Union with its European laws and lingua francas.

26 The forces of transmission can be studied as diffusion; discovery and innovation can be modeled as brokerage (see Chapters 6 and 7); and environmental selection by competition can be modeled as a bipartite network, equivalent to niche overlap. Only natural selection without competition falls outside the network perspective.

27 In large-scale processes of identification and disidentification, not only networks but also mass media play a crucial role. Cohesion by itself is not necessarily related to a sense of common identity. Some communities, in particular elites such as the aristocracy, construct their identity with great care, and consciously increase their cohesion through marriages that in turn yield strategic advantages for the families involved (Padgett and Ansell 1993). Many other communities, in contrast, become self-aware mostly under external pressure (H. White 1992).

6 Social inequality

1 Before the notion of social capital existed, Uriel Foa (1971) distinguished resources (benefits) according to the dimensions of concreteness and particularism, which yielded a typology of six resources. Relating these resources to social capital, (1) status requires power centrality, (2) affection (Foa's "love") requires strong ties, and (3) information, (4) money, (5) goods, and (6) services require brokerage to yield individual benefits, or cohesion for collective benefits.

2 "Macht bedeutet jede Chance, innerhalb einer socialen Beziehung den eigenen Willen auch gegen Widerstreben durchzusetzen, gleichviel worauf diese Chance beruht" (Weber 1922: 28). According to this definition, power can also be passive, e.g. letting someone wait for a long time. The case of applying force at a distance, e.g. shooting someone with a rifle without any social relation to the victim, falls somewhat out of the ordinary network approach, which could be expanded to incorporate this case.

3 It is possible that a prestigious person attracts more (powerful) friends than a non-prestigious person and thereby becomes powerful in turn, but this strongly depends on the kind of prestige. It seems more often the case that high-status persons have prestige due to their status. If there is a strong discrepancy between power and prestige, as between high-power–low-prestige politicians and a low-power–high-prestige journalists, the more powerful might feel tempted to act against those who overshadow them in prestige; "power tends to corrupt and absolute power corrupts absolutely," said Lord Acton. What will happen then depends on the institutions that control the network, e.g. if there are checks and balances, and on how individuals are socialized.

4 Network *centralization* expresses the extent to which "centrality" is concentrated in one or few actors. It is measured as variability of individual centrality (Freeman 1979), i.e. the summed

difference between the highest centrality score and all other centrality scores, subsequently normalized by dividing by the maximum possible summed difference (which for most centrality measures is in a star network of the same order).

5 Anyone with social skills may be able to restore agreement between two antagonists, but, in general, high-status actors have a better chance to succeed, and at lower cost (Flack, de Waal, and Krakauer 2005). Intervention can be more complex than direct intervention by a third party individual, and can consist of organized police on behalf of (possibly organized) superiors against (possibly organized) norm violators.

6 Weber distinguishes (1) legal, or rational, authority in modern organizations from (2) charismatic authority and (3) traditional authority (e.g. belonging to an aristocracy). Notice that, among humans, power leads to a hierarchical structure, but not so among all animals, e.g. every kea in a group is dominant to some other kea (Brosnan and de Waal 2002: 133), which in a hierarchy is impossible.

7 One can set a parameter to have power diminish steeply with path length rather than slowly, but then power centrality becomes (almost) indistinguishable from degree.

8 Although a consensus is not reached under all parameter settings, one can interpret the current models as models of *selection* of a dominant opinion, for a fixed network and an exogenously given initial variety of opinions (Friedkin 1993, 1999; Marsden and Friedkin 1993; Friedkin and Johnsen 1997, 2003). Even under the tight constraint of a fixed network over some time period, the models are quite interesting, and we may hope that in the future they will be generalized to include network dynamics. Notice that, if a cross-sectional study features homogeneity of opinion, this result does not imply a network cause, and may also be caused by prior selection of similar friends (Marsden and Friedkin 1993). To distinguish empirically influence from selection of similar people, see the approach of Steglich, Snijders, and Pearson (2004). Finally, in some cases the influence of mass media on opinion is larger than that of networks.

9 For *n* vertices each with an arc to focal actor a_i, and outdegree denoted as $O(a)$ (which in an undirected net will indicate degree), *page rank* $PR(a_i)$ of the focal actor is

$$PR(a_i) = (1 - d) + d(PR(a_1)/O(a_1) + \ldots + PR(a_n)/O(a_n))$$

with a damping factor d in between 0 and 1 (Brin and Page 1998). In the software we use (Chapter 8), the default value for d is 0.85, which gives good results for quite a variety of network topologies. The data used should be binary and, if weighted ties are used, any value above 0 will be interpreted by the computer as a tie and be set to 1.

10 In the original paper, a rather complicated entropy-like measure was used, but a far more simple power law can do the job.

11 Bounded rationality implies, among other things, that, depending on the framing of information, humans either avoid risks or are overconfident, even in situations where they have enough information to make better decisions than they do (Kahneman 2003). The limitations of rationality are unequally distributed, and some humans are considerably more rational than others (Camerer and Fehr 2006), net of network position. In contrast to what many scholars thought till recently, the importance of consciousness in decision making is lower for complex decision problems than for simple ones, and choices of products with many different aspects, such as cars and houses, are viewed more favorably in retrospect when they are made largely unconsciously (Dijksterhuis *et al.* 2006).

12 In African actuality, the chain of reselling is more complex than the didactic example suggests, and *démarcheurs* ("market runners"), not treated in the example, have language advantages more often than resellers have (Beuving 2006). This doesn't matter for the example, though. What does matter is that Hamidou's culture obliges him to hide negative news from his superior, in

this case his father, and to cover up financial losses. The latter has a strong negative effect on his business, and shows that the negative effect of relatively low status can undo the positive effect of brokerage. Strategic advantages from a language intermediary position were discussed and formalized earlier in the literature (de Swaan 1988) but not cast in a predictive model until Burt (1992).

13 Some scholars argue that not all new ideas spring from recombining existing ideas, for example because some ideas embody the discoveries of empirical regularities previously unknown. However, empirical generalizations are combinations of less general observations which in their turn have to be made first before cumulative knowledge development is possible. The discovery of DNA, for example, could not have been made by Charles Darwin, who despite his genius did not have access to the body of knowledge, including technology, that the discoverers of DNA had at their disposal. Recombination is a crucial mechanism of any knowledge growth beyond accumulation of facts, an insight that dates back to Ramon Lull's system of concentric circles in the thirteenth century (Gardner 1982).

14 A potentially interesting alternative to Burt's measure is Ernesto Estrada's *subgraph centrality* (Estrada 2007), which is a hybridization of brokerage and power centrality. The subgraph centrality value depends on the number of subgraphs ego is related to, and is inversely related to the path lengths from these subgraphs to ego. It thereby takes into account (to some degree) the diversity of information that is important for brokerage, as well as the reliability of shorter distances, but it does not take into account the timing of information, a third hallmark of brokerage, although perhaps not in all cases. It appears that the productivity of scientists depends more strongly on their comprehension of a diverse set of ideas and of the potential new combinations thereof than on being the first and only person to know about these ideas (see Estrada and Rodríguez-Velázquez 2005: 6). However, more empirical applications should demonstrate the usefulness and validity of this measure before it can be lifted to the main text.

15 The Dutch language has the beautiful expression "op het vinkentouw zitten."

16 There is a measure of flow-betweenness that can handle valued ties, but its underlying assumption that stronger ties carry more relevant information is empirically false (Granovetter 1973, 1983).

17 An equivalence relation is reflexive, symmetric, and transitive (Devlin 2003).

18 For a complementary network approach to international relations, as a product space, see Hidalgo *et al.* (2007).

19 This measure is equivalent to the Herfindahl index used in economics.

7 Organizations as networks

1 Bruce Kogut and Udo Zander (1992: 390) said that "Complex organizations exist as communities within which varieties of functional expertise can be communicated and combined by a common language and organizing principles." Arthur Stinchcombe (1965: 145) spoke about "special purpose organizations." The purposes, or goals, of organizations vary in explicitness and clarity, e.g. firms usually have clearer goals than governments, and all organizations contrast with "non-purposive corporations" such as family, village, and nation (Coleman 1974: 29).

2 For detailed practical guidelines, e.g. how to negotiate in dyads, there is other literature available (e.g. Fisher, Ury, and Patton 1981). After all, this book is an introduction to networks, not a practical course on management. For managerial guidelines from a network perspective, recommended reading is *The Hidden Powers of Social Networks* (Cross and Parker 2004).

3 Hofstede's pioneering research suggested that all national cultures can be characterized on a small number of dimensions, among others (1) large versus small *power distance*, and (2) *individualism* versus *collectivism* (Hofstede 1980). These two dimensions were also found if the questionnaire was developed by Chinese instead of Western scholars (Hofstede 1994), whereas

another dimension (uncertainty avoidance) was not. Another interesting dimension is low versus high context; in high-context, or explicit, cultures, most information is verbalized explicitly (US, Germany, Scandinavia) and in low-context, or implicit, cultures, metaphors or suggestions in a given context hint at what is being meant (China, Arab countries, Brazil, France). Members of the latter understand members of the former more easily than the other way around.

4 As the biological roots of emotions, decisions, and cognitions are now being discovered, the final choice between the terms *engagement*, *commitment*, and similar notions will ultimately depend on future brain research.

5 Rob Cross, Wayne Baker, and their colleagues went into organizations to map out networks of collaboration, for which they distinguished "energizing" from "de-energizing" social contacts (Baker and Dutton 2007; Baker, Cross, and Wooten 2003; Cross, Baker, and Parker 2003), which led to surprising discoveries for these organizations.

6 Notice that task variety is related non-monotonically with commitment, and too much variety, or complexity, exceeds the limits of individual rationality and is demotivating (Gardner 1990).

7 For the disasters that can happen if managers don't listen to their subordinates at all, see Perrow (2005).

8 Tasks and their workflow relations can also be represented as a network, abstracting away from the people performing the tasks, called a Petri net (van der Aalst 1998). Workflow relations often coincide with working relations in the social network, but not necessarily so. If one wants to be strict, the discussion about modularity applies to workflow relations. For a representation of organizations wherein people, positions, and tasks are precisely kept apart, see Oeser and Harary (1964). Notice that in their representation, in contrast to ours, one person can have several positions, and each position can have only a single occupant.

9 Like many social abilities (Chapter 5), social coordination too has a biological basis (Tognoli *et al.* 2007).

10 Ordering relations – partial orderings to be precise – are (1) *reflexive* (e.g. each set is a subset of itself), in contrast to social relations, which are not reflexive; (2) *antisymmetric* (e.g. if A is a subset of B and B is a subset of A, then A and B are equivalent), whereas friendship relations are not antisymmetric, and some are not symmetric either; and (3) *transitive* (e.g. if A is a subset of B and B is a subset of C, then A is a subset of C), whereas, for friendship, transitivity is statistically true but not a universal rule.

11 A hierarchy is a directed acyclic graph (DAG) that is connected. Not all connected DAGs are hierarchies, though, because there can be multiple paths from the top to a given element "below," for example someone having two different bosses in the same organization.

12 A recent contribution building on Simon's (1962) insight is that many hierarchical networks feature self-repeating patterns at different scales of their structure (Strogatz 2005; Song, Havlin, and Makse 2005). Guimerà *et al.* (2003) conjecture that this self-similarity might be due to people trading off a need for cooperation and costs of tie maintenance.

13 In the division of labor, some members, or units, of an organization will have different specializations from others, each working in a different local environment. Some members, or units, in a boundary-spanning role may then specialize in searching external information and transforming it into a useful form for the organization. However, they need some level of shared knowledge to be able to communicate well across the organization (Cohen and Levinthal 1990: 132–133).

14 By means of a different measure of cohesion from ours, although broadly consistent with it, it turned out that transfer of complex knowledge in organizations is enhanced by cohesion (Reagans and McEvily 2003).

15 The learning curve in its simplest form, without forgetting, is a power law, $y = ax^{-b}$, in which y denotes labor costs, usually in hours, x is the rank number of the unit produced, starting at 1, and b equals approximately 1/3, for a wide variety of products (Argote and Epple 1990; Huberman 2001; Thompson 2007).

16 Biased cultural selection is based on the scarcity of cognitive resources of the culture bearers, and has to be distinguished from natural, or environmental, selection, which is (largely) independent of their cognition and desires. Organizations' consumers are culturally influenced, and one might therefore argue that the selection of organizations is also cultural, seemingly different from natural selection (while keeping in mind that ultimately also culture is part of nature). However, competition between organizations is based on the resources of the consumers, not on those of the employees who establish and transmit the organizational routines. Because of this (near) independence, environmental selection by consumers should be distinguished from selection due to biased transmission of routines.

17 On complexity theory applied to organizations and other economic phenomena, see Durlauf (2005).

18 Citation patterns of scientific papers and of patents are excellent data for knowledge networks (De Solla Price 1965; Podolny and Stuart 1995, 1996; Henderson, Jaffe, and Trajtenberg 2005).

19 Exploitation, or specialization, is similar to, but not identical with, Burt's constraint, with reflexive ties being the main difference; accordingly, Equation 6.5 gets an additional term (p_{ii}) that accounts for the percentage of ideas that the focal actor re-uses. Another difference is that actor A can exploit the knowledge of actor B while B is not exploiting A, whereas in Burt's model A and B would mutually constrain each other. This can be accounted for by slightly modifying the definition of terms p_{ij} in Burt's model (Carnabuci 2005). The specialization-brokerage model was initially tested on technology domains (Carnabuci and Bruggeman 2007a), but is also true at the organizational level (Carnabuci, unpublished). Be aware that in the diffusion literature, arcs point in the direction of information transmission, while in the cognitive literature and in our model, arcs point in the opposite direction, toward information search.

20 On the important but often overlooked difference between oscillation and cyclical change, see Turchin (2003). In contrast to organizations, individuals have different parts of their brain dealing with exploration and exploitation, respectively (Daw *et al.* 2006), and for regulating the dynamic balance between the two they have a chemical (noradrenaline) helping them to choose (Cohen and Aston-Jones 2005). Both individuals and organizations feature learning curves in repeated tasks. Notice that even routinely following a learning curve involves some modest degree of exploration, which becomes clear once learning is modeled as a search space wherein a shorter path to a given goal state has to be found (Huberman 2001), and new paths have to be explored. This is then a *local search*, close to current knowledge of paths, whereas for a new goal state a more *distant search* is required, which does not follow a learning curve. As a matter of fact, exploitation in its extreme state involves no learning at all.

21 Currently, there is a debate about what kind of institution could prevent top managers from having too much influence on their own salary, against the interest of the shareholders (Bebchuk and Fried 2006). Also in this case reciprocity is a key mechanism, here between directors and top executives.

22 Older organizational literature opposed non-routine tasks to routine, pointing to aerospace as an example of non-routine in the 1960s, which misses the point that, to achieve mastery in any kind of job at all, some decisions must be routine, including in aerospace.

23 One might protest that mathematical theorems need no authority if their proofs are correct, but then authority is still needed for the definitions.

24 Knowledge of organizational rules is a source of power in itself. Rule masters can slalom faster than their opponents in between rules and exceptions, defending themselves with reasons and excuses that have shown their usefulness in previous cases (Luhmann 1964: 186).

25 At different moments, e.g. during a night and a day shift, employees can have different managers, but at each moment they should only have one. Attempts to organize otherwise, e.g. in matrix organizations, have always failed in the longer run, as far as I know.

26 Power differences further increase by decreasing public awareness of or interest in top decision making, which in turn becomes opaque to outsiders.

27 See the wonderful network images in Powell *et al.* (2005), which for copyright reasons could not be reproduced in this book.

28 Organizations as dance partners is an older metaphor; see for example Richardson (1972: 896).

8 Methods

1 For sampling of difficult-to-access populations, e.g. drug users, see Salganik and Heckathorn (2004).

2 If there is an error message and igraph won't start, go to the "modules" folder (in the R folder), and copy the file "iconv.dll" into the folder . . .\library\igraph\libs.

3 Density as defined can be maximally 1. However, if in a computer simulation (see barabasi.game) the parameter of average degree is set beyond the maximum possible value, in a clique of the given order, then the computed density value will be above 1.

4 For additional information, type the command help("mle-class")

Bibliography

Abbott, Andrew (2004) *Methods of discovery: heuristics for the social sciences*. New York, Norton.

Abrahamson, Eric (1991) Managerial fads and fashions: the diffusion and rejection of innovations. *Academy of Management Review* 16: 586–612.

Adamic, Lada and Adar, Eytan (2003) Friends and neighbors on the web. *Social Networks* 25(3): 211–230.

Adamic, Lada and Adar, Eytan (2005) How to search a social network. *Social Networks* 27(3): 187–203.

Adamic, Lada and Huberman, Bernardo A. (2002) Zipf's law and the Internet. *Glottometrics* 3: 143–150.

Ahmed, Akbar S. (2005) Ibn Khaldun and anthropology. *Contemporary Sociology* 34: 591–599.

Aigner, Martin and Ziegler, Günter M. (2003, 3rd ed.) *Proofs from THE BOOK*. Berlin, Springer.

Albert, R., Jeong, H., and Barabási, A.L. (1999) The diameter of the World Wide Web. *Nature* 401: 130–131.

Albert, R., Jeong, H., and Barabási, A.L. (2000) Error and attack tolerance of complex networks. *Nature* 406: 378–381.

Alderson, Arthur and Nielsen, François (2002) Globalization and the great U-turn: Income inequality trends in 16 OECD countries. *American Journal of Sociology* 107: 1244–1299.

Almroth, Lars *et al.* (2005) Primary infertility after genital mutilation in girlhood in Sudan: A case-control study. *Lancet* 366: 385–391.

Alon, U. (2003) Biological networks: The tinkerer as an engineer. *Science* 301: 1866.

Amaral, L.A.N. *et al.* (2000) Classes of small-world networks. *Proceedings of the National Academy of Sciences* 97: 11149–11152.

Anderson, Benedict (1991) *Imagined communities*. London, Verso.

Andrews, Kenneth T. and Biggs, Michael (2006) The dynamics of protest diffusion: Movement organizations, social networks, and news media in the 1960's sit-ins. *American Sociological Review* 71: 752–777.

Antal, T., Krapivsky, P.L., and Redner, S. (2005) Dynamics of social balance on networks. *Physical Review E* 72: 036121.

Anthonisse, Jac M. (1971) *The rush in a directed graph: Technical report*. Amsterdam, Mathematisch Centrum.

Argote, Linda and Epple, Dennis (1990) Learning curves in manufacturing. *Science* 247: 920–924.

Argote, Linda and Ingram, Paul (2000) Knowledge transfer: A basis for competitive advantage of firms. *Organizational Behavior and Human Decision Processes* 82: 150–169.

Argote, Linda *et al.* (2000) Knowledge transfer in organizations: Learning from the experience of others. *Organizational Behavior and Human Decision Processes* 82: 1–8.

Arrow, Kenneth J. (1962) The implications of learning by doing. *Review of Economic Studies* 29: 155–173.

Arrow, Kenneth J. (1974) *The limits of organization*. New York, W.W. Norton.

Arthur, Brian W. (1989) Competing technologies, increasing returns, and lock-in by historical events. *Economic Journal* 99: 116–131.

Artzy-Randrup, Yael *et al.* (2004) Comment on "Network motifs." *Science* 305: 1107c.

Axelrod, Robert and Hamilton, William D. (1981) The evolution of cooperation. *Science* 211: 1390–1396.

Axtell, R.L. (2001) Zipf distribution of U.S. firm sizes. *Science* 293: 1818–1820.

Bailey, Stefanie and Marsden, Peter V. (1999) Interpretation and interview context: Examining the General Social Survey name generator using cognitive methods. *Social Networks* 21: 287–309.

Bainbridge, William Sims (2007) The scientific research potential of virtual worlds. *Science* 317: 472–476.

Baker, Wayne E. and Dutton, Jane E. (2007) Enabling positive social capital in organizations, in Dutton, Jane E. and Ragins, Belle Rose (eds.) *Exploring positive relationships at work*. Mahwah, NJ, Lawrence Erlbaum.

Baker, Wayne E. and Faulkner, Robert R. (1993) The social organization of conspiracy: Illegal networks in the heavy electrical equipment industry. *American Sociological Review* 58: 837–860.

Baker, Wayne, Cross, Rob, and Wooten, Melissa (2003) Positive organizational network analysis and energizing relationships, in Cameron, K.S., Dutton, J.E., and Quinn, R.E. (eds.) *Positive organizational scholarship*. San Francisco, Berrett-Koehler.

Ball, Philip (2004) *Critical mass: How one thing leads to another*. London, Arrow.

Ballester, Coralio, Calvó-Armengol, Antoni, and Zenou, Yves (2006) Who's who in networks. *Econometrica* 74: 1403–1417.

Barabási, Albert-László (2002) *Linked*. Cambridge, MA, Perseus.

Barabási, Albert-László (2005) The origin of bursts and heavy tails in human dynamics. *Nature* 207: 435.

Barabási, Albert-László and Albert, Réka (1999) Emergence of scaling in random networks. *Science* 286: 509–512.

Barabási, Albert-László and Bonabeau, Eric (2003) Scale-free networks. *Scientific American* 288–5: 50–59.

Barabási, Albert-László *et al.* (2002) Evolution of the social network of scientific collaborations. *Physica A* 311: 590–614.

Barnett, William P. (1997) The dynamics of competitive intensity. *Administrative Science Quarterly* 42: 128–160.

Barnett, William P. and Carroll, Glenn R. (1987) Competition and mutualism among early telephone companies. *Administrative Science Quarterly* 32: 400–421.

Barnett, William P. and Carroll, Glenn R. (1995) Modeling internal organizational change. *Annual Review of Sociology* 21: 217–236.

Barnett, William P. and Hansen, Morten T. (1996) The red queen in organizational evolution. *Strategic Management Journal* 17: 139–157.

Barrat, A., Barthélemy, M., Pastor-Satorras, R., and Vespignani, A. (2004) The architecture of complex weighted networks. *Proceedings of the National Academy of Sciences* 101: 3747–3752.

Batty, Michael (2006) Rank clocks. *Nature* 444: 592–596.

Baum, Joel A.C., Shipilov, Andrew V., and Rowley, Tim J. (2003) Where do small worlds come from? *Industrial and Corporate Change* 12: 697–725.

Baum, Joel A.C. *et al.* (2005) Dancing with strangers: Aspiration performance and the search for underwriting syndicate partners. *Administrative Science Quarterly* 50: 536–575.

Baumol, William (2004) *Education for innovation: Entrepreneurial breakthroughs vs. corporate incremental improvements*. NBER, technical report.

Bavelas, Alex (1950) Communication patterns in task-oriented groups. *Journal of the Acoustic Society of America* 22: 725–730.

Bearman, Peter S., Moody, James, and Faris, Robert (2003) Networks and history. *Complexity* 8: 61–71.

Bearman, Peter S., Moody, James, and Stovel, Katherine (2004) Chains of affection: The structure of adolescent romantic and sexual networks. *American Journal of Sociology* 110(1): 44–91.

Bebchuk, Lucian A. and Fried, Jesse M. (2006) Pay without performance. *Academy of Management Perspectives* 20: 5–24.

Bendix, Reinhard (1956) *Work and authority in industry: Ideologies of management in the course of industrialization*. New York, Harper and Row.

Bernard, H. Russell *et al.* (1984) The problem of informant accuracy: The validity of retrospective data. *Annual Review of Anthropology* 13: 495–517.

Bernard, H. Russel, Killworth, Peter D., and Sailer, Lee (1982) Informant accuracy in social network data: An experimental attempt to predict actual communication from recall data. *Social Science Research* 11: 30–66.

Bernhard, Helen, Fischbacher, Urs, and Fehr, Ernst (2006) Parochial altruism in humans. *Nature* 442: 912–915.

Beuving, Joost. (2006) Cotonou's Klondike: Nigerian second-hand car traders in Cotonou: A sociocultural analysis of economic decision-making. *African Affairs* 105: 353–373.

Bian, Yanjie (1997) Bringing strong ties back in: Indirect ties, network bridges, and job searches in China. *American Sociological Review* 62: 366–385.

Biggs, Michael (2005) Strikes as forest fires: Chicago and Paris in the late nineteenth century. *American Journal of Sociology* 110: 1684–1714.

Blau, Peter (1964) *Exchange and power in social life*. New York, Wiley.

Boccaletti, S. *et al.* (2006) Complex networks: structure and dynamics. *Physics Reports* 424: 175–308.

Boehm, Christopher (1993) Egalitarian behavior and reverse dominance hierarchy. *Current Anthropology* 34: 227–240.

Boissevain, Jeremy (1966) Patronage in Sicily. *Man* 1: 18–33.

Boissevain, Jeremy (1968) The place of non-groups in the social sciences. *Man* 3: 542–556.

Boissevain, Jeremy (1974) *Friends of friends*. Oxford, Blackwell.

Boissevain, Jeremy (1979) Network analysis: A reappraisal. *Current Anthropology* 20(2): 392–394.

Boissevain, Jeremy and Mitchell, J. Clyde (eds.) (1973) *Network analysis studies in human interaction*. The Hague, Mouton.

Bonacich, Phillip (1987) Power and centrality: A family of measures. *American Journal of Sociology* 92(5): 1170–1182.

Bonacich, Phillip (2007) Some unique properties of eigenvector centrality. *Social Networks* 29: 555–564.

Bonacich, Phillip and Lloyd, Paulette (2001) Eigenvector-like measures of centrality for asymmetric relations. *Social Networks* 23: 191–201.

Bonacich, Phillip and Lloyd, Paulette (2004) Calculating status with negative relations. *Social Networks* 26: 331–338.

Boon, Jean Pierre and Tsallis, Constantino (2005) Special issue overview, Non-extensive statistical mechanics: new trends, new perspectives. *Europhysics News* November–December: 185–186.

Borgatti, Stephen P., Carley, Kathleen M., and Krackhardt, David (2006) On the robustness of centrality measures under conditions of imperfect data. *Social Networks* 28: 124–136.

Borgatti, Stephen P. and Cross, Rob (2003) A relational view of information seeking and learning in social networks. *Management Science* 49: 432–445.

Borgatti, Stephen P. and Everett, Martin G. (1992) Notions of position in social network analysis. *Sociological Methodology* 22: 1–35.

Bott, Elizabeth (1955) Urban families: conjugal roles and social networks. *Human Relations* 8: 345–383.

Bourdieu, Pierre (1980) Le capital social: notes provisoires. *Actes de la Recherche en Sciences Sociales* 31: 2–3.

Bourdieu, Pierre and Wacquant, Loïc J.D. (1992) *An invitation to reflexive sociology*. Chicago, University of Chicago Press.

Bowles, Samuel and Gintis, Herbert (2002) *Homo reciprocans*. Nature 415: 125–128.

Boyd, Robert and Lorberbaum, Jeffrey P. (1987) No pure strategy is stable in the repeated prisoners' dilemma game. *Nature* 327: 58–59.

Boyd, Robert and Richerson, Peter J. (1985) *Culture and the evolutionary process*. Chicago, University of Chicago Press.

Brañas-Garza, Pablo, Cobo-Reyes, Ramón, and Jimenez, Natalia (2006) *An experimental device to elicit social networks*. Alicante, technical report.

Brass, Daniel J. (1984) Being in the right place. *Administrative Science Quarterly* 29: 518–539.

Braun, Tibor (2004) Frigyes Karinthy. *Science* 304: 1745.

Braverman, Harry (1974) *Labor and monopoly capital*. New York, Monthly Review Press.

Breiger, Ronald L. (1974) The duality of persons and groups. *Social Forces* 53(2): 181–190.

Brewer, D.D. (2000) Forgetting in the recall-based elicitation of personal and social networks. *Social Networks* 22: 29–43.

Brin, Sergey and Page, Lawrence (1998) The anatomy of a large-scale hypertextual Web search engine, http://infolab.stanford.edu/~backrub/google.html

Brockmann, D., Hufnagel, L., and Geisel, T. (2006) The scaling laws of human travel. *Nature* 439: 462–465.

Broder, A., *et al.* (2000) Graph structures in the Web. *Computer Networks* 33: 309–320.

Brosnan, Sarah F. and de Waal, Frans B.M. (2002) A proximate perspective on reciprocal altruism. *Human Nature* 13: 129–152.

Burns, Tom and Stalker, G.M. (1961) *The management of innovation*. Oxford, Oxford University Press.

Burt, Ron. S. (1992) *Structural holes*. Cambridge, MA, Harvard University Press.

Burt, Ron. S. (1998) The gender of social capital. *Rationality and Society* 10: 5–46.

Burt, Ron. S. (2001) Bandwidth and echo: Trust, information, and gossip in social networks, in Casella, Alessandra and Rauch, James E. (eds.) *Networks and markets*. New York, Russell Sage Foundation.

155

Burt, Ron. S. (2002) Bridge decay. *Social Networks* 24: 333–63.

Burt, Ron. S. (2004) Structural holes and good ideas. *American Journal of Sociology* 110: 349–399.

Burt, Ron. S. (2007) Secondhand brokerage. *Academy of Management Journal* 50: 119–148.

Burt, Ron S. and Knez, Marc (1995) Kinds of third-party effects on trust. *Rationality and Society* 7: 255–292.

Buskens, Vincent and Raub, Werner (2008) Rational choice research on social dilemmas, in Wittek, R., Snijders, T.A.B., and Nee, V. (eds.) *Handbook of rational choice social research*. New York, Russell Sage, forthcoming.

Buskens, Vincent and Yamaguchi, Kazuo (1999) A new model of information diffusion in heterogeneous social networks. *Sociological Methodology* 29: 281–325.

Camerer, Colin F. and Fehr, Ernst (2006) When does "economic man" dominate social behavior? *Science* 311: 47–52.

Campbell, Donald T. (1960) Blind variation and selective retention in creative thought as in other knowledge processes. *Psychological Review* 67: 380–400.

Campbell, Donald T. (1976) On the conflicts between biological and social evolution and between psychology and moral tradition. *Zygon* 11: 167–192.

Carley, Kathleen M. (1994) Extracting culture through textual analysis. *Poetics* 22: 291–312.

Carley, Kathleen M. and Krackhardt, David (1996) Cognitive inconsistencies and non-symmetric friendships. *Social Networks* 18: 1–29.

Carnabuci, Gianluca (2005) *A theory of knowledge growth: Network analysis of US patents, 1975–1999*. Amsterdam, unpublished PhD thesis.

Carnabuci, Gianluca and Bruggeman, Jeroen (2007a) Explaining knowledge growth: Knowledge specialization and knowledge brokerage. Draft paper.

Carnabuci, Gianluca and Bruggeman, Jeroen (2007b) Why do technology domains grow at different rates? The competitive network of knowledge domains. Draft paper.

Carrington, P.J., Scott, J., and Wasserman, S. (eds.) (2005) *Models and methods in social network analysis*. Cambridge, Cambridge University Press.

Carroll, G.R. (1985) Concentration and specialization: Dynamics of niche width in populations of organizations. *American Journal of Sociology* 90: 1262–1283.

Cartwright, Dorwin and Harary, Frank (1956) Structural balance: a generalization of Heider's theory. *Psychological Review* 63: 277–293.

Casciaro, T. and Piskorski, M.J. (2005) Power imbalance, mutual dependence, and constraint absorption. *Administrative Science Quarterly* 50: 167–199.

Cavalli-Sforza, L.L. and Feldman, M.W. (1981) *Cultural transmission and evolution*. Princeton, NJ, Princeton University Press.

Cavalli-Sforza, L.L., Menozzi, P., and Piazza, A. (1993) Demic expansions and human evolution. *Science* 259: 639–646.

Cavalli-Sforza *et al.* (1982) Theory and observation in cultural transmission. *Science* 218: 19–27.

Chandler, Alfred D. (1992) Organizational capabilities and the economic history of the industrial enterprise. *Journal of Economic Perspectives* 6: 79–100.

Chase, Ivan D. (1980) Social process and hierarchy formation in small groups. *American Sociological Review* 45: 905–924.

Chase, Ivan D. (1982) Behavioral sequences during dominance hierarchy formation in chickens. *Science* 216: 439–440.

Clauset, Aaron, Shalizi, Cosma Rohilla, and Newman, Mark E.J. (2007) Power-law distributions in empirical data, http://arxiv.org/abs/0706.1062v1

Clauset, Aaron, Young, Maxwell, and Gleditsch, Kristian Skrede (2007) On the frequency of severe terrorist events. *Journal of Conflict Resolution* 51: 58–87.

Clutton-Brock, Tim (2002) Breeding together: Kin selection and mutualism in cooperative vertebrates. *Science* 296: 69–72.

Cohen, Jonathan D. and Aston-Jones, Gary (2005) Decision amid uncertainty. *Nature* 436: 471–472.

Cohen, Michael D. and Bacdayan, Paul (1994) Organizational routines are stored as procedural memory: Evidence from a laboratory study. *Organization Science* 5: 554–568.

Cohen, Wesley M. and Levinthal, Daniel (1990) Absorptive capacity: A new perspective on learning and innovation. *Administrative Science Quarterly* 35: 128–152.

Coleman, James S. (1974) *Power and the structure of society.* New York, W.W. Norton.

Coleman, James S. (1988) Social capital in the creation of human capital. *American Journal of Sociology* 94: S95–S120.

Collins, J.J. and Chow, C.C. (1998) It's a small world. *Nature* 393: 409–410.

Collins, Randall (2000) The sociology of philosophies: A précis. *Philosophy of the Social Sciences* 30: 157–201.

Collins, Randall (2004) *Interaction ritual chains.* Princeton, NJ, Princeton University Press.

Conlisk, John (1996) Why bounded rationality? *Journal of Economic Literature* 34: 669–700.

Constant, E.W. (1980) *The origins of the turbojet revolution.* Baltimore, Johns Hopkins University Press.

Conyon, Martin and Muldoon, Mark. (2006) The small world of corporate boards. *Journal of Business Finance and Accounting* 33: 1321–1343.

Cook, Karen S. and Emerson, Richard M. (1978) Power, equity and commitment in exchange networks. *American Sociological Review* 43: 721–739.

Cook, Karen S. *et al.* (1983) The distribution of power in exchange networks: Theory and experimental results. *American Journal of Sociology* 89: 275–305.

Coser, Lewis (1971, 2nd ed.) *Masters of sociological thought.* New York, Harcourt Brace Jovanovich.

Couzin, Iain (2007) Collective minds. *Nature* 445: 715.

Couzin, Iain *et al.* (2005) Effective leadership and decision making in animal groups on the move. *Nature* 433: 513–516.

Cox, T.F. and Cox, M.A.A. (2001, 2nd ed.) *Multidimensional scaling*. London, Chapman and Hall.

Cross, Bob and Parker, Andrew (2004) *The hidden powers of social networks*. Boston, Harvard Business School Publishing.

Cross, Bob, Baker, Wayne, and Parker, Andrew (2003) What creates energy in organizations? *MIT Sloan Management Review* 44: 51–56.

Cross, Bob *et al.* (2001). Knowing what we know: Supporting knowledge creation and sharing social networks. *Organizational Dynamics* 30: 100–120.

Crozier, Michel (1963) *Le phénomène bureaucratique*. Paris, Seuil.

Csikszentmihalyi, Mihalyi (1990) *Flow, the psychology of optimal experience*. New York, Harper Collins

Cyert, Richard M. and March, James G. (1963, 2nd ed. 1992) *A behavioral theory of the firm*. Oxford, Blackwell.

Damasio, Antonio (2005) Brain trust. *Nature* 435: 571–572.

Darwin, Charles (1874) *The descent of man and selection in relation to sex*. New York, American Home Library.

David, Paul A. (1985) Clio and the economics of QWERTY. *American Economic Review* 75: 332–337.

Davis, James A. (1963) Structural balance, mechanical solidarity, and interpersonal relations. *American Journal of Sociology* 68: 444–462.

Davis, James A. (1967) Clustering and structural balance in graphs. *Human Relations* 20: 181–187.

Davis, Gerald and Greve, Henrich (1997) Corporate elite networks and governance changes in the 1980's. *American Journal of Sociology* 103: 1–37.

Davis, Gerald and Marquis, Christopher (2005) Prospects for organization theory in the early twenty-first century: Institutional fields and mechanisms. *Organization Science* 16: 332–343.

Davis, Gerald, Yoo, Mina, and Baker, Wayne (2003) The small world of the American corporate elite, 1982–2001. *Strategic Organization* 1: 301–326.

Davis, James A. (1979) The Davis/Holland/Leinhardt studies: An overview, in Abelson, R.P. *et al.* (eds.) *Theories of cognitive consistency*. Chicago, Rand McNally.

Daw, Nathaniel D. *et al.* (2006) Cortical substrates for exploratory decisions in humans. *Nature* 441: 876–879.

de Nooy, Wouter, Mrvar, Andrej, and Batagelj, Vladimir. (2005) *Exploratory social network analysis with Pajek*. Cambridge: Cambridge University Press.

De Sola Pool, Ithiel and Kochen, Manfred (1978) Contacts and influence. *Social Networks* 1: 5–51.

De Solla Price, D.J. (1965) Network of scientific papers. *Science* 149: 510–515.

de Swaan, Abram (1988) *In care of the state*. New York, Oxford University Press.

de Swaan, Abram (1995) Hogere weetnietkunde. *NRC Handelsblad*, August 12.

de Swaan, Abram (2001) *Human societies: An introduction*. Bristol, Policy Press.

de Swaan, Abram (2007) *Bakens in niemandsland*. Amsterdam, Bert Bakker.

Della Porta, Donatella and Diani, Mario (2006, 2nd ed.) *Social movements, an introduction*. Oxford, Blackwell.

Devereux, George (1967) *From anxiety to method in the behavioral sciences*. The Hague, Mouton.

Devlin, Keith. (2003, 3rd ed.) *Sets, functions, and logic*. London, Chapman and Hall.

de Waal, Frans B.M. (2000) Primates: A natural heritage of conflict resolution. *Science* 289: 586–590.

de Waal, Frans B.M. (2003) Silent invasion: Imanishi's primatology and cultural bias in science. *Animal Cognition* 6: 293–299.

de Waal, Frans B.M. (2005) How animals do business. *Scientific American* 292–4: 72–79.

Diamond, Jared (1997) *Guns, germs, and steel: The fates of human societies*. New York and London, W.W. Norton.

Diamond, Jared (2001) Unwritten knowledge. *Nature* 410: 521–522.

Diamond, Jared (2002) Evolution, consequences and future of plant and animal domestication. *Nature* 418: 700–707.

Diamond, Jared and Bellwood, Peter (2003) Farmers and their languages: The first expansions. *Science* 300: 597–603.

Dijksterhuis, Ap *et al.* (2006) On making the right choice: The deliberation-without-attention effect. *Science* 311: 1005–1007.

DiMaggio, Paul J. and Powell, Walter W. (1983) The iron cage revisited. *American Sociological Review* 48: 147–160.

Dodds, Peter Sheridan, Muhamad, Roby, and Watts, Duncan (2003) An experimental study of search in global social networks. *Science* 301: 827–829.

Dodds, Peter Sheridan, Watts, Duncan, and Sabel, Charles F. (2003) Information exchange and the robustness of organizational networks. *Proceedings of the National Academy of Sciences* 100: 12516–12521.

Doreian, Patrick (1989) Models of network effects on social actors, in Freeman, L.C., White, D.R., and Romney, K. (eds.) *Research methods in social analysis*. Fairfax, VA, George Mason University Press.

Doreian, Patrick *et al.* (1996) A brief history of balance through time. *Journal of Mathematical Sociology* 21: 113–131.

Dorogovtsev, S.N. and Mendes, J.F.F. (2002) Evolution of networks. *Advances in Physics* 51: 1079–1187.

Dow, Marcom M. *et al.* (1984) Galton's problem as network autocorrelation. *American Ethnologist* 11: 754–770.

D'Souza, Raissa *et al.* (2007) Emergence of tempered preferential attachment from optimization. *Proceedings of the National Academy of Sciences* 104: 6112–6117.

Dunbar, R.I.M. and Schultz, Suzanne (2007) Evolution of the social brain. *Science* 317: 1344–1347.

159

Durkheim, Emile (1893) *De la division du travail social*. Paris, Presses Universitaires de France.

Durkheim, Emile (1895) *Les Règles de la méthode sociologique*. Paris, Presses Universitaires de France.

Durkheim, Emile (1912) *Les Formes élémentaires de la vie religieuse*. Paris, Presses Universitaires de France.

Durlauf, Steven N. (2005) Complexity and empirical economics. *Economic Journal* 115: F225–F243.

Ehrlich, Paul R. and Levin, Simon A. (2005) The evolution of norms. *PloS Biology* 3: e194.

Elias, Norbert (1939) *Über den Prozess der Zivilisation*. Basel, Haus zum Falken.

Elias, Norbert (1970) *Was ist Soziologie?* Munich, Juventa Verlag.

Elias, Norbert and Scotson, John L. (1965) *The established and the outsiders*. London, Frank Cass.

Emirbayer, Mustafa (1997) Manifesto for a relational sociology. *American Journal of Sociology* 103: 281–317.

Entwisle, Barbara *et al.* (2007) Networks and contexts. *American Journal of Sociology* 112: 1495–1533.

Erickson, Bonnie H. (1996) Culture, class, and connections. *American Journal of Sociology* 102: 217–251.

Eshel, Ilan and Cavalli-Sforza, L.L. (1982) Assortment of encounters and evolution of cooperativeness. *Proceedings of the National Academy of Sciences* 79: 1331–1335.

Estrada, Ernesto (2007) Topological structural classes of complex networks. *Physical Review E* 75: 016103.

Estrada, Ernesto and Rodríguez-Velázquez, Juan A. (2005) Subgraph centrality in complex networks. *Physical Review E* 71: 056103.

Ethiraj, Sendil K. and Levinthal, Daniel (2004) Modularity and innovation in complex systems. *Management Science* 50: 159–173.

Farquharson, Robin (1969) *Theory of voting*. Oxford, Blackwell.

Fayol, Henri (1916, trans. 1949) *General and industrial management*. London, Pitman.

Fehr, Ernst (2002) The economics of impatience. *Nature* 415: 269–272.

Fehr, Ernst and Fischbacher, Urs (2003) The nature of human altruism. *Nature* 425: 785–791.

Fehr, Ernst and Fischbacher, Urs (2004) Social norms and human cooperation. *Trends in Cognitive Sciences* 8(4): 185–190.

Fehr, Ernst and Gächter, Simon (2002) Altruistic punishment in humans. *Nature* 415: 137–140.

Feld, Scott L. (1981) The focused organization of social ties. *American Journal of Sociology* 86: 1015–1035.

Feld, Scott L. (1991) Why your friends have more friends than you do. *American Journal of Sociology* 96: 1464–1477.

Fischer, Claude S. (1982) *To dwell among friends*. Chicago, Chicago University Press.

Fisher, Roger, Ury, William, and Patton, Bruce (1981) *Getting to yes*. Boston, Houghton Mifflin.

Flache, A. and Macy, M.W. (1996) The weakness of strong ties: Collective action failure in highly cohesive groups. *Journal of Mathematical Sociology* 21: 3–28.

Flack, J.C. *et al.* (2006) Policing stabilizes construction of social niches in primates. *Nature* 439: 426–429.

Flack, J.C., de Waal, F.B.M., and Krakauer, D.C. (2005) Social structure, robustness, and policing cost in a cognitively sophisticated species. *American Naturalist* 165: E126–E139.

Flament, Claude (1963) *Applications of graph theory to group structure*. Prentice-Hall, London.

Fleming, Lee (2001) Recombinant uncertainty in technological search. *Management Science* 47: 117–132.

Fliessbach, K. *et al.* (2007) Social comparison affects reward-related brain activity in the human ventral stratum. *Science* 318: 1305–1308.

Foa, Uriel G. (1971) Interpersonal and economic resources. *Science* 171: 345–351.

Form, William (1987) On the degradation of skills. *Annual Review of Sociology* 13: 29–47.

Forsé, Michel and Chauvel, L. (1995) L'évolution de l'homogamie en France. *Revue Française de Sociologie* 36: 123–142.

Freeman, Linton C. (1977) A set of centrality measures based on betweenness. *Sociometry* 40(1): 35–41.

Freeman, Linton C. (1979) Centrality in social networks: Conceptual clarification. *Social Networks* 1: 215–239.

Freeman, Linton C. (1992) Filling in the blanks: a theory of cognitive categories and the structure of social affiliation. *Social Psychology Quarterly* 55: 118–127.

Freeman, Linton C. (2004) *The development of social network analysis*. Vancouver, Booksurge.

Freeman, Linton C., Romney, A. Kimball, and Freeman, Sue C. (1987) Cognitive structure and informant accuracy. *American Anthropologist* 89: 310–325.

Friedkin, Noah E. (1983) Horizons of observability and limits of informal control in organizations. *Social Forces* 62: 54–77.

Friedkin, Noah E. (1991) Theoretical foundations for centrality measures. *American Journal of Sociology* 96: 1478–1504.

Friedkin, Noah E. (1993) Structural bases of interpersonal influence in groups. *American Sociological Review* 58: 861–872.

Friedkin, Noah E. (1999) Choice shift and group polarization. *American Sociological Review* 64: 856–875.

Friedkin, Noah E. and Johnsen, Eugene C. (1997) Social positions in influence networks. *Social Networks* 19: 209–222.

Friedkin, Noah E. and Johnsen, Eugene C. (2003) Attitude change, affect control, and expectation states in network formation of influence networks. *Advances in Group Processes* 20: 1–29.

Gama Oliveira, João and Barabási, Albert-László (2005) Darwin and Einstein correspondence patterns. *Nature* 437: 1251.

Gama Oliveira, João and Barabási, Albert-László (2006) Reply to Kentsis. *Nature* 441: E5–6.

Gardner, D.G. (1990) Task complexity effects on non-task-related movements. *Organizational Behavior and Human Decision Processes* 45: 209–231.

Gardner, Martin (1982, 2nd ed.) *Logic machines and diagrams*. Brighton, Harvester Press.

Geertz, Clifford (1973) *The interpretation of cultures*. New York, Basic books.

Geertz, Clifford (1978) The bazaar economy: Information and search in peasant marketing. *American Economic Review* 68: 28–32.

Gelissen, J. (2000) Popular support for institutionalised solidarity: A comparison between European welfare states. *International Journal of Social Welfare* 9: 285–300.

Gelman, Andrew (2006) *Methodology as ideology: Mathematical modeling of trench warfare*. New York, technical report.

Gerlach, Michael L. (1992) The Japanese corporate network. *Administrative Science Quarterly* 37: 105–139.

Gersick, Connie J. and Hackman, J. Richard (1990) Habitual routines in task-performing groups. *Organizational Behavior and Human Decision Processes* 47: 65–97.

Gigerenzer, G. and Goldstein, D.G. (1996) Reasoning the fast and frugal way: Models of bounded rationality. *Psychological Review* 103: 650–669.

Gilbert, Daniel T. and Wilson, Timothy D. (2007) Prospection: Experiencing the future. *Science* 317: 1351–1354.

Gintis, Herbert (2007) A framework for the unification of the behavioral sciences. *Behavioral and Brain Sciences* 30: 1–61.

Girard, René (1961) *Mensonge romantique et vérité romanesque*. Paris, Grasset.

Glimcher, Paul W., Kable, Joseph and Louie, Kenway (2007). Neuroeconomic studies of impulsivity: Now or just as soon as possible? *American Economic Review* 97: 142–147.

Glimcher, Paul W. and Rustichini, Aldo (2004) Neuroeconomics: The consilience of brain and decision. *Science* 306: 447–452.

Gluckman, Max (1963) Gossip and scandal. *Current Anthropology* 4: 307–316.

Gobet, Fernand *et al.* (2001) Chunking mechanisms in human learning. *Trends in Cognitive Sciences* 5: 236–243.

Goffman, Erving (1959) *The presentation of self in everyday life*. New York, Doubleday.

Goffman, Erving (1963) *Behavior in public places*. New York, Free Press.

Goldenfeld, Nigel and Kadanoff, Leo P. (1999) Simple lessons from complexity. *Science* 284: 87–89.

Goodman, Nelson (1961) The test of simplicity. *Science* 128: 1064–1069.

Gordon, Deborah M. (2007) Control without hierarchy. *Nature* 446: 143.

Gould, Roger V. (1991) Multiple networks and mobilization in the Paris commune, 1871. *American Sociological Review* 56: 716–729.

Gould, Roger V. (1993) Collective action and network structure. *American Sociological Review* 58: 182–196.

Gould, Roger V. (1999) Collective violence and group solidarity: Evidence from a feuding society. *American Sociological Review* 64: 356–380.

Gould, Roger V. (2002) The origins of status hierarchies. *American Journal of Sociology* 107: 1143–1178.

Goyal, Sanjeev (2007) *Connections: An introduction to the economics of networks*. Princeton, NJ, Princeton University Press.

Grabowski, A. and Kosiński, R.A. (2006) Evolution of a social network: The role of cultural diversity. *Physical Review E* 73: 016135.

Granovetter, Mark (1973) The strength of weak ties. *American Journal of Sociology* 78–6: 1360–1380.

Granovetter, Mark (1983) The strength of weak ties: A network theory revisited. *Sociological Theory* 1: 201–233.

Granovetter, Mark (1985) Economic action and social structure: The problem of embeddedness. *American Journal of Sociology* 91: 481–510.

Granovetter, Mark (1995, 2nd ed.) *Getting a job: A study of contacts and careers*. Chicago, University of Chicago Press.

Granovetter, Mark (2003) Ignorance, knowledge and outcomes in a small world. *Science* 301: 773–774.

Granovetter, Mark (2005a) The impact of social structure on economic outcomes. *Journal of Economic Perspectives* 19–1: 33–50.

Granovetter, Mark (2005b) Business groups and social organization, in Smelser, N.J. and Swedberg, R. (eds.) *The handbook of economic sociology*. Princeton, NJ, Princeton University Press.

Greif, Avner (1994) Cultural beliefs and the organization of society: A historical and theoretical reflection on collectivist and individualist societies. *Journal of Political Economy* 102: 912–950.

Greve, Henrich R. (2003) *Organizational learning from performance feedback*. Cambridge, Cambridge University Press.

Guimerà, Roger *et al.* (2003) Self-similar community structure in a network of human interactions. *Physical Review E* 68: 065103.

Guimerà, Roger *et al.* (2005) Team assembly mechanisms determine collaboration network structure and team performance. *Science* 308: 697–702.

Guimond, Serge, Begin, Guy, and Palmer, Douglas L. (1989) Education and causal attributions: The development of "person-blame" and "system-blame" ideology. *Social Psychology Quarterly* 52: 126–140.

Gulati, Ranjay and Gargiulo, Martin (1999) Where do interorganizational networks come from? *American Journal of Sociology* 104: 1439–1493.

Gürerk, Ő., Irlenbusch, B., and Rockenbach, B. (2006) The competitive advantage of sanctioning institutions. *Science* 312: 108–111.

Haidt, Jonathan (2007) The new synthesis in moral psychology. *Science* 316: 998–1002.

Hamilton, Gary G. and Biggart, Nicole Woolsey (1988) Market, culture and authority: A comparative analysis of management and organization in the Far East. *American Journal of Sociology* 94: S52–S94.

Hamilton, W.D. (1964) The genetical evolution of social behavior. *Journal of Theoretical Biology* 7: 1–16.

Hammersley, M. and Atkinson, P. (1995, 2nd ed.) *Ethnography: Principles in practice.* London, Routledge.

Handcock, Mark *et al.* (2003) statnet: An R package for the statistical modeling of social networks, www.csde.washington.edu/statnet

Handel, Michael J. (ed.) (2003) *The sociology of organizations.* Thousand Oaks, CA, Sage.

Hannan, Michael T. (2005) Ecologies of organizations: Diversity and identity. *Journal of Economic Perspectives* 19: 51–70.

Hannan, Michael T. and Freeman, John (1984) Structural inertia and organizational change. *American Sociological Review* 49: 149–164.

Hansen, M.T. (1999) The search-transfer problem: The role of weak ties in sharing knowledge across organization subunits. *Administrative Science Quarterly* 44: 82–111.

Harary, Frank (1969) *Graph theory.* Reading, MA, Perseus.

Hardin, Garrett (1968) The tragedy of the commons. *Science* 162: 1243–1248.

Hargadon, Andrew B. (2002) Brokering knowledge: Linking learning and innovation. *Research in Organizational Behavior* 24: 41–85.

Hartwell, Leland H. *et al.* (1999) From molecular to modular cell biology. *Nature* 402: c47–c52.

Hauser, Marc D., Chomsky, Noam, and Fitch, W. Tecumseh (2002) The faculty of language: What is it, who has it, and how did it evolve? *Science* 298: 1569–1579.

Hayek, F.A. (1945) The use of knowledge in society. *American Economic Review* 35: 519–530.

Hedberg, Bo L.T., Nystrom, Paul C., and Starbuck, William H. (1976) Camping on seesaws. *Administrative Science Quarterly* 21: 41–65.

Hedström, Peter (1994) Contagious collectivities: on spatial diffusion of Swedish trade unions, 1890–1940. *American Journal of Sociology* 99: 1157–1179.

Hedström, Peter (2006) Experimental macro sociology. *Science* 311: 786–787.

Heemskerk, Eelke (2007) *Decline of the corporate community*. Amsterdam, Amsterdam University Press.

Heider, Fritz (1946) Attitudes and cognitive organization. *Journal of Psychology* 21: 107–112.

Helbing, Dirk, Farkas, Illés, and Vicsek, Tamás (2000) Simulating dynamical features of escape panic. *Nature* 407: 487–490.

Henderson, Rebecca M. and Clark, Kim B. (1990) Architectural innovation: The reconfiguration of existing product technologies and failure of established firms. *Administrative Science Quarterly* 35: 9–30.

Henderson, Rebecca, Jaffe, Adam, and Trajtenberg, Manuel (2005) Patent citations and the geography of knowledge spillovers: A reassessment: Comment. *American Economic Review* 95, 461–464.

Henrich, Joseph (2003) Cultural group selection, coevolutionary processes and large-scale cooperation. *Journal of Economic Behavior and Organization* 53: 3–35.

Henrich, Joseph (2006) Cooperation, punishment, and the evolution of human institutions. *Science* 312: 60–61.

Henrich, Joseph *et al.* (2001) In search of homo economicus. *American Economic Review* 91: 73–78.

Henrich, Joseph *et al.* (2006) Costly punishment across human societies. *Science* 312: 1767–1770.

Henrich, Joseph and Gil-White, Francisco J. (2001) The evolution of prestige. *Evolution and Human Behavior* 22: 165–196.

Herrmann, Esther *et al.* (2007) Humans have evolved specialized skills of social cognition: The cultural intelligence hypothesis. *Science* 317: 1360–1366.

Herzberg, Frederick (1968) One more time: How do you motivate employees? *Harvard Business Review* January–February: 53–62.

Hess, Nicole H. and Hagen, Edward H. (2006) Psychological adaptations for assessing gossip veracity. *Human Nature* 17: 337–354.

Hidalgo, C.A. *et al.* (2007) The product space conditions the development of nations. *Science* 317: 482–487.

Hlebec, Valentina and Ferligoj, Anuška (2002) Reliability of network measurement instruments. *Field Methods* 14: 288–306.

Hofstede, Geert (1980) *Culture's consequences*. Beverly Hills, CA, Sage.

Hofstede, Geert (1994) Management scientists are human. *Management Science* 40: 4–13.

Hofstede, Geert *et al.* (1990) Measuring organizational cultures. *Administrative Science Quarterly* 35: 286–316.

Holme, Petter, Edling, Christofer R., and Liljeros, Fredrik (2004) Structure and time evolution of an internet dating community. *Social Networks* 26: 155–174.

Homans, George (1950) *The human group*. New York, Harcourt Brace.

165

Horowitz, D.L. (2001) *The deadly ethnic riot*. Berkeley, University of California Press.

Huber, George P. (1991) Organizational leaning: the contributing processes and the literatures. *Organization Science* 2: 88–115.

Huberman, Bernardo (2001) The dynamics of organizational learning. *Computational and Mathematical Organization Theory* 7: 145–153.

Huberman, Bernardo and Glance, Natalie (1993) Evolutionary games and computer simulations. *Proceedings of the National Academy of Sciences* 90: 7716–7718.

Huberman, Bernardo and Adamic, Lada (1999) The growth dynamics of the World Wide Web. *Nature* 401:131.

Huizinga, Johan (1938, transl. 1964) *Homo ludens*. Boston, Beacon.

Ingram, Paul and Roberts, Peter W. (2000) Friendships among competitors in the Sydney hotel industry. *American Journal of Sociology* 106: 387–423.

Ijiri, Y. and Simon, Herbert A. (1977) *Skew distributions and the sizes of business firms*. Amsterdam, North Holland.

Ioannides, Yannis M. and Datcher Loury, Linda (2004) Job information networks, neighborhood effects, and inequality. *Journal of Economic Literature* 42: 1056–1093.

Jaffe, Adam, Trajtenberg, Manuel, and Henderson, Rebecca (1993) Geographic localization of knowledge spillovers as evidenced by patent citations. *Quarterly Journal of Economics* 108: 577–598.

Janicik, Gregory A. and Larrick, Richard P. (2005) Social network schemas and the learning of incomplete networks. *Journal of Personality and Social Psychology* 88(2): 348–364.

Jensen, Keith, Call, Josep, and Tomasello, Michael (2007) Chimpanzees are rational maximizers in an ultimatum game. *Science* 318: 107–109.

Kadushin, Charles (1995) Friendship among the French financial elite. *American Sociological Review* 60: 202–221.

Kadushin, Charles (2004) Too much investment in social capital? *Social Networks* 26: 75–90.

Kadushin, Charles (2005) Review of Freeman (2004). *Journal of Social Structure*, www.cmu.edu/joss/

Kahneman, Daniel (2003) Maps of bounded rationality. *American Economic Review* 93: 1449–1475.

Kalish, Yuval and Robins, Garry (2006) Psychological predispositions and network structure. *Social Networks* 28: 56–84.

Katz, Leo (1953) A new status index derived from sociometric analysis. *Psychometrika* 18(1): 39–43.

Kearns, Michael, Suri, Siddharth, and Montfort, Nick (2006) An experimental study of the coloring problem on human subject networks. *Science* 313: 824–827.

Kentsis, Alex (2006) Mechanisms and models of human dynamics. *Nature* 441(7092): E5.

Kilduff, Martin and Krackhardt, David (1994) Bringing the individual back in. *Academy of Management Journal* 37: 87–108.

Kilduff, Martin and Tsai, Wenpin (2003) *Networks and organizations*. London, Sage.

Killworth, Peter D. and Bernard, H. Russel (1978) The reversal small-world experiment. *Social Networks* 1: 159–192.

Killworth, Peter D. *et al.* (2005) The accuracy of small world chains in social networks. *Social Networks* 28: 85–96.

Kilpatrick, S., Gelatt, C.D., and Vecci, M.P. (1983) Optimization by simulated annealing. *Science* 220: 671–680.

Kleinberg, Jon (2000) Navigation in a small world. *Nature* 406: 845.

Kleinberg, J. and Lawrence, S. (2001) The structure of the Web. *Science* 294: 1849–1850.

Knoch, Daria *et al.* (2006) Diminishing reciprocal fairness by disrupting the right prefrontal cortex. *Science* 314: 829–832.

Knoke, David (2001) *Changing organizations*. Boulder, CO, Westview Press.

Knutson, Brian (2004) Sweet revenge? *Science* 305: 1246–1247.

Kogovšek, Tina and Ferligoj, Anuška (2005) Effects on reliability and validity of egocentered network measurements. *Social Networks* 27: 205–229.

Kogut, Bruce and Walker, Gordon (2001) The small world of Germany and the durability of national networks. *American Sociological Review* 66: 317–335.

Kogut, Bruce and Zander, Udo (1992) Knowledge of the firm, combinative capabilities, and the replication of technology. *Organization Science* 3: 283–397.

Kosfeld, Michael (2003) *Network experiments*. Zurich, working paper, www.iew.uzh.ch/wp/iewwp152.pdf

Kosfeld, Michael *et al.* (2005) Oxytocin increases trust in humans. *Nature* 435: 673–676.

Kossinets, Gueorgi and Watts, Duncan (2006) An empirical analysis of an evolving social network. *Science* 311: 88–90.

Krackhardt, David (1987) Cognitive social structures. *Social Networks* 9: 109–134.

Krackhardt, David (1990) Assessing the political landscape: Structure, cognition, and power in organizations. *Administrative Science Quarterly* 35: 342–369.

Krackhardt, David and Hanson, Jeffrey R. (1993) Informal networks: The company behind the chart. *Harvard Business Review*, July–August, 104–111.

Krackhardt, David and Kilduff, Martin (2002) Structure, culture, and Simmelian ties in entrepreneurial firms. *Social Networks* 24: 279–290.

Krapivsky, P.L. and Redner, S. (2001) Organization of growing random networks. *Physical Review E* 63: 066123.

Kumbasar, Ece, Romney, A. Kimball, and Batchelder, William H. (1994) Systematic biases in social perception. *American Journal of Sociology* 100: 477–505.

Kunda, Gideon (1992) *Engineering culture: Control and commitment in a high-tech corporation*. Philadelphia, Temple University Press.

Labianca, Guiseppe and Brass, Daniel J. (2006) Exploring the social ledger: Negative relationships and negative asymmetry in social networks in organizations. *Academy of Management Review* 31: 596–614.

Labianca, Guiseppe, Brass, Daniel J., and Gray, Barbara (1998) Social networks and perceptions of intergroup conflict. *Academy of Management Journal* 41: 55–67.

Lakatos, Imre (1976) *Proofs and refutations*. Cambridge, Cambridge University Press.

Laumann, Edward O. (2006) A 45-year retrospective on doing networks. *Connections* 27(1): 65–90.

Laumann, Edward O. *et al.* (1989) Monitoring the AIDS epidemic in the United States: A network approach. *Science* 244: 1186–1189.

Laumann, Edward O., Marsden, Peter and Prensky, David (1983) The boundary specification problem, in Burt, R.S. and Minor, M.J. (eds.) *Applied network analysis: A methodological introduction*. London, Sage.

Lawler, Edward J. and Yoon, Jeongkoo (1996) Commitment in exchange relations: Test of a theory of relational cohesion. *American Sociological Review* 61: 89–108.

Lawrence, Paul R. and Lorsch, Jay W. (1967) *Organization and environment*. Boston, Harvard University Press.

Lee, Sang Hoon, Kim, Pan-Jun, and Jeong, Hawoong (2006) Statistical properties of sampled networks. *Physical Review E* 73: 016102.

Leenders, Roger Th.A.J. (2002) Modeling social influence through network autocorrelation. *Social Networks* 24: 21–47.

Lévi-Strauss, Claude (1949, trans. 1969) *The elementary structures of kinship*. Boston, Beacon.

Lewin, K. (1945) The research center for group dynamics at Massachusetts Institute of Technology. *Sociometry* 8: 126–135.

Liljeros, Fredrik *et al.* (2001) The web of human sexual contacts. *Nature* 411: 907–908.

Liljeros, Fredrik *et al.* (2003) Reply to Holland Jones and Handcock. *Nature* 423: 606.

Lin, Nan (2001) *Social capital*. Cambridge, Cambridge University Press.

Lipset, M., Trow, M.A., and Coleman, J.S. (1956) *Union democracy*. New York, Free Press.

Lorrain, Francois and White, Harrison (1971) Structural equivalence of individuals in social networks. *Journal of Mathematical Sociology* 1: 49–80.

Lotka, Alfred. J. (1926) The frequency distribution of scientific productivity. *Journal of the Washington Academy of Science* 16: 317–323.

Luhmann, Niklas (1964) *Funktionen und Folgen formaler Organisation*. Berlin, Duncker und Humblot.

Lusseau, David and Newman, Mark E.J. (2004) Identifying the role that animals play in their social networks. *Proceedings of the Royal Society B* 271: S477–S481.

McCarty, Christopher and Govindaramanujam, Sama (2005) A modified elicitation of personal networks using dynamic visualization. *Connections* 26: 61–69.

McCarty, Christopher, Killworth, Peter D., and Rennell, James (2007) Impact of methods for reducing respondent burden on personal network structural measures. *Social Networks* 29: 300–315.

McElreath, Richard and Boyd, Robert (2007) *Mathematical models of social evolution.* Chicago, Chicago University Press.

McGregor, Douglas (1960) *The human side of the enterprise.* New York, McGraw Hill.

McPherson, Miller, Smith-Lovin, Lynn, and Cook, James M. (2001) Birds of a feather: Homophily in social networks. *Annual Review of Sociology* 27: 425–444.

March, James G. (1991) Exploration and exploitation in organizational learning. *Organization Science* 2: 71–87.

March, James G. (2005) Parochialism in the evolution of a research community: The case of organization studies. *Management and Organization Review* 1: 5–22.

March, James G. and Simon, Herbert A. (1958, 2nd ed. 1993) *Organizations.* Oxford, Blackwell.

March, James G., Sproull, Lee S., and Tamuz, Michal (1991) Learning from samples of one or fewer. *Organization Science* 2: 1–13.

Marsden, Peter V. (1982) Brokerage behavior in restricted exchange networks, in Marsden, Peter V. and Lin, Nan (eds.) *Social structure and network analysis.* Beverly Hills. Sage.

Marsden, Peter. V. (2005) Recent developments in network measurement, in Carrington, P.J., Scott, J., and Wasserman, S. (eds.) *Models and methods in social network analysis.* Cambridge, Cambridge University Press.

Marsden, Peter V. and Campbell, Karen E. (1984) Measuring tie strength. *Social Forces* 63(2): 482–501.

Marsden, Peter. V. and Friedkin, Noah E. (1993) Network studies of social influence. *Sociological Methods and Research* 22: 127–151.

Marwell, Gerald, Oliver, Pamela E., and Prahl, Ralph (1988) Social networks and collective action: A theory of critical mass III. *American Journal of Sociology* 94: 502–534.

Massey, Douglas S. (2002) A brief history of human society. *American Sociological Review* 67: 1–29.

Mattick, John S. and Gagen, Michael J. (2005) Accelerating networks. *Science* 307: 856–858.

Mead, George Herbert (1934) *Mind, self, and society.* Chicago, University of Chicago Press.

Melis, Alicia P., Hare, Brian, and Tomasello, Michael (2006) Chimpanzees recruit the best collaborators. *Science* 311: 1297–1300.

Merton, Robert (1940) Bureaucratic structure and personality. *Social Forces* 18: 560–568.

169

Merton, Robert (1947) The machine, the worker, and the engineer. *Science* 105: 79–84.

Merton, Robert (1968a) The Matthew effect in science: The reward and communication systems of science are considered. *Science* 159:56–63.

Merton, Robert (1968b) *Social theory and social structure*. New York, Free Press.

Meyer, John W. and Rowan, Brian (1977) Institutionalized organizations: Formal structure as myth and ceremony. *American Journal of Sociology* 83: 340–363.

Michels, Robert (1915; 1962) *Political parties: A sociological study of the oligarchical tendencies of modern democracy*. New York, Free Press.

Milgram, Stanley (1967) The small world problem. *Psychology Today* 22: 61–67.

Milinski, Manfred and Rockenbach, Bettina (2007) Spying on others evolves. *Science* 317: 464–465.

Miller, Greg (2006) Signs of empathy seen in mice. *Science* 312: 1860–1861.

Milo, R. *et al.* (2002) Network motifs: Simple building blocks of complex networks. *Science* 298: 824–827.

Milo, Ron *et al.* (2004a) Superfamilies of evolved and designed networks. *Science* 303: 1538–1542.

Milo, Ron *et al.* (2004b) Response to comments. *Science* 305: 1107d.

Mische, Ann and White, Harrison (1998) Between conversation and situation: Public switching dynamics across network domains. *Social Research* 65: 695–724.

Mitchell, Clyde (ed.) (1969) *Social networks in urban situations*. Manchester, Manchester University Press.

Mitzenmacher, M. (2003) A brief history of generative models for power law and lognormal distributions. *Internet Mathematics* 1(2): 226–251.

Mizruchi, Mark S. and Stearns, Linda B. (2001) Getting deals done. *American Sociological Review* 66: 647–671.

Mohr, John W. (1996) Measuring meaning structures. *Annual Review of Sociology* 24: 345–370.

Mokken, Robert J. and Stokman, Frans N. (1978) Corporate–governmental networks in the Netherlands. *Social Networks* 1: 333–358.

Mokyr, Joel (2002) *The gifts of Athena: Historical origins of the knowledge economy*. Princeton, NJ, Princeton University Press.

Monge, P. and Contractor, N. (2003) *Theories of communication network*. New York, Oxford University Press.

Moody, James (2002) The importance of relationship timing for diffusion. *Social Forces* 81: 25–56.

Moody, James (2004) The structure of a social science collaboration network. *American Sociological Review* 69: 213–238.

Moody, James and White, Douglas R. (2003) Structural cohesion and embeddedness. *American Sociological Review* 69: 103–127.

Moore, Michael (1979) Structural balance and international relations. *European Journal of Social Psychology* 9: 323–326.

Moreno, Jacob Levi (1934) *Who shall survive? Foundations of sociometry, group psycho-therapy, and sociodrama*. Washington, DC, Nervous and Mental Disease Publishing Co.

Mutz, Diana C. (2002) Cross-cutting social networks. *American Political Science Review* 96(1): 111–126.

Nee, Sean (2005) The great chain of being. *Nature* 435: 429.

Nelson, R.R. and Winter, S.G. (1982) *An evolutionary theory of economic change*. Cambridge, MA, Harvard University Press.

Nelson, R.R. and Winter, S.G. (2002) Evolutionary theorizing in economics. *Journal of Economic Perspectives* 16(2): 23–46.

Newman, Mark E.J. (2001) The structure of scientific collaboration networks. *Proceedings of the National Academy of Sciences* 98(2): 404–409.

Newman, Mark. E.J. (2003) The structure and function of complex networks. *SIAM Review* 45: 167–256.

Newman, Mark E.J. (2004) Analysis of weighted networks. *Physical Review E* 70: 056131.

Newman, Mark E.J. (2005) Power laws, Pareto distributions and Zipf's law. *Contemporary Physics* 46: 323–351

Newman, Mark E.J. (2006a) Modularity and community structure in networks. *Proceedings of the National Academy of Sciences* 103: 8577–8582.

Newman, Mark E.J. (2006b) Finding community structure in networks using the eigenvectors of matrices, *Physical Review E* 74: 036104.

Newman, Mark E.J. and Girvan, Michelle (2004) Finding and evaluating community structure in networks. *Physical Review E* 69: 026113.

Newman, Mark E.J. and Park, Juyong (2003) Why social networks are different from other types of networks. *Physical Review E* 68: 036122.

Newman, Mark E.J., Watts, Duncan, and Strogatz, Steven (2002) Random graph models of social networks. *Proceedings of the National Academy of Sciences* 99: 2566–2572.

Nohria, N. and Eccles, R.G. (1992) *Networks and organizations*. Boston, Harvard Business School Press.

North, Douglass C. (1990) *Institutions, institutional change and economic performance*. Cambridge, Cambridge University Press.

Nowak, Martin A. (2006) Five rules for the evolution of cooperation. *Science* 314: 1560–1563.

Nowak, Martin A. and Sigmund, Karl (1993) A strategy of win–stay, lose–shift that outperforms tit-for-tat in the prisoner's dilemma game. *Nature* 364: 56–58.

Nowak, Martin A. and Sigmund, Karl (2005) Evolution of indirect reciprocity. *Nature* 437: 1291–1298.

Oeser, O.A. and Harary, Frank (1964) A mathematical model for structural role theory, II. *Human Relations* 17: 3–17.

Öhman, Arne (2005) Conditioned fear of a face: A prelude to ethnic enmity? *Science* 309: 711–713.

Oliver, Pamela E. and Marwell, Gerald (2001) Whatever happened to critical mass theory? *Sociological Theory* 19: 292–311.

Olson, Mancur (1965) *The logic of collective action*. Cambridge, MA, Harvard University Press.

Olsson, A. *et al.* (2005) The role of social groups in the persistence of learned fear. *Science* 309: 785–787.

Oltvai, Zoltán and Barabási, Albert-László (2002) Life's complex pyramid. *Science* 298: 763–764.

Onnela, J.P. *et al.* (2007) Structure and tie strengths in mobile communication networks. *Proceedings of the National Academy of Science* 104: 7332–7336.

Padgett, J.F. and Ansell, C.K. (1993) Robust action and the rise of the Medici, 1400–1434. *American Journal of Sociology* 98: 1259–1319.

Palla, G., Barabási, A.-L., and Vicsek, T. (2007). Quantifying social group evolution. *Nature* 446: 664–667.

Palla, Gergely *et al.* (2005) Uncovering the overlapping community structure of complex networks in nature and society. *Nature* 435: 814–818.

Panchanathan, Karthik and Boyd, Robert (2004) Indirect reciprocity can stabilize cooperation without the second-order free rider problem. *Nature* 432: 499–502.

Pareto, V. (1966) *Sociological writings*. New York, Praeger.

Parkinson, C. Northcote (1957) *Parkinson's law*. Boston, MA, Houghton Mifflin.

Parsons, Talcott (1964) Evolutionary universals in society. *American Sociological Review* 29: 339–357.

Pastor-Satorras, Romualdo and Vespignani, Alessandro (2001) Epidemic spreading in scale-free networks. *Physical Review Letters* 86: 3200.

Peirce, Charles Sanders (1878) How to make our ideas clear. *Popular Science Monthly* 12: 286–302.

Pennisi, Elizabeth (2005) How did cooperative behaviour evolve? *Science* 309: 93.

Perrow, Charles (1984) *Normal accidents*. New York, Basic Books.

Perrow, Charles (1986, 3rd ed.) *Complex organizations*. New York, McGraw-Hill.

Perrow, Charles (1991) A society of organizations. *Theory and Society* 20: 725–762.

Perrow, Charles (2005) Organizational or executive failure? *Contemporary Sociology* 34(2): 99–107.

Pfeffer, Jeffrey (1997) *New directions for organization theory*. New York, Oxford University Press.

Pfeffer, Jeffrey (2007) Human resources from an organizational behavior perspective. *Journal of Economic Perspectives* 21: 115–134.

Pfeffer, Jeffrey and Salancik, Gerald R. (1978) *The external control of organizations*. New York, Harper and Row.

Podolny, Joel M. (1993) A status-based model of market competition. *American Journal of Sociology* 98–4: 829–872.

Podolny, Joel M. (1994) Market uncertainty and the social character of economic exchange. *Administrative Science Quarterly* 39: 458–483.

Podolny, Joel M. (2001) Networks as the pipes and prisms of the market. *American Journal of Sociology* 107: 33–60.

Podolny, Joel M. and Baron, James N. (1997) Resources and relationships: Social networks and mobility in the workplace. *American Sociological Review* 62: 673–693.

Podolny, Joel M. and Page, Karen L. (1998) Network forms of organization. *Annual Review of Sociology* 24: 57–76.

Podolny, Joel M. and Stuart, Toby E. (1995) A role-based ecology of technological change. *American Journal of Sociology* 100: 1224–1260.

Podolny, Joel M. and Stuart, Toby E. (1996) Networks, knowledge, and niches. *American Journal of Sociology* 102: 659–689.

Podolny, J.M., Stuart, T.E., and Hannan, M.T. (1996) Networks, knowledge, and niches: Competition in the worldwide semiconductor industry, 1984–1991. *American Journal of Sociology* 102: 659–689.

Poincaré, Henri (1902) *La science et l'hypothèse*. Paris, Flammarion.

Portes, Alejandro (1998) Social capital: Its origins and applications in modern sociology. *Annual Review of Sociology* 24: 1–24.

Powell, W. (1990) Neither market nor hierarchy: Network forms of organization. *Research in Organizational Behavior* 12: 295–336.

Powell, W.W., Koput, K.W., and Smith-Doerr, Laurel (1996) Interorganizational collaboration and the locus of innovation: Networks of learning in biotechnology. *Administrative Science Quarterly* 41: 116–145.

Powell, W.W., White, D.R., Koput, K.W., and Owen-Smith, J. (2005) Network dynamics and field evolution: The growth of interorganizational collaboration in the life sciences. *American Journal of Sociology* 110: 1132–1205.

Quervain, Dominique *et al.* (2004) The neural basis of altruistic punishment. *Science* 305: 1254–1258.

Quine, Willard Van Orman (1990) *Pursuit of truth*. Cambridge, MA, Harvard University Press.

Quine, Willard Van Orman and Ullian, J.S. (1978, 2nd ed.) *The web of belief*. New York, Random House.

Radicchi, Filippo *et al.* (2007) Social balance as a satisfiability problem of computer science. *Physical Review E* 75: 026106.

Radner, Roy (1992) Hierarchy: The economics of managing. *Journal of Economic Literature* 30: 1382–1415.

Ramasco, J.J. and Morris, S.A. (2006) Social inertia in collaboration networks. *Physical Review E* 73: 016122.

173

Randall, Donna M. (1987) Commitment and the organization. *Academy of Management Review* 12: 460–471.

Rapoport, Anatol (1953) Spread of information through a population with socio-structural bias: Parts I and II. *Bulletin of Mathematical Biophysics* 15: 523–546.

Rapoport, Anatol (1957) Contribution to the theory of random and biased nets. *Bulletin of Mathematical Biophysics* 19: 257–277.

Raub, Werner and Buskens, Vincent (2006) Spieltheoretische Modellierungen und empirische Anwendungen in der Soziologie. *Kölner Zeitschrift für Soziologie und Sozialpsychologie* 44: 560–598.

Raub, Werner and Weesie, Jeroen (1990) Reputation and efficiency in social interactions: An example of network effects. *American Journal of Sociology* 96: 626–654.

Ravasz, E. *et al.* (2002) Hierarchical organization of modularity in metabolic networks. *Science* 297: 1551–1555.

Ravasz, Erzsébet and Barabási, Albert-László (2003) *Physical Review E* 67: 026112.

Reagans, Ray and McEvily, Bill (2003) Network structure and knowledge transfer. *Administrative Science Quarterly* 48: 240–267.

Reichardt, Jörg and Bornholdt, Stefan (2004) Detecting community structures in complex networks with a Potts model. *Physical Review Letters* 93: 218701.

Reichardt, Jörg and Bornholdt, Stefan (2006a) Statistical mechanics of community detection. *Physical Review E* 74: 016110.

Reichardt, Jörg and Bornholdt, Stefan (2006b) When are networks truly modular? *Physica D* 224: 20–26.

Reichardt, Jörg and Bornholdt, Stefan (2007) Clustering of sparse data via network communities. *Journal of Statistical Mechanics* 07: P06016.

Reichardt, Jörg and White, Douglas R. (2007) Role models for complex networks. *European Physical Journal B*, 60: 217–224, also at http://arxiv.org/PS_cache/arxiv/pdf/0708/0708.0958v1.pdf

Richardson, G.B. (1972) The organisation of industry. *Economic Journal* 82: 883–896.

Richardson, L.F. (1948) Variation of the frequency of fatal quarrels with magnitude. *American Statistical Association Journal* 43: 523–546.

Richerson, Peter J. and Boyd, Robert (2005) *Not by genes alone*. Chicago, Chicago University Press.

Richerson, Peter J., Collins, Dwight, and Genet, Russell M. (2006) Why managers need an evolutionary theory of organizations. *Strategic Organization* 4: 201–211.

Ridgeway, Cecilia and Diekema, David (1989) Dominance and collective hierarchy formation in male and female task groups. *American Sociological Review* 54: 79–93.

Robins, G. *et al.* (2007) An introduction to exponential random graph ($p*$) models for social networks. *Social Networks* 29: 192–215.

Robins, Garry, Pattison, Philippa, and Wollcock, Jodie (2005) Small and other worlds: Global network structures from local processes. *American Journal of Sociology* 110: 894–936.

Rockenbach, Bettina and Milinski, Manfred (2006) The efficient interaction of indirect reciprocity and costly punishment. *Nature* 444: 718–723.

Rogers, E. (2003, 5th ed.) *The diffusion of innovations*. New York, Free Press.

Rousseau, D.M. *et al.* (1998) Not so different after all: A cross-discipline view of trust. *Academy of Management Review* 23: 393–404.

Salgado, Sebastião (1993) *Workers: An archaeology of the industrial age*. New York, Aperture.

Salganik, Matthew J., Dodds, Peter Sheridan, and Watts, Duncan (2006) Experimental study of inequality and unpredictability in an artificial cultural market. *Science* 311: 854–856.

Salganik, Matthew J. and Heckathorn, Douglas D. (2004) Sampling and estimation in hidden polulations using respondent-driven sampling. *Sociological Methodology* 34: 193–239.

Sampson, Robert, J., Morenoff, Jeffrey D., and Earls, Felton (1999) Beyond social capital: Spatial dynamics of collective efficacy for children. *American Sociological Review* 64: 633–660.

Sampson, Robert, J., Raudenbush, Stephen W., and Earls, Felton (1997) Neighborhoods and violent crime: A multilevel study of collective efficacy. *Science* 277: 918–924.

Sanchez, Ron and Mahoney, Joseph T. (1996) Modularity, flexibility, and knowledge management in product and organization design. *Strategic Management Journal* 17: 63–76.

Sanfey, Alan G. (2007) Social decision-making: Insights from game theory and neuroscience. *Science* 318: 598–602.

Sanfey, Alan G. *et al.* (2003) The neural basis of economic decision-making in the ultimatum game. *Science* 300: 1755–1758.

Santos, F.C. and Pacheco, J.M. (2005) Scale-free networks provide a unifying framework for the emergence of cooperation. *Physical Review Letters* 95: 098104.

Sapolsky, Robert M. (2005) The influence of social hierarchy on primate health. *Science* 308: 648–652.

Schelling, Thomas (1978) *Micromotives and macrobehavior*. New York, W.W. Norton.

Schneeberger, Anne *et al.* (2004) Scale-free networks and sexually transmitted diseases. *Sexually Transmitted Diseases* 31: 380–387.

Schumpeter, Joseph A. (1942) *Capitalism, socialism, and democracy*. London, Routledge.

Schütz, Alfred (1932) *Der sinnhafte Aufbau der sozialen Welt*. Vienna, Springer.

Schweizer, Thomas (1997) Embeddedness of ethnographic cases. *Current Anthropology* 38: 739–759.

Scott, John (1991) Networks of corporate power. *Annual Review of Sociology* 17: 181–203.

Scott, W. Richard and Davis, Gerald F. (2007) *Organizations and organizing*. Upper Saddle River, NJ, Pearson.

Seibel, Wolfgang and Raab, Jörg (2003) Verfolgungsnetzwerke. *Kölner Zeitschrift für Soziologie und Sozialpsychologie* 55: 197–230.

Shi, Xiaolin, Adamic, Lada A., and Strauss, Martin J. (2007) Networks of strong ties. *Physica A* 378: 33–47.

Silk, Joan B. (2007) Social components of fitness in primate groups. *Science* 317: 1347–1351.

Silk, Joan B., Alberts, Susan C., and Altmann, Jeanne (2003) Social bonds of female baboons enhance infant survival. *Science* 302: 1231–1234.

Simmel, Georg (1890, 1908, trans. 1950) *The sociology of Georg Simmel*. New York, Free Press.

Simmel, Georg (1910) How is society possible? *American Journal of Sociology* 16: 372–391.

Simon, Herbert A. (1954) Some strategic considerations in the construction of social science models, in Lazersfeld, P.F (ed.) *Mathematical thinking in the social sciences*. Glencoe, IL, Free Press.

Simon, Herbert A. (1962) The architecture of complexity. *Proceedings of the American Philosophical Society* 106: 467–482.

Simon, Herbert A. (1990) A mechanism for social selection and successful altruism. *Science* 250: 1665–1668.

Simon, Herbert A. (1991) Bounded rationality and organizational learning. *Organization Science* 2: 125–134.

Simon, Herbert A. (1996, 3rd ed.) *The sciences of the artificial*. Cambridge, MIT Press.

Simon, Herbert A. (1945, 4th ed. 1997) *Administrative behavior*. New York, Free Press.

Simonton, D. K. (2000) Creativity: Cognitive, developmental, personal, and social aspects. *American Psychologist* 55: 151–158.

Singer, Tania and Fehr, Ernst (2005) The neuroeconomics of mind reading and empathy. *American Economic Review* 95: 340–345.

Singer, Tania *et al.* (2006) Empathic neural responses are modulated by the perceived fairness of others. *Nature* 439: 466–469.

Singh, Jasjit (2005) Collaborative networks as determinants of knowledge diffusion patterns. *Management Science* 51: 756–770.

Skvoretz, John, Fararo, Thomas J., and Agneessens, Filip (2004) Advances in biased net theory. *Social Networks* 26: 113–139.

Smelser, Neil, J. (1998) The rational and the ambivalent in the social sciences. *American Sociological Review* 63: 1–15.

Smethurst, D.P. and Williams, H.C. (2001) Power laws: Are hospital waiting lists self-regulating? *Nature* 410: 652–653.

Smith, Adam (1986) *The essential Adam Smith*, ed. R.L. Heilbroner. New York, Norton.

Smith, David A. and White, Douglas R. (1992) Structure and dynamics of the global economy. *Social Forces* 70: 857–893.

Snijders, Tom A.B., Pattison, Philippa E., Robins, Garry L., and Handcock, Mark S. (2006) New specifications for exponential random graph models. *Sociological Methodology* 36: 99–153.

Solomonoff, Ray and Rapoport, Anatol (1951) Connectivity of random nets. *Bulletin of Mathematical Biophysics* 13: 107–117.

Sommerfeld, Ralf D. *et al.* (2007) Gossip as an alternative for direct observation in games of indirect reciprocity. *Proceedings of the National Academy of Sciences* 104: 17435–17440.

Song, Chaoming, Havlin, Shlomo, and Makse, Hernán A. (2005) Self-similarity of complex networks. *Nature* 433: 392–395.

Sorge, Arndt and van Witteloostuijn, Arjen (2004) The (non)sense of organizational change: An essai about universal management hypes, sick consultancy metaphors, and healthy organization theories. *Organization Studies* 25: 1205–1231.

Spencer Brown, George (1957) *Probability and scientific inference*. London, Longman.

Stanley, M.H.R. *et al.* (1996) Scaling behavior in the growth of companies. *Nature* 379: 804–806.

Staw, Barry M. and Epstein, Lisa D. (2000) What bandwagons bring: Effects of popular management techniques on corporate performance, reputation, and CEO pay. *Administrative Science Quarterly* 45: 523–556.

Staw, Barry M. and Ross, Jerry (1989) Understanding behavior in escalation situations. *Science* 246: 216–220.

Steglich, C., Snijders, T.A.B., and Pearson, M. (2004) *Dynamic networks and behavior: Separating selection from influence*. Technical report, available via http://stat.gamma.rug.nl/snijders/publ.htm

Stinchcombe, Arthur (1965) Social structure and organizations, in March, J.G. (ed.) *Handbook of organizations*. Chicago, Rand McNally.

Stinchcombe, Arthur (2001) *When formality works*. Chicago, University of Chicago Press.

Strang, David and Soule, Sarah A. (1998) Diffusion in organizations and social movements. *Annual Review of Sociology* 24: 265–290.

Strogatz, Steven H. (2001) Exploring complex networks. *Nature* 410: 268–276.

Strogatz, Steven H. (2005) Romanesque networks. *Nature* 433: 365–366.

Suppes, Patrick (1968) The desirability of formalization in science. *Journal of Philosophy* 65: 651–664.

Sutton, R.I. and Hargadon, A. (1997) Technology brokering and innovation in a product development firm. *Administrative Science Quarterly* 42: 716–717.

Szabó, György and Fáth, Gábor (2007) Evolutionary games on graphs. *Physics Reports* 446: 97–216.

Tangney, June Price (1995) Recent advances in the empirical study of shame and guilt. *American Behavioral Scientist* 38: 1132–1145.

Taylor, Frederick W. (1911) *The principles of scientific management*. New York, Harper and Brothers.

Teece, David J. (1977) Technology transfer by multinational firms: the resource cost of transferring technological know-how. *Economic Journal* 87: 242–261.

Teece, David J. (2007) Explicating dynamic capabilities. *Strategic Management Journal* 28: 1319–1350.

Terracciano, A. *et al.* (2005) National character does not reflect mean personality trait levels in 49 cultures. *Science* 310: 96–100.

Thompson, Peter (2007) How much did the liberty shipbuilders forget? *Management Science* 53: 908–918.

Tilly, Chris and Tilly, Charles (1998) *Work under capitalism*. Boulder, CO, Westview Press.

Tinbergen, Nikolaas (1968) On war and peace in animals and man. *Science* 160: 1411–1418.

Tognoli, Emmanuelle *et al.* (2007) The phi complex as a neuromarker of human social coordination. *Proceedings of the National Academy of Sciences* 104: 8190–8195.

Travers, Jeffrey and Milgram, Stanley (1969) An experimental study of the small world problem. *Sociometry* 32: 425–443.

Trivers, Robert L. (1971) The evolution of reciprocal altruism. *Quarterly Review of Biology* 46: 35–57.

Turchin, Peter (2003) Evolution in population dynamics. *Nature* 424: 257–258.

Uzzi, Brian (1996) The sources and consequences of embeddedness for the economic performance of organizations: the network effect. *American Sociological Review* 61: 674–698.

Uzzi, Brian (1997) Social structure and competition in interfirm networks: The paradox of embeddedness. *Administrative Science Quarterly* 42: 35–67.

Uzzi, Brian and Spiro, Jarrett (2005) Collaboration and creativity: The small world problem. *American Journal of Sociology* 111: 447–504.

Valente, Thomas W. (2005) Network models and methods for studying the diffusion of innovations, in Carrington, P.J., Scott, J., and Wasserman, S. (eds.) *Models and methods in social network analysis*. Cambridge, Cambridge University Press.

van Dalen, Dirk (2004, 4th ed.) *Logic and structure*. Berlin, Springer.

Van den Bulte, Christophe and Lilien, Gary L. (2001) Medical innovation revisited: Social contagion versus marketing effort. *American Journal of Sociology* 106: 1409–1435.

van der Aalst, W.M.P. (1998) The application of Petri nets to workflow management, http://is.tm.tue.nl/staff/wvdaalst/publications/p53.pdf

van der Gaag, Martin and Snijders, Tom A.B. (2005) The resource generator: Social capital quantification with concrete items. *Social Networks* 27: 1–29.

Van Rossem, Ronan (1996) The world system paradigm as general theory of development: A cross-national test. *American Sociological Review* 61: 508–527.

van Schaik, Carel P. *et al.* (2003) Orangutan cultures and the evolution of material culture. *Science* 299: 102–105.

Völker, Beate and Flap, Henk (2007) *Foes at work: On the evolution of negative work relations*. Utrecht, technical report.

Vaughan, Diane (1999) The dark side of organizations. *Annual Review of Sociology* 25: 271–305.

Warneken, Felix and Tomasello, Michael (2006) Altruistic helping in human infants and young chimpanzees. *Science* 311: 1301–1303.

Wasserman, Stanley and Faust, Katherine (1994) *Social network analysis*. Cambridge, Cambridge University Press.

Watts, Duncan (1999a) Networks, dynamics, and the small world phenomenon. *American Journal of Sociology* 105: 493–527.

Watts, Duncan (1999b) *Small worlds*. Princeton, NJ, Princeton University Press.

Watts, Duncan (2003) *Six degrees: The science of a connected age*. New York, Norton.

Watts, Duncan (2004) The "new" science of networks. *Annual Review of Sociology* 30: 243–270.

Watts, Duncan, Dodds, Peter Sheridan, and Newman, Mark E.J. (2002) Identity and search in social networks. *Science* 296: 1302–1305.

Watts, Duncan and Strogatz, Steven (1998) Collective dynamics of small-world networks. *Nature* 393: 440–442.

Weber, Eugen (1976) *Peasants into Frenchmen*. Palo Alto, CA, Stanford University Press.

Weber, Max (1922) *Wirtschaft und Gesellschaft*. Tübingen, Mohr.

Weber, Max (1949) *The methodology of the social sciences*. New York, Free Press.

Wegener, B. (1991) Job mobility and social ties. *American Sociological Review* 56: 60–71.

Weick, Karl E. (1976) Educational organizations as loosely coupled systems. *Administrative Science Quarterly* 21: 1–19.

Weitzman, M.L. (1996) Hybridizing growth theory. *American Economic Review* 86: 207–212.

Weitzman, M.L. (1998) Recombinant growth. *Quarterly Journal of Economics* 113: 331–360.

Wellman, Barry (2001) Computer networks as social networks. *Science* 293: 2031–2034.

Wellman, Barry and Wortley, Scott (1990) Different strokes from different folks: Community ties and social support. *American Journal of Sociology* 96: 558–588.

White, Douglas R. (forthcoming) Innovations in the context of networks, hierarchies, and cohesion, in Lane, David *et al.* (eds.) *A new perspective on innovation and social change*. Dordrecht, Springer.

White, Douglas R. *et al.* (2004) Networks, fields and organizations: Micro-dynamics, scale and cohesive embeddings. *Computational and Mathematical Organization Theory* 10: 95–117.

White, Douglas R. *et al.* (2006) Generative model for feedback networks. *Physical Review E* 73: 016119.

White, Douglas R. and Harary, Frank (2001) The cohesiveness of blocks in social networks: Node connectivity and conditional density. *Sociological Methodology* 31: 305–359.

White, Douglas R. and Houseman, Michael (2003) The navigability of strong ties. *Complexity* 8(1): 72–80.

White, Douglas R. and Johansen, Ulla (2005) *Network analysis and ethnographic problems: Process models of a Turkish nomad clan*. Oxford, Lexington. A summary is at http://en.wikipedia.org/wiki/Network_Analysis_and_Ethnographic_Problems

White, Douglas R. and Reitz, Karl P. (1983) Graph and semigroup homomorphisms on networks of relations. *Social Networks* 5: 193–234.

White, Harrison (1970) Search parameters for the small world problem. *Social Forces* 49(2): 259–264.

White, Harrison (1981) Where do markets come from? *American Journal of Sociology* 87: 517–547.

White, Harrison (1992) *Identity and control*. Princeton, NJ, Princeton University Press.

White, Harrison (2000) Parametrize! Notes on mathematical modeling for sociology. *Social Theory* 18(3): 505–509.

White, Harrison, Boorman, S.A., and Breiger, R.L. (1976) Social structure from multiple networks: I. Blockmodels of roles and positions. *American Journal of Sociology* 81: 730–779.

Whiten, A. (2005) The second inheritance system of chimpanzees and humans. *Nature* 437: 52–55.

Whiten, A. *et al.* (1999) Cultures in chimpanzees. *Nature* 399: 682–685.

Whiten, A., Horner, V., and De Waal, F.B.M. (2005) Conformity to cultural norms of tool use in chimpanzees. *Nature* 437: 737–740.

Whyte, W.H. (1956) *The organization man*. New York, Doubleday.

Winter, Sidney G. (2003) Understanding dynamic capabilities. *Strategic Management Journal* 24: 991–995.

Wolfe, Alvin (2006) Review of D. White and Johansen (2005) *International Journal of Middle East Studies* 38: 603–605.

Wolfe, Eric (1982) *Europe and the people without history*. Berkeley, University of California Press.

Wu, Shali and Keysar, Boaz (2007) The effect of culture on perspective taking. *Psychological Science* 18: 600–606.

Wuchty, Stefan, Jones, Benjamin F., and Uzzi, Brian (2007) The increasing dominance of teams in production of knowledge. *Science* 316: 1036–1039.

Xiao, Zhixing and Tsui, Anne S. (2007) When brokers may not work: The cultural contingency of social capital in Chinese high-tech firms. *Administrative Science Quarterly* 52: 1–31.

Zachary, W.W. (1977) An information flow model for conflict and fission in small groups. *Journal of Anthropological Research* 13: 452–473.

Zhang, Guo-Quing, Wang, Di, and Li, Guo-Jie (2007) Enhancing the transmission efficiency by edge deletion in scale-free networks. *Physical Review E* 76: 017101.

Zheng, Rian, Salganik, Matthew J., and Gelman, Andrew (2006) How many people do you know in prison? *Journal of the American Statistical Association* 101(474): 409–423

Zimmer, Carl (2003) How the mind reads other minds. *Science* 300: 1079–1080.

Zollo, Maurizio and Winter, Sidney G. (2002) Deliberate learning and the evolution of dynamic capabilities. *Organization Science* 13: 339–351.

Zuckerman, Ezra W. (2003) *On Networks and Markets* by Rauch and Casella, eds. *Journal of Economic Literature* 41: 545–565.

Index

Sociology, Work and Industry
Fifth edition

Tony J. Watson, Nottingham University Business School, UK

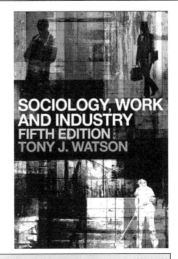

This popular text effectively explains and justifies the use of the sociological imagination to understand the nature of institutions of work, occupations, organizations, management and employment, and how they are changing in the twenty-first century. With outstanding breadth of coverage, it provides an authoritative overview of both traditional and emergent themes in the sociological study of work; explains the basic logic of sociological analysis of work and work-related institutions and provides an appreciation of different theoretical traditions.

It considers:
- the direction and implications of trends in technological change, globalization, labour markets, work organization, managerial practices and employment relations
- the extent to which these trends are intimately related to changing patterns of inequality in modern societies and to the changing experiences of individuals and families
- the ways in which workers challenge, resist and make their own contributions to the patterning of work and shaping of work institutions.

New features include an easy to read layout, key issues questions, mini case studies, chapter summaries, and a fantastic Companion Website which is packed full of useful resources (for students and teachers). All of these elements – and much more – provide the reader with a text unrivalled in the field.

Contents
Introduction 1. Studying Work and Society 2. The Sociological Analysis of Work and Industry 3. Work, Society and Globalisation 4. Work Organisations 5. The Changing Organisation and Management of Work 6. Occupations, Inequality and Varieties of Work 7. Work Experiences, Identities and Meanings 8. Conflict, Challenge and Resistance in Work

April 2008 PB: 978-0-415-43555-0: £23.99 HB: 978-0-415-43554-3: £80.00

VISIT www.routledge.com **TELEPHONE: 01264 343071**